IN THE FOOTSTEPS OF MARCO POLO

IN THE
FOOTSTEPS OF MARCO POLO

Being the Account of a Journey Overland from Simla to Pekin

BY

MAJOR CLARENCE DALRYMPLE BRUCE

LATE COMMANDING THE CHINESE REGIMENT OF INFANTRY

WITH ILLUSTRATIONS

GYAN

Published by

Gyan Publishing House
5, Ansari Road
Daryaganj, New Delhi-110002
Phone: 011-47034999, 9811692060
E-mail: books@gyanbooks.com

Distribution Network
gyanbooks.com
India, USA, Canada, UK, Australia, France

ISBN : 978-81-212-3577-8 (PB)
First Published, 1907

2nd Impression 2020

Printed at: Gyan Press, Delhi.

In the Footsteps of Marco Polo
Author: Major Clarence Dalrymple Bruce

IN THE FOOTSTEPS OF MARCO POLO

Being the Account of a Journey Overland from Simla to Pekin

BY

MAJOR CLARENCE DALRYMPLE BRUCE

LATE COMMANDING THE CHINESE REGIMENT OF INFANTRY

WITH ILLUSTRATIONS

WILLIAM BLACKWOOD AND SONS

EDINBURGH AND LONDON

MCMVII

TO MY BROTHER OFFICERS, AS WELL AS TO THE EUROPEAN NON-COMMISSIONED OFFICERS, OF THE LATE CHINESE REGIMENT, THIS BOOK IS DEDICATED, IN MEMORY OF MANY HAPPY YEARS ENJOYED TOGETHER, AND OF HARD TIMES CHEERFULLY SHARED.

PREFACE.

MY sole excuse for venturing to lay before a long-suffering public such a book as this lies in the hope that it may afford a few hours of interest and amusement to those less fortunate than the author in the opportunities they may have had for gratifying that passion for wandering which is inherent in the Anglo-Saxon race.

Many whose fate is the busy city were born for the wilds. All honour to them for stifling the innate craving. It is as a humble offering to such kindred spirits that this book is written.

My thanks are first of all due to Mr William Blackwood for much kind help in the production of this book. To the proprietors of 'The Cornhill Magazine,' 'The Standard,' and 'Blackwood's Magazine' I am indebted for permission to make use of articles and letters. To the Council of the Royal Geographical Society I owe help in the production of my map; and finally, to my friend John Swire, for more material help in enabling me partly to meet the heavy expenses connected with such a journey.

C. D. BRUCE.

Wynters Grange,
Harlow, Essex.

CONTENTS.

CHAPTER V.

CHAPTER VI.

CHAPTER VII.

CHAPTER VIII.

CHAPTER IX.

CHAPTER X.

CHAPTER XI.

CHAPTER XII.

CHAPTER XIII.

CHAPTER XIV.

CHAPTER XV.

CHAPTER XVI.

LIST OF ILLUSTRATIONS.

IN THE FOOTSTEPS OF MARCO POLO.

CHAPTER I.

THE AVOIDANCE OF BEATEN PATHS—A BUSY WEEK AT SRINAGAR—"MR COOK"—A VALLEY OF LOVELINESS—THE ZOJI PASS—THE RELIGION OF THE LADAKIS—PRAYER CYLINDERS—POLYANDRY—AN ELABORATE COIFFURE—LEH—A LAMA TEMPLE.

In the endeavour to see as much of the world as possible, a good general rule through life is never to travel twice by the same route when there is an alternative. Although the present is a restless age, there is no inconsiderable number of people travelling who are content to follow the same path, however well beaten.

In the course of nearly twenty-five years' soldiering in most parts of the world, acceptance of the above rule has thrown open to me many byways and little known tracks, particularly during the last eight years. Throughout this latter period my service has been spent for the most part in China, or in passing to and fro to the Far East, and on no two occasions has the same route been followed. A glance at any map of the world will show that there are only two ordinary routes. But to any one bent on wandering there are many, and it is the account of one such journey that it is proposed to offer to readers of the following pages.

I left England in June 1905 for India by the usual sea-route. Traversing the Red Sea in July is not a pleasure to be dwelt upon. But for the distraction offered by the kindness of the captain of the P. and O. vessel, in allowing me to improve a scanty knowledge of solar observations, the voyage would have been marked as so much time wasted.

My previous experience of India had been in the early 'eighties, so that the idea of a renewal of acquaintance with Anglo-Indian society and customs was not without interest.

Bombay in the rains is no place to linger at, as those who have not become acclimatised to its somewhat humid atmosphere know well. As soon as the much-improved railway service would allow, I was speeding north over the then brazen plains in the height of the hot weather to the more salubrious atmosphere of the summer capital at Simla. There, the final arrangements regarding a surveyor to accompany the expedition, as well as those connected with the necessary permission to travel through certain portions of Central Asia, occupied another ten days. Thanks to the kindly interest taken by the late Viceroy in all matters connected with Asiatic travel, these arrangements presented no difficulty. The only other possible source of delay—that of obtaining a companion to accompany me on the journey—was also at once removed by the no less ready sympathy of the present Commander-in-chief with the aim of our journey. Permission to accompany me having been granted to a former brother officer, Captain W. T. Layard, who had served in the now defunct Chinese regiment with which I had also been connected, we left Simla together at the end of July, our immediate destination being Srinagar the capital of Kashmir.

The beauties of Kashmir have so often been described, and that exquisite country is now so well known to visitors to India, that it is unnecessary to follow this portion of the journey in detail.

After a busy week at Srinagar, where the various native shops provide every want the traveller may have, we were glad to be done with the endless bargaining, and to find our lists of stores more or less complete.

It is said that the occasion will always produce the man, and in our case at Srinagar the adage certainly was true. We had begun our chaffering under the wing of a well-known merchant who, as the Eastern does, had entirely taken possession of us upon our arrival. Everything we required he, of course, had, and protestations flowed as they only can from the mouth of a would-be seller and he a native. It was not until two days' patient waiting had produced nothing more than words that we became alive to the character of our friend. Sallying out in despair into the picturesque slums bordering the many-bridged Jhelum river, we visited in turn the various puttoo-makers, leather-workers, and others, at each endeavour becoming more depressed at the length of time required to fulfil our orders. At last, worn out with protesting that we might be at least half-way to Leh by the time the requisite goods were to be ready in Srinagar, we had nearly confessed ourselves beaten, when the sudden appearance of a bland and smiling native entirely changed the position of affairs.

If the National Congress is ever to take the place of the Viceroy's Council in the endeavour to smooth the path of those whose cry is India for the Indians, the president of that congress will undoubtedly be the man whom fate threw in our path that day at Srinagar. Blessed with an imperturbable manner which no outpourings of rival purveyors could disturb, with a glib tongue far too clever to entangle its owner in the usual meaningless string of polite affirmatives, our new friend possessed also the most valuable gift which nature can bestow, that of inspiring personal confidence at once and in a marked degree. From the moment we set eyes upon "Mr Cook,"—for so we named our friend out of compliment to a Western counterpart he had never heard of,—he became our sole Universal Provider, and nobly he fulfilled the self-assumed task.

Difficulties, which a moment before appeared insuperable, dissolved like magic. Prices all round—except Mr Cook's own—at once fell as unaccountably as have our own Consols; and that night, for the first time, we laid our weary heads upon the pillows of Mr Nedous' comfortable beds, with a future assuming a complexion altogether *couleur de rose.*

Upon the 29th of July preparations were finally completed, and we were able to leave the capital. The country traversed in the march from Srinagar to the confines of the Zoji Pass appeared a veritable paradise after the scorching plains of Lower India. One of the most beautiful spots at which the traveller halts during the daily marches through the wealth of lovely forest is the little valley of Sonamarg. This peaceful spot has been so well described by one who thoroughly appreciated its natural charm, that his own words can best enable my readers to draw the mental picture.

"Sonamarg is a narrow grassy flat extending some two miles between the hillside and the river-bank. Connected with it is a wider tract at the meeting of a side valley from the south-west. This latter is beautiful undulating ground, known as Tahjwaz, a succession of dells surrounded by hillocks or grassy mounds, which are sometimes connected more or less into a line and sometimes isolated. The dells are covered with long thick grass and numerous wild-flowers, while the slopes of the hillocks have a growth of silver fir, with sycamore, birch, and other bright green trees beautifully intermingled. Surrounded by forests and great rocky mountains, divided into hollows, in each of which lies a glacier, nature has combined to form in the lonely meadows of Sonamarg a grandeur and beauty that can hardly be exceeded."

Such is the charm of this little valley that it was once intended to use it as a summer abode for the British Resident in Kashmir. A log church was even built, but was afterwards destroyed by fire. This did not, however, prevent us from enjoying an open-air service, the day being Sunday. A travelling friend, a pâdre from the plains, was encamped a short distance away. One or two other camps also rested in quiet contentment farther up the valley, and as it was the last Sunday we were likely to spend in such a manner for many months, we gladly accepted our friend's invitation to the simple service he had prepared outside his little camp. A more ideal spot could hardly be desired even by the most imaginative of men; and to my companion and myself this chance service seemed to foretell what is known to the dwellers in the far-off land which was our goal, as a "good joss."

Between the Zoji-la (11,300 feet) and Leh there is to be found some hard and excessively dull marching. At the time our party crossed the pass it was still covered with ice, a somewhat unusual experience for the month of August. As a pass it is by no means an easy ascent. It has been described by Sven Hedin, who crossed it in January, as one of the worst he had ever been over.

From Baltal, in the valley below, the track commences at once to ascend. Six hundred feet up, it runs out on to a small ice slide or miniature glacier, where the foothold, to say the least of it, is precarious. One slip for man or beast would mean a fall into the stream-bed below, with little or no chance of recovery; and once fallen, the victim would have no personal interest in his recovery.

Above the Zoji-la, although the heavy forest which covers the lower mountain-slopes is entirely absent, the valleys still hold good grass. We found in one a fine herd of ponies, the property of his Highness the Maharajah, guarded by some of his people living in tents. It is the custom to send into the higher valleys of Kashmir not only ponies, but also sheep and goats, in order that they may profit by a summer on the luscious grass. Large herds of the latter are driven from as far away as Dhera-gazi-khan.

Between the Zoji-la and Leh, the track follows various mountain streams, tributaries of the Indus river, through rocky bare gorges, where the heat in August is by no means pleasant. Rest-houses have been erected at the end of each day's march, and a small payment by those travellers who use them helps towards their upkeep.

The Ladakis who inhabit this country differ considerably from the Kashmiris. The former profess Buddhism, but, be it said at once, a form which bears hardly any resemblance to the elevating and mystic faith which Buddha once taught.

The actual religion of Ladak is a modified form of Indian Buddhism, and was introduced more than 2000 years ago. It is contained in a voluminous work called the 'Kah-Gyur' or 'Translation of Precepts,' because it is a version of the precepts of "Sakya" made from the Indian language. Sakyamuni, the founder of the Buddhist faith, is called "Chom-dan-das" by the Lamas, but "Sakya-

Thubba," or the mighty Sakya, by the people. As is well known, there are various sects of Lamas, the most ancient being the Nyiampa, who wear red robes. This sect was founded in the eighth century. In the fourteenth was founded the great sect of the Geluk-Pa. These wear yellow robes, and are now the most numerous in Tibet. Both the Dalai Lama of Lhasa and the Tashi-Lama of Tashi-Luhn-Po belong to it. There is besides a third sect who also wear yellow robes. All who have taken vows of celibacy are called by the collective name of *gedun* (clergy). A monk is styled a *lama*, a nun *djomu*, *tsomu*, or *ani*.

With nuns the monastic life is apparently optional, and is only adopted by the friendless and homeless. A woman merely shaves her head, goes to a monastery, and becomes a nun. Should she wish to quit the life, her hair is allowed to grow again, and, after paying a small fine to the Lamas, she may emerge.

Most Lamas shave their heads and go bareheaded. The higher ones wear semicircular red caps. There are three ritualistic instruments — the bell, the sceptre or thunderbolt, and the prayer cylinder. The sceptre is called *sera-pun-dze;* it is said to have flown away from India and to have alighted at Sera in Tibet. An annual festival is held in its honour.

The prayer cylinder, *mani-chus-khor*, or "the precious religious wheel," is an ingenious instrument—a metal cylinder 3 inches high and 2 inches to 2½ inches in diameter. The axis is prolonged to form a handle. The cylinder is filled with rolls of printed prayers and charms, which revolve with the instrument. Every Lama is supposed to carry a *chus-khor*. Some of the cylinders have the sacred sentences, "Om-mani-pad-mi-hun," "oh, the jewel in the lotus," graven on them. Cylinders are also placed near the doors of *gonpas* (literally a solitary place), which votaries turn as they enter. Other cylinders are sometimes seen near villages, turned perpetually by the water of some stream.

The monasteries are known as *gonpas*. It is the custom in most large monasteries to have two head Lamas,—one being the leader in spiritual matters and the other the manager of temporal affairs. In the monasteries are *lha-khang* (God's House or Temple), consisting of single rooms, square and unadorned, filled with images and pictures. The former are usually nearly life-size, made of unburnt clay, and painted in gaudy colours.

Where no monasteries exist, a *labrang* (Lama House) is used. The Lamas then live in separate houses. Other Buddhistical erections are the *chorten* (offering receptacle), which is a dedicatory pyramid erected in honour of Sakya-Thubba or of some of the holy Buddhas. It consists of a square base surrounded by steps, upon which stands the dome, the principal part of the edifice. In shape this is an inverted truncated cone. The dome is surmounted by a lofty pinnacle crowned by a sacred crescent-shaped emblem. These pyramids vary from 15 to 30 feet in height, and are constructed of mud brick plastered over and painted.

A *kagani* is a magnified *chorten* with a roadway leading through it. They are frequently found at the entrance to villages, as at Lamayuru near Leh, and at the entrance to houses.

Another religious requisite is the *dungten* (bone-holder). It is a pyramid erected over the corpse of a Lama, or over the ashes of a person of consequence. Inside the urn are the ashes with numerous relics. The most common of all religious emblems everywhere in evidence are the *mani*. A *mani* is a dyke of stones varying in length, but usually some 5 feet by 6 to 8 feet wide. On the road to Leh *mani* over 250 yards in length are to be seen, whose sides, tops, and ends are all covered with flat stones of varying sizes, but every one bearing cut upon its surface the "Om-mani-pad-mi-hun."

The *mani* are made by the contributions of the faithful, each person placing on the mound a stone, some of which in the carving of the characters are of considerable artistic merit. As an offering the idea may appear childish, yet the principle is one common to our own religion in early days. The idea embodied in the action of devout Buddhists is somewhat doubtful. By some authorities it is said to be merely the act of those desiring a special favour, such as a son born to them. Another, and on the part of the superstitious peasant it would seem a more likely reason for the act, is, that upon the last day when a certain recording angel, Khurjidal by name, appears on earth, any one who has placed a stone on the *mani* will have his name read by the angel, and be accorded "value for goods received," or, in less prosaic language, salvation or at least intervention by the recording angel with the great Judge.

At each *mani* the track divides to pass on both sides of the dyke in order that travellers may always keep the *mani* on their right in whichever direction they are going.

I have frequently watched the behaviour of the caravan men under the circumstances, and found as a rule that the animals, from habit more often than not, appeared to take the proper side. On the occasions when they did not, no one seemed to pay any attention to the fact.

Hlato (cairns) may be seen on any pass or high solitary spot. Sôme merely consist of stones and a rag or two: others are more picturesque, and offer landmarks for a considerable distance round. These latter have poles inserted into the cairns, from which long streamers flutter in the breeze. Besides the streamers, boughs of trees are sometimes found wedged among the stones, and on these are stuck the horns of ibex or other wild sheep.

It is well known that polyandry is the custom among the Ladakis. The elder brother marries a wife, and she *de facto* becomes the wife of all his brothers. The children of such marriages always take the name of and obey the eldest brother, who is called the big father, a younger brother being spoken of as the little father. The system of polyandry is chiefly due to the advantage which, in cases of extreme poverty, brothers gain by being able to live together and jointly till the small property they have inherited. The Ladaki women are undoubtedly finer than the men, and this is partly proved by the intermarriages between Yarkandi and other traders and Ladaki women. The offspring, called "Arghuns," are generally fine men of notable physique, but their mothers are wife to one man only.

The Ladaki women wear the usual loose robes of the East, and follow the customary rule as to outdoor work. One curious custom in common use among them is the making up of their complexions with a process called "Shogolo." This consists in smearing the cheeks and forehead with the juice and seeds of the belladonna plant. Great pains are bestowed in arranging the bright-yellow seeds effectively upon the brown skin, and the result is that the face appears as if sprinkled with grains of gold.

The method of wearing the hair indulged in by the women of Ladak is also peculiar. That they become accustomed to the weight of the ornamental head-dress is no doubt the case, but that such an inconvenient and cumbersome style should be adopted by people who work largely out of doors, only affords one more example of the tyranny of fashion even in remote countries. Having plaited the hair down the back, they work into it a long strip of red or black cloth. This is some 24 inches long by 5 inches wide at the top, but tapering at the lower end to a width of 1½ to 2 inches. Upon this bit of cloth are fastened, at times, as many as five vertical rows of small stones of lapis-lazuli. The stones vary in size from some as small as a pea up to others larger than a big walnut, and what the weight is can easily be imagined. They are fastened to the strip of cloth in even rows, usually having the largest stone in the centre, from which to both ends they decrease in size. The top portion of the cloth covers the head like a flat cap, coming down to the roots of the hair in front. As seen in gala dress the effect is not unpleasing. Unfortunately, cleanliness of person is usually a difficulty with natives who dwell at high altitudes, and the Ladaki men and women are no exception either in person or in the matter of their clothes.

The approach to Leh from the valley of the Indus river is a striking one, nor does nearer acquaintance, as is usual in the East, tend to obliterate first impressions. From Pitak, a village on the banks of the river, the track turns to mount gently for five miles across a bare stony plain until green trees, fields, and small grassy gardens or "baghs," as they are locally called, mark the limits of the area under cultivation.

The town stands five miles from the right bank of the Indus river and at the commencement of the ascent which leads to the Khardong-la on the Yarkand route. It also commands the track which leads up the right bank of the Indus river as far as Chimray, thirteen miles beyond Leh. Here the track quits the river and crosses the Chang-la and other passes into Tibet. Thirdly, Leh commands the main track *viâ* Pitak down the Indus river to Srinagar.

The only attempt at defence is in the fort, which stands a mile nearer to Pitak than the town itself and three-quarters of a mile from the mountain ridges which command its interior.

The fort is a rectangular one, built of wood and mud. It has a fosse from 10 to 12 feet deep and

20 feet wide, which could be filled if necessary from the stream-bed, upon whose bank the fort is built. Being the point of departure for all the Yarkand trading caravans as well as for the private expeditions which purpose crossing the Chang-Chenmo valley and penetrating into Tibet, the population of Leh is a very mixed one. The inhabitants depend for their livelihood almost entirely upon the caravan trade. The shopkeepers, who provide all and every article used by natives for pack transport, in their turn offer work for the actual makers of such goods. To provide subsistence for all is again the work of other stall-keepers, who find the grain, fodder, and daily necessities of bazar life.

Among the many types of this polyglot population may be mentioned Ladakis, Baltis, men from the Zanskar district south-west of Leh, Yarkandis, dwellers round Khotan, Turkis, half-bred Tibetans and Tibetans from the Rudok district, Hindoo shopkeepers, Mussulmans, Lamas, and last but not least, a large population of "Arghuns." The last, as already mentioned, are the offspring of intermarriages or temporary cohabitation between Yarkandi traders and Ladaki women. As a class they are usually fine men of extra good physique, and as caravan men frequently make useful servants.

The cultivated portion of the Leh valley proper is, roughly, three miles by one mile in area, equal to some 2000 acres.

Grazing for animals in such a place, where caravans are for ever arriving and starting, is a matter of importance. After as well as before facing the hardships of the Yarkand route, it is the custom to feed up the animals upon the grass or hay which grows in the *baghs* or wooded gardens surrounding the town. In extent these *baghs* vary from 50 to 150 yards square, and are sometimes let for grazing for as much as Rs. 45 (£3) per *bagh.* Naturally, the price varies with the state of the grass. We paid Rs. 18 for a fortnight's grazing in one of the biggest, the Magna Bagh, but the grass was not at its best.

The castle of the *gyalpo*—literally king—is, together with the Lama temples, the most striking building in Leh. It stands perched upon a precipitous spur immediately above the town, and is the point which attracts the eye in any view of the latter.

The walls are of solid stone, and, in security of position and massive strength, yield little in defensive power to the castles of our own feudal times. Inside, the area consists of a labyrinth of semi-dark passages, steep stairways, and trap-door-like exits. The stairways appear to lead to nowhere in particular, but pass from one empty vault to another. In the old days it can easily be imagined that nothing short of starvation or want of water would cause the garrison to succumb. To assault, or even to being set on fire, the castle appears impregnable.

Perched some 2000 feet above the town, the Lama temple overrides the castle itself. The buildings consist of a warren of crumbling rooms built of mud, of precipitous flights of stone steps, and of small courtyards on different levels, joined by goat-tracks overhanging sheer drops many hundreds of feet down. At odd corners and outside dilapidated doorways are many prayer-wheels; whilst tattered flags and rags for warding off the ever-to-be-feared demons adorn the roofs and equally tumble-down walls.

Nor can the interior be said to be any more prepossessing. In the inner holy of holies is the Buddhist shrine. The room or hall in which it stands is usually kept so darkened that nothing can be seen but the immediate front of the altar; upon the latter burn one or two miserable oil-wicks, and behind these, and partly screening the hideous figure itself, are heavy faded hangings, which may have once been clean. Upon either side of the altar stand silver *manis*, and behind these some of the flat oblong-shaped wood-covered books which contain the sacred writings.

In another hall, some thirty feet square, is a large figure of Chamba. Three-quarters of its length stands erect within the chamber but not the whole; the upper portion is continued outside, above, and so to speak through the roof, in order that the eyes of the figure may rest afar upon the snow-clad mountain-ranges surrounding its picturesque abode.

The roof, walls, and pillars of the hall are covered with various representative figures and scenes in what was formerly bright red, blue, and yellow paint. Among these figures are many used by the Chinese in their Buddhist temples: traced in colour upon the walls are also what appear to be Chinese characters. It may be thought that, for the people for whom they are intended, both the figures and the religion they teach are sufficient inducements to moral improvement; and did the present-day

Buddhism of Ladak even faintly retain the teaching of its great master there might be some hope. But we know it is not so. Priest-ridden and terrorised over by means of threats as to his future state, the Ladaki peasant has no real religion. His one and only thought is the propitiation of his unseen yet none the less dreaded demons, and such religion as he has is merely used as a means to rob and degrade him by those whose bounden duty it is to help him upwards.

CHAPTER II.

PREPARING THE CARAVAN—LADAK SLIMNESS—HORSE-BUYING BY ARBITRATION—A GRAND POLO-MATCH IN THE STREET AT LEH—THE LAPCHACK MISSION—THE DIFFICULTIES ATTENDING A START—TRAINING AS A CURE FOR MOUNTAIN SICKNESS—A PRIMITIVE PAIR OF SCALES—THE SILENT LAND—HOW TO DRIVE A YAK—HUNTING THE TIBETAN HARE.

At Leh the serious preparations for the journey to Peking commenced. So far as could be calculated, we did not expect to reach that capital until the following spring. And throughout all this distance there was little or no chance for renewing the few European stores we intended to carry.

Previous experience had made us only too well aware how the necessities of civilisation become the luxuries of such journeys as we contemplated, yet it was not without inward qualms that such daily commodities as butter, milk, jam, potatoes, and vegetables were one by one erased from the list. In the end the staff of life, in the shape of flour, formed by far the largest portion of our transport. Meat it was unnecessary to trouble about, even in the compressed form, as our rifles could supply what was necessary; but army rations, Bovril lozenges, sardines, sugar, and a little jam and some tapioca, made up our luxuries. Baking-powder, tea, coffee, and cocoa we looked upon as necessities; and I also brought from home a small store of the best French (Marquis) chocolate, without which it is unwise ever to quit civilisation. For liquor there was of course no room, with the exception of four bottles of the best brandy for medicinal purposes.

Having made out the lists of food, the most difficult problem of all had then to be faced, in the shape of deciding how much, or rather how little, grain must be taken to feed all the animals of which our caravan was composed. In Tibet the daily ration that can be carried is extremely limited. It might seem at first thought that the difficulty is merely one of numbers, and that if more grain is required, the traveller has only to buy more animals,—supposing, that is, that there happen to be any to buy. A moment's reflection, however, will show that the problem is not so simple. Assume, as we did, that twenty-five ponies would carry all our kit and surveying instruments, and afford us each an animal to ride when necessary. There are then so many pounds of grain for each of these animals to feed upon, which must be carried somewhere. A three months' supply was the least we dared to start with, and at 2 lb. a pony per day, a slight calculation will show that three months' supplies soon run into four figures. Again the matter becomes one of simple calculation. Each pony can carry a load of about 150 lb. To load over 4000 lb. weight of grain thirty more ponies must be bought. Suppose that they are available and are purchased, where are we now? Unfortunately at exactly the point where we started, for the thirty fresh ponies must each have 2 lb. of grain a-day, and who is to carry that?

It was with such and similar trifling problems as these that our stay in Leh was beguiled. By the help of the Assistant British Commissioner, to whom we owe a debt of gratitude not easily paid, we eventually triumphed over all obstacles, and after this manner. The original number of twenty-five ponies was bought. To carry the grain, thirty yak were also purchased, with the intention that they might drop out as their work was done. One of the few good points these animals possess is that they themselves require no grain; and besides the yak a certain number of ponies were hired to go as far with us into Tibet as their owners would.

The main question being settled, we turned to what was to my companion and myself a labour of love—viz., the purchase of the ponies. A few hours spent in the *serai* soon showed us that the word "slimness" is not unknown even in far Ladak. No sooner did we select some less ragged-looking hill-pony than the rest but he at once became the possessor of every virtue horseflesh is heir to.

It was useless to point to a barely healed sore back, or to teeth that made him at least a score of years old; we were assured that this was merely Western prejudice, and even if things were as we suggested, what matter! To such Eastern logic the West, if it be wise, pays no attention. Argument is merely breath wasted. Freedom of speech a native vendor must have, and granted his right to talk incessantly, and sufficient patience on the part of the buyer, the odds are not so very great in favour of the Asiatic. After playing to the gallery for some hours, we began to look for the way round, and it was soon discovered.

As in London so in Leh, when in doubt appoint a committee. In London the latter means blue books. In Leh it means more conversation and much tea. For our purchasing committee we suggested four of the local greybeards to act as referees.

The sellers were to state their price: we stated our price, and the greybeards struck the happy medium. In two days the choicest of horseflesh then in Leh became our property at an average price of about £5 a head, the previous figure having been more than double.

During those two days of the sale the compound of the little "rest-house" knew no peace. Swarms of wild-looking ruffians with equally ragged ponies hung round all day, and during the hours that the committee figuratively sat, Barnet fair was a joke to it. Thanks to the Assistant Commissioner, all this time our yak were being collected for us at Tankse, a village we had to pass through soon after quitting Leh. But bad fortune for once met us over the yak, for the previous spring and autumn had seen a bad outbreak of cattle plague, which had carried off hundreds of these beasts, causing heavy losses to the poor villagers, and making even inferior animals exceedingly scarce. Curiously, neither ponies nor mules suffered at all from the outbreak.

Having purchased the animals, it was necessary

to provide all the remaining impedimenta, such as pack-saddles, extra shoes, hobbles, feeding-bags, and many other minor articles, and also to engage more caravan men.

Once more we were indebted to the kind assistance of the Assistant Commissioner, and our following was soon complete. It consisted, all told, of six pony men—not including the hired men—with a caravan *bashi* or headman, and later on five yak men. Our own party was made up of Captain Layard, Lall Singh, our Sikh surveyor, and his servant, Abdull, a young Mohammedan servant of Layard's, and Ramzani, a Punjaubi servant, who had afterwards to be sent back, and myself.

Each day at Leh was fully occupied with final preparations. Not until the necessity actually arises is it possible to remember everything required; and more than once, when lists seemed finally completed and final orders given, was it found that there yet remained another day's work in the bazars.

During the summer months there are few more delightful spots in India than Leh. The British Joint Commissioner is provided with a fairly good house, and the efforts of succeeding occupants have made its immediate surroundings still more pleasing. A charming garden, shaded with fine old trees, and lawns which remind the exile of his own English grass, are the chief attractions to a perpetual open-air life, itself so delightful. Magnificent views are obtained of the higher snow-ranges on the far side of the Indus; and there in the well-earned intervals of a busy summer the

Commissioner can usually find the sport and the heads for which Northern Kashmir is so justly famed.

One afternoon during our stay at Leh we were invited to an entertainment to be given by the Wazir Sahib, the chief attraction of which was to be the marriage of his son. Incidentally the rejoicings were to include polo,—a game which, strange as it may seem, the people of these mountain regions are very fond of.

Arrived at our host's house, situated in a prettily shaded garden, we found a tent pitched, whence, after the usual courtesies, the party adjourned to the upper storey of one of the houses situated upon the main street of the town. This street, said to be the work of a particularly enterprising former British Joint Commissioner, is about 350 to 400 yards long and 50 to 60 feet wide. It is bordered on both sides by fine rows of trees, which give shade to the lines of shops stretching without break throughout three parts of its entire length. Gazing down into the street below from our balconies, we were surprised to see that both sides of the street held a large number of the townspeople, also groups of ponies, and men with mallets, who appeared to be setting saddles, girths, and their own costumes in readiness for some unusual display.

Immediately opposite the balconies we were in, and across the street, a dozen ancient musicians were seated on a small raised platform under the trees. Their instruments were a quaint collection of horns and drums, and of such as one's childish mind recalls as remotely connected with the fall of the walls of Jericho.

Inquiring in our innocence what the preparations in progress below betokened, we were surprised to hear that we were about to witness the royal game of polo.

"But polo," we said, "up and down the streets of the town?"

"Yes, sahib," said the Wazir; "and why not?"

And as the Joint Commissioner whispered, "There is no County Council here," we faintly began to wonder why we suffered such things to exist at home. But the moment was not one for reflection upon such matters.

Led by a good-looking man on a grey at least fourteen hands high, the players were beginning to take up their positions.

In the twentieth century it is a little difficult at times to realise all that the improvements in modern methods of travel have done for this generation. But it was forcibly brought home that afternoon as visions of the last time I had watched polo crossed my mind. Shortly before leaving England, about the middle of June, Hurlingham, in all the freshness and beauty of the early summer, was in full swing, and there I had seen the pick of the world for ponies and men hard at work in a first-class match. Barely eight weeks later I was again watching polo, but under conditions so changed as to make Hurlingham almost a dream.

Of the Leh game, from the expert point of view, criticism is not easy. Though the players

A Group at Leh.

In centre, British Joint Commissioner, Captain Patterson; on his right, the Wazir of Ladak and Captain Layard.

Preparing for Polo in the Street at Leh.

numbered five a-side, and were mounted for the most part on tiny hill-ponies about twelve hands high, there seemed to be less hustling and go about the game than might be expected. Possibly the presence of the Wazir's son, and the size of the pony he rode, which turned out to be the big grey, had something to do with this: it may also have been connected with the general apparent insecurity of straps, girths, and even bridles,—for anything like the collection which covered the little ponies is not often seen outside a gipsy camp.

Whatever the reason was, the game *quâ* polo resolved itself into repeated runs down by one player after another,—whoever, in fact, happened at the time to be in possession of the ball. Very slight was the attempt ever to stop him; and as ponies became blown it was no unusual thing to see the last runner-down dismount and breathe his animal, while taking little if any notice of the game. The one point about the latter which did attract attention was when, after a pause, it was necessary to make a fresh start. Then a player would pick up the ball, and holding it in one hand, with his stick in the other, start at full gallop down the street. When about half-way—a liberal interpretation of the half-way mark being usually allowed—he threw up the ball and, still galloping, endeavoured to strike it in the air. If successful in doing so, which was not often the case, a good run down and a goal into a butcher's shop at the town end of the street was usually the result. This was the signal for general applause and, what was as amusing as any part of the game, a fearful tom-tomming and blowing of horns by the antiquated performers opposite our stand. In between-whiles these ancients appeared to take no interest in the game—at least not until, as sometimes happened, a ball came ricochetting into the middle of them off some neighbouring tree.

After about an hour the match was declared at an end. Not having been able always to follow the sequence of goals, and anxious not to congratulate the wrong people, I inquired of the courteous native gentleman by my side which team had won. So evidently upset did he appear to be that I felt at once such a detail was considered unworthy of notice. In Leh, as with ourselves, polo is still one of the purest forms of sport, and that it may long remain so was our inward and earnest wish.

As has already been said in the early portion of this chapter, Leh is the starting-point for most of the Central Asiatic expeditions into Tibet or into Chinese Turkestan.

From Leh also is still sent a curious mediæval mission to Lhasa, known as the Lapchack Mission, of which in its present-day guise some account may be of interest.

The Lapchack commercial embassy is said to be of very old standing. Before the time of the Dogra conquest of Ladak, in 1841, it was the means of transmitting tribute as well as of cementing mutual trade, but is now considered both by the Kashmir and British authorities to have no political significance. It was established on its present footing in 1842, when a treaty was concluded between Lhasa and Ladak to demarcate the north-east frontier of the latter country. The arrangement was, and, so far as the despatch of the caravan, still is, that every third year a *kafila* should leave Ladak for Lhasa, consisting of 270 yak- or pony-loads of goods, and that it should be conducted by a representative of the Maharajah of Kashmir, chosen by the Wazir of Ladak. For just that number of loads is carriage provided by the Lhasa authorities from Ghur—a lamasery near Rudok in Tibet—to Lhasa on the outward journey, and from Lhasa to the first villages or encampments in Ladak on the return journey.

The Maharajah's representative used to be taken from a Ladak family of eminence, as no other person, not even a Dogra of high rank from the Maharajah's own court, would be welcomed—probably, indeed, would not be received into the capital of Tibet. The post of leader of the Lapchack Mission, though held only for one term, was much valued, as the profits generally enriched the family between whom and the Maharajah's government they used to be divided. The goods sent from Ladak are dried apricots — the most bulky portion of the consignment,—currants, saffron, and textile fabrics from European and Indian looms. On the return journey the chief goods are shawls, wool, and tea. Complimentary letters were sent to the Grand Lama and his Ministers, and also to the heads of certain of the monasteries; and with each went a small present, the nature of which is laid down and did not vary. The embassy, which is absent nearly a year, brought back corresponding letters and presents.

The leader transacted his business with the Ministers, but paid ceremonial visits to the Dalai Lama.

In addition to the presents, there is reason to believe that the Lapchack Embassy was also provided with the following, which was paid by it to the treasurer at Lhasa :—

10 small bags of gold-dust, value each Rs. 8 .	Rs. 80
1½ seers of saffron	50
5 pieces of native cloth, each of a separate value of Rs. 1	5
	Rs. 135

These three items are known as *sahtal* or ground-tax, and a receipt was given by the treasurer at Lhasa, which the Lapchack brought back to Ladak.

Even so great an authority as Ney Elias has written that it is difficult to estimate how far the *sahtal* or ground-tax, paid or presented to the treasurer of Lhasa, was regarded by the Tibetan authorities as *nazar* or tribute; but by the government of Kashmir it was certainly looked upon in the light of a present only, and as the return for the provisions, &c., with which the agent and his party were supplied during a part of their stay in Lhasa. Again, the treasurer at Lhasa was a servant of the native government, and was appointed by the Deva Jung or Grand Lama, not by the Chinese officials, and his receipt set forth that the *sahtal* had been paid into the Deva Jung's treasury. The fact of the treasurer giving a formal receipt while the other recipients of presents gave none; secondly, that he sent no return presents; thirdly, that the word *sahtal* means literally land-tax, would be reasons in favour of regarding the presents or payments, which were made to the Lhasa treasury, as tribute paid by Ladak to Chinese Tibet. But against this must be placed the following considerations: first, that *sahtal* of similar value was given by the Lapchack for many years before the agreement was made; and secondly, that in those years when no Lapchack went to Lhasa no *sahtal* was paid.

The distinction between presents of friendship on the one hand, and tribute as a sign of dependency on the other, is always very loosely drawn by Asiatics; nor do the names of taxes, duties, &c., always designate accurately the purpose for which they are levied.

Whatever the Ladakis may now think of the meaning of the *sahtal* and presents, I have no doubt that the Chinese authorities at Lhasa still look upon them, and—if they considered it to be of any advantage to themselves—would describe them as tribute.

Before quitting Leh mention must be made of the Karakoram route, which is the main highway for such trade as exists between Chinese Turkestan and British India.

This route leads to Yarkand, over the Kadongla, a glacier pass 17,500 feet above sea-level. After surmounting this difficult ascent, the track runs for thirty-two days' march over a barren desolate country, devoid of all supplies, to Yarkand.

That the trade with Chinese Turkestan is never likely to become of anything but local importance may be accepted as a fact. During the time spent at Leh, I had the opportunity of being present at a meeting between the British Joint Commissioner and some native merchants interested in this trade-route.

Among other topics, one subject of discussion was tea, which some of the merchants were sanguine enough to hope might be exported from Bombay as brick tea, at such prices as would enable it to compete favourably at Yarkand with the Chinese article. A very brief comparison of the prices at which the tea could be placed on the market at the latter place sufficed to show that those engaged in the export of the Indian article would be un likely to make a fortune.

On the 29th August our caravan left Leh. A first march-out is invariably a difficulty, no matter how careful the overnight arrangements may be; and we considered ourselves lucky to have got the twenty-eight animals loaded-up and away by 7.30 A.M. But our self-congratulation was somewhat premature.

During the last week at Leh we had hired one of the grassy *baghs* on the outskirts of the town, for the purpose of feeding up our stud. Unfortunately, the route at starting, on the morning of the 29th, lay for some distance in the same direction as that with which the ponies were so familiar, and which led to their beloved *bagh*. All went well until the parting of the ways was reached, and then the trouble began. First one pony and then another kept breaking away towards the garden; loads began to shift as the ponies broke into a canter in response to our efforts to round them up; and the final catastrophe came when a little black, more headstrong than any of them, completely dislodged the two *yakdans* he carried. Down crashed all the methylated spirit, carefully stored for use with the hypsometer; also our four bottles of "medical comforts."

Having called a halt, loads were replaced. Thanks to the excellence of the Srinagar *yakdans*, nothing was broken, and to enable him to work off his superabundant spirits, the black pony became from that moment my own riding animal. It is but fair to his memory to state that he carried me daily many a weary mile over the forsaken wastes of North-West Tibet, as well as through the dreadful gorges in the Kuen Lun mountains. Starved by day and frozen by night, his gallant little spirit never failed him. And it was not until completely worn out, some months later, that he finally broke down, dying by a water-hole in the edge of the Takla Makan desert in Chinese Turkestan.

It is not until Leh is left behind that the traveller feels he has cut the painter which has so far bound him to civilisation. And even after quitting that place, for a few days villages and cultivation are still found. Tankse is a poor hamlet situated on the far side of the Chang-la from Leh, lying at the opposite end of a small valley leading to another hamlet, Durgu by name. The Chang-la,

17,000 feet high, is the most severe of the three passes separating Leh from the Tibet border. It is approached up the Chimray valley, in which stands a picturesque lamasery, and also a village of the same name.

Crossing the Chang-la was the first experience our party had of such heights, and we were prepared to feel the effects of the rarefied air in the form of the usual mountain sickness. We had endeavoured, so far as it is possible to do so, to prepare ourselves and the men for these high altitudes by walking all the intermediate passes from the Zoji on to Leh. Not only did we train ourselves gradually uphill, but we also carried our theory so far as by degrees to increase the pace up some of the easier passes. Whether the theory of previous training is of universal application or not it is impossible to say, but the fact remains that neither my companion nor myself was ever affected with either headache or nausea during the whole time spent in North-West Tibet, and that, too, living at an average of 16,000 to 17,000 feet for about two months.

In addition to the physical training referred to, we made use of all the usual palliatives—feeding sparsely, eating pieces of chocolate at frequent intervals, and taking pinches of chlorate of potash. That the natives are not immune we found to our cost; for the Punjaubi servant who had arranged to accompany me throughout the whole journey collapsed, and had to be sent back to India. Some of our caravan men were also affected, but they, perhaps, had more physical strain in helping the animals than we had. To carry a load, or in any way to interfere with the action of the heart and lungs, is, I believe, sufficient to bring on an attack, when otherwise no ill effect would be felt. So far can this be proved, that we found, from watching the natives, that the best position to assume while climbing was to hold the body upright, and, as they did, carry one's *khud* stick held across the small of the back through the elbow joints. Although, as has been said, we experienced no difficulty in becoming used to the rarity of the air, any but the most ordinary exertion will soon remind the traveller that he can take no liberties at these altitudes. To talk while climbing the Chang-la very soon reduced the rate of progress to a standstill. Later on, at greater heights, in blowing the nose, to cover the mouth with the handkerchief and to continue walking produced a choking effect. To smoke and face even a gentle incline were two actions quite incompatible. To crawl while stalking is most exhausting and cannot be continued, while any attempt to run, even though it be only a hundred yards, is to fall down gasping. Strange as these unusual experiences may sound to those who dwell almost at sea-level, the cause is no secret in spite of native theories. The explanation is simple and natural. At such heights the amount of air and oxygen taken into the lungs at each inhalation is considerably less than what would enter them at sea-level. To right this state of affairs the climber endeavours to inhale more oxygen, unconsciously, perhaps, breathes quickly and more powerfully, and so makes matters worse.

The actual causes of these symptoms are thus easily defined, being first the deficiency of oxygen in the air; secondly, a diminished atmospheric pressure; thirdly, deficient moisture.

Towards the summit of the Chang-la, my pony, which I was leading, stopped every fifty yards. Though not so distressed as those carrying loads, he continued to heave great gasps, and his heart could be felt thumping painfully against his ribs. Our caravan ponies showed no particular signs of distress beyond what might have been expected, but three of the hired animals collapsed exhausted immediately upon gáining the summit of the pass.

Having reached Tankse, we found the man from Leh who had been sent ahead to arrange for the purchase of the necessary yak.

We had hoped to find everything ready, and that there would be no necessity to camp more than the night; but as usual, where time and an Asiatic come in contact, our hopes were vain. A conclave of the elders revealed the fact that a severe epidemic had raged all over the country the previous year,—over 2000 yak had succumbed to a species of foot-and-mouth disease, and of that number 300 in the Tanske-Durgu valley alone. As for selecting from a mob, as we had hoped to do, it was with the utmost difficulty, after a fortnight's scouring of the few surrounding hamlets, that thirty-five could be collected for us. We finally purchased thirty, pack saddles included, the price proportionately increased by the unusual scarcity.

From Tankse it had also been arranged by the British Commissioner at Leh that we should draw from the Government store the greater part of our grain.

The Tankse granary is a quaint spot even in that far-away hamlet, and consists of a small block of adobe buildings set inside a tiny grove of trees, which afford the only shade in the valley.

Going to inspect the grain, we stumbled from the glaring sunlight into a dark room, and before the eye could discern anything, were invited to climb to an upper storey by means of a crooked and very irregular ladder. In the centre of the upper room we found our grain spread out, a trifle of some seventy maunds.[1]

In order to weigh the grain—a very necessary proceeding—an antiquated arrangement was produced, consisting of two old skin scales hung by bits of mended string to a crooked stick. Together, these held 2 lb., and as we had to weigh between five and six thousand pounds, the prospect of our ever getting beyond Tankse appeared for the moment somewhat remote.

We all know the copy-book maxim, and the invention finally did appear, in the shape of a wooden pot, thirteen of which it was soon ascertained went to one maund.

This in the hands—and very dirty ones—of an ancient greybeard, eventually solved the problem. Squatting on the floor, half covered by the grain which he proceeded to measure, he incessantly sang the various number of pots in such a monotonous chant that we were soon driven below again, leaving the grain to Lall Singh to finish.

[1] 1 maund=82 pounds.

Between Tankse and the next pass, the Masemick, the Poongoon lake is passed. This considerable sheet of water forms the border line between Kashmir and the Chang-Chenmo. The lake lies at an elevation of nearly 14,000 feet above the sea-level, and though of a lovely deep blue colour is brackish to the taste.

On the western shores high snow-capped peaks reach over 18,000 feet, though these do not rise abruptly from the lake edge. An older lake level is clearly discernible, especially on the eastern shore, where indications show a previous height thirty feet above the present.

Our route lay past the north end of the lake, turning aside from a track leading along it to Rudok, at the southern end of the chain.

The Chang-Chenmo valley is a forerunner of the uninhabited plateaux which, with their surrounding higher mountain ranges, go to make up North West Tibet. Geographically it belongs to Kashmir, but in its physical characteristics it is part and parcel of that other lone land into which we were about to venture. To this sense of loneliness must be added the depressing effect produced by an entire absence of any kind of vegetation—for the few spots where tufts of grass afford scanty grazing for herds of antelope and kyang cannot be called by that name—or of any sign of human habitation.

By the time we had traversed the Chang-Chenmo, a highland waste composed of uninhabited valleys, the spell of that lonesome land was upon us. I have frequently been asked to describe that portion of Tibet through which our route lay, but have invariably failed to satisfy myself by the answer given. The main characteristic it undoubtedly possesses gives the key to its general description, and that is its vast solitariness. Who does not know the feeling of one's own insignificance and impotence in the face of stupendous natural surroundings? In Northern Tibet that feeling is never absent. Encircled on all sides by the eternal snows of those sublime regions, which stretch apparently without end as far as human vision can reach, What is man? Range upon range, peak behind peak, spotless in its intense purity, brilliant in the dazzling sunshine, the illimitable panorama stretches before him. How small and insignificant in comparison appears the existence of mere human beings!

It was upon the summit of the Masemick-la, slightly under 18,000 feet above sea-level, that we met the last European we were to see for nearly eight months. Though natural enough on the confines of India that he should be an Englishman, in this case an officer of the 15th Hussars in quest of heads, it was somewhat curious that the first European met by us in the far north-west of China should also have been an Englishman, in the latter case a gentleman in the service of the Bible Society. Exchanging greetings, and declining the kindly offer to empty his cigarette-case, we bade good-bye to our friend and set our faces towards the Tibet border now only a few miles distant.

Before reaching the last of the three high passes leading into Tibet we camped one night by some natural hot springs. These springs serve to break the deadly monotony in a valley which only differed from scores like it in the possession of a little grazing.

Already our yak began to require a rest; for one of the drawbacks attending the use of these patient but slow-moving beasts is that they are easily over-marched and then go off their feed. Their favourite pace can only be described as funereal, nor will anything on earth induce them to mend it. Great skill is required to handle them, and little short of a lifetime to learn the peculiar shrill whistle, the only noise to which they pay any attention. If, in addition to these accomplishments, the traveller is as expert as David was in the use of stones as missiles, he may hope, if he is sufficiently mis-guided, to take some share in the driving of his own yak.

Other and more engrossing details occupied our daily attention. The only help we could ever offer was to make certain that those beasts which did succumb to the hardships of the march should not be left to a lingering death.

While halting one day to rest the caravan, we explored the hot springs. The highest temperature discovered in any of the various pools did not exceed 65° Fahrenheit. The water in them is generally of a creamy white colour, but in some places a peaty brown. Slime of the same white colour oozes up continually, but the bottoms of the pools when disturbed show black mud. There is a slight salt-like deposit round some of the holes, but to the taste they are more sulphurous than salt. Short grass grows in the vicinity in hummicks. It is unsafe to try to cross the surface of the ground in the vicinity of the pools. In attempting to do so, the pony I was riding was engulfed over his knees.

In this valley we made our first acquaintance with the Tibetan hare. The attraction which drew them, no doubt, was the grass. A five-mile tramp produced five hares, though to maintain even that average it was necessary to have recourse to methods which partook more of the poacher than the sportsman.

The Tibetan hare has a woolly coat, rather long ears, and a long grey scut. The hind quarters are of a greyer tinge than the rest of the coat, which, as usual, nature had coloured to local surroundings. He is smaller than our English species, and though, owing to his woolly coat, he appears a fairly substantial beast, we found what appeared to be a heavy animal to be only five pounds. Fired by the hare hunt, we had arranged to look for larger game in the vicinity of camp the following morning. After an early meal we walked uphill in a side nullah for three miles, the equivalent perhaps of a nine-mile tramp on flat ground at sea-level. The nullah contained no tracks, nor did there appear to be any sign of game about. Asking one of our men what chance he thought there was, he calmly pointed to a snow-clad range eight miles beyond, saying that that was where he intended to begin, and adding that we might get back by 7 P.M. Having come out for a stroll, and being without food or ponies, we thought discretion the better part, so decided to return to camp and more pressing duties. Thus may a thirst for big game be temporarily quenched by the difficulty of combating the rarefied atmosphere on one's own feet.

A week of bad weather with rain and hail storms had caused us to fear the early approach of winter, but as we neared the last of the three high passes which lead into Tibet, a change in the weather took place. To say that North-West Tibet is, at any time, a cheerful climate, is to go beyond the truth, but to deny that it has its softer moments would be equally misleading.

The early portion of the day frequently raises hopes of favours to come. But a very slight acquaintance with the country is sufficient to induce a less optimistic view. Up to 9.30 A.M. we found it occasionally possible to sit outside our tents, basking in a sun of sufficient strength to warm the body thoroughly. Within half an hour, as often as not, it was hailing and snowing or both, while a westerly wind cut like a razor, chilling one to the bone. Were it not for the wind, the remorseless west wind, the country might just be bearable, but when Nature automatically switches on the daily sample at 9.30 A.M., and when that sample is such that no amount of skin coats can withstand it, mere human endurance must in the long-run succumb.

On September 16 we crossed the Lanak-la, which we made to be just under 18,000 feet above sea-level. It is the easiest of the three passes already referred to, so long as snow has not fallen, and in this respect we had timed our crossing well.

CHAPTER III.

ENTERING TIBET—THE DETECTION OF "THE LAMA"—ROBBERS—STALKING UNDER DIFFICULTIES—A HEAVY SLEEPING-SUIT—THE CURZON RANGE AND KITCHENER GROUP—CHARACTER OF THE LADAKI—HINTS ON TRANSPORT—THE HISTORY OF TIBET.

ONCE over the Lanak-la the traveller has entered Tibet proper, and may be forgiven for not being able to repress something of the feeling which must have crossed the minds of early ocean navigators when they found themselves far from any base, dependent for their very existence upon the favour of wind and weather. To carry our simile farther is to increase its force. In Tibet not only is the voyager dependent upon the favour of the climate for his actual safety, but his caravan is his ship, and the loss of the former to him is as the loss of the latter to the navigator. In either case the chances of surviving are small.

Among the discomforts attendant upon travelling in North-West Tibet, the entire absence of wood, or even brushwood, is not the least. What this means in ordinary camp-life everybody who has ever tried it knows. At the altitudes at which we were forced to live the discomfort caused by the absence of all fuel save *boortsa* and yak dung is easily imagined. *Boortsa* is a close-growing wormwood which has long roots. It is found in most parts of North-West Tibet, but not everywhere. At such altitudes man's hourly craving is for warmth, and it remains always unsatisfied.

Over the Lanak-la the country in places contained large herds of antelope. To obtain food is not difficult, but the attempt to add a good head to the collection is. So much so—owing partly to the physical difficulty of creeping and crawling at such a height, also to the fact that one might equally well endeavour to stalk on a billiard-table,—that the sportsman is soon content to spy without stalking.

One week after crossing the Lanak-la the hired men and their ponies who had accompanied us so far from Tankse had had enough of it. It was only by bribery that we had induced them to stick to us so far, and as they were becoming every morning less willing to leave camp we decided to pay them off. From the very start we had found that the men hired to look after the yak caravan were not to be trusted, and our suspicions were again aroused by their eagerness to drop a yak—not forgetting his load—without any valid reason. It did not at first occur to us that there was anything more in this than the usual laziness of the caravan men where their master's and not their own interests are concerned. But a circumstance which happened the day it became known the hired men were shortly to return, completely gave away the yak men and their little plot. Before quitting Leh strict instructions had been issued that a report of either ponies or yak having dropped out on the march should invariably be made as soon as those in charge reached camp.

At the daily inspection of animals one afternoon we found three yak missing, and no report had been made. Calling up the head driver, known in the caravan as "the Lama," from the filthy red robe he never took off, we questioned him as to the missing animals. The usual string of excuses and evasions was the only answer which could be got; so as it was necessary to make an example, we ordered out our tired ponies, and with "the Lama" in attendance on foot, rode back six miles to find just what we had expected. Quietly grazing within a short distance of one another were the three yak, and near to them their three loads of precious grain, a coat, and some other odds and ends. There could be little doubt now as to the meaning of what we had found. All had been carefully left behind, to be picked up by the hired men on their return towards Leh next day.

Of course "the Lama," falling on his knees, protested ignorance of everything, but as we had fairly caught him, it was a time to assert our authority. Collecting the yak and reloading them, we gave him to understand that he must drive them into camp that night, or nothing short of annihilation would atone for his wickedness. Then we ourselves mounted our ponies and rode back the six weary miles in a blinding snow-storm, finding our only consolation in the fact that "the Lama" was at that moment even more miserable than ourselves.

During the next few days one other *contretemps* occurred before we made it clear to our following that we intended to run our own show, and it happened thus: Having arranged one morning for an earlier start than usual, we were greeted on awakening with the depressing announcement that sixteen of the ponies were missing. The full significance of the loss did not at first strike us, owing to the fact that it was not unusual for the ponies to stray during the night in search of ground to graze upon.

Unless the weather was very bad, it was our custom to turn all the animals loose at dusk after their evening pound of grain had been eaten. Their own instinct usually kept them in some more or less sheltered nullah, and being, as we were, nightly camped by whatever water there was, the scattered tufts of grazing were as a rule to be found close at hand.

With the comforting reflection that nothing worse than a prolonged stray had happened, the pony-men not already away were sent to help in the search, while the daily packing of camp proceeded. Up till ten o'clock we possessed our souls in patience, with no news of the runaways. But as hour after hour passed, the situation began to appear serious. At 4 o'clock in the afternoon, as we were about to get on our ponies to join in the search, great was our relief to see first the caravan *bashi*, then all the ponies and the men descending the stony hillside behind the camp.

What happened was this. At about three in the morning the man on watch in camp dozed, as he afterwards confessed, overcome by the cold, and unable to keep awake. Finding their nearer approach unnoticed, the *chapkas* or robbers, who must for some nights have been waiting their opportunity, stole in and drove off seven of the best ponies. By the selection made there could be little doubt that they were in collusion with some one in the caravan. Not content with this haul, and their presence being still undiscovered, the robbers then removed nine more ponies, leaving behind only eight of the worst and least serviceable.

So far we probably learnt the true story of our loss, but to this day I am by no means certain that we were ever fully informed as to the true story of the recovery. The account given by the caravan *bashi*, and of course confirmed by the rest of the men, was that they found the tracks and had started to trace the ponies up one of the side nullahs. After fifteen miles they began to overtake the *chapkas*, but the latter, seeing that the game was up, and that the chances of escape with the proceeds of their midnight raid became momentarily less, gave over the attempt to drive off the mob of ponies, and themselves vanished among the network of surrounding nullahs.

Cross-questioned by us, the men individually stuck to their story, and being once more in possession of our animals we accepted the lesson with inward gratitude for their recovery, at the same time vowing by the Providence that watches over travellers such a thing should not occur again.

After parting with our hired men and purchasing from them a few of the best of their ponies, we turned our steps north towards the Kuen Lun mountains.

Previous accounts given by travellers who have penetrated into Central and Southern Tibet agree always in referring to the numberless herds of animals—antelope, yak, and kyang—which swarmed over the country through which they passed. It may be of interest from the point of view of natural history to state that the reverse was found to be the case in North-West Tibet. During the period spent by us in that inhospitable region, the only animals which could in any sense of the term be considered common were the Tibetan antelope, and these, never in large herds, practically disappeared as we approached the southern side of the Kuen Lun range.

Of yak and kyang we saw hardly any, and the bagging of our first and, as it turned out, only yak was marked as a red-letter day.

In order to provide meat for the followers, to enjoy a better chance of sport, and to select a spot to camp at in the evening, it was our custom for one of us to ride each day ahead of the caravan. The other always remained with it to keep an eye upon stragglers, to watch that the pedometer wheel was properly run, and to exercise a general supervision.

One day I had been lucky enough to knock over a fair antelope head at a height of 17,300 feet and at a somewhat long range, and, as usually happens in fulfilment of the adage that to him who hath shall be given, fortune decreed that it was again my turn for advance-guard when we came across the first yak. It was a bright and, for Tibet, windless morning when one of the men, who was with me some distance ahead of the caravan, suddenly uttered the word *doong* (yak), pointing at the same time to a black speck upon the nearest ridge to our left. A glance through a 12-power Zeiss glass soon confirmed the man's statement, and I turned my pony back as quickly as possible towards the caravan, in order to exchange the light .303 rifle I was carrying for a .500 express. In ten minutes, joined by the caravan *bashi*, I had started on the hardest stalk I have ever attempted. The difficulty of crawling and creeping at such altitudes has already been noticed. When to the physical disability is added the fact that one is clad in a heavy skin coat, also that one has to carry with one's own hand a .500 express rifle, those who have shot in the higher ranges in Kashmir will not need to be reminded how helpless the stalker feels.

Before we reached the first ridge, three-quarters of a mile from the caravan, the yak had disappeared. Guessing at the direction in which he had fed, I succeeded in gaining the far side of a low valley without exposure, but only just in time to see the yak once more disappear slowly over the next ridge ahead. So far the wind was in my favour, but it was very apparent that human powers were no match in the way of climbing for those of a yak born and bred at such heights. Should the beast continue to feed on, even as slowly as he was doing, I felt that no efforts I could make would suffice to get me a shot, but for an hour and five minutes I stuck to my yak.

At the end of that time, after the usual checks and disappointments, by luck I managed to get into position within 200 yards, on a rocky knoll rather above him. Up the last rise, a fairly stiff one, but not over 150 feet high, I was obliged to stop every twenty-five yards gasping for breath, the heavy rifle carried being the final straw. It was over two minutes before I dared take the shot, even after crawling into position, and then, so heavily did my heart thump, that it required four bullets, all of which went home, but not all in the right place, before my follower dared run in to perform the last rites according to Mohammedan custom.[1]

Reference has already been made to the cruel effect of the daily west wind in Northern Tibet. In its wearing monotony it is ably seconded by the equally piercing cold at night. As the middle of October came, and the thermometer fell still lower, so our dread of the twelve hours after sundown increased. By 3 or 4 P.M. the daily march was usually ended, and by 6 P.M. the day's work finished. After pitching the tents and seeing to the animals, the next most important matter was the collection of such fuel as could be secured. A pile of *boortsa* was generally available, and about sufficed to boil the water for tea, to fry some antelope steak, and to make the half-dozen chupatties we could afford to allow ourselves.

The evening meal disposed of, a pipe followed, and then the worst portion of the twenty-four

[1] Mohammedans will not eat meat unless killed by a Mohammedan. *Halalling* is the cutting of the animal's throat.

hours was before us. Hitherto, like the rest of the world, we had been in the habit of undressing at bed-time. But in Tibet yet another new experiment had to be faced. In civilised countries the lighting of bedroom candles denotes that the time to undress for bed is approaching. But Tibet has no pretensions to be considered civilised. There, on the contrary, it is the signal for donning all the available clothing which could by any means be squeezed into the sleeping-bags with which we were provided. During the daytime the thickest English shooting clothes, with an extra jersey, formed the foundation of our kit. Over these each of us wore a coat — warm — British, — incidentally be it remarked, the best article of clothing our army ever possessed, — a puttoo muffler, fur cap and gloves, or, according to the state of the weather, a huge skin coat. To add to such a costume might seem difficult: to sleep in it absurd: yet I must so far trespass on the credulity of my readers as to ask them to believe that we did both.

The tents we occupied were provided by the well-known Elgin Mills at Cawnpore, and were some eight feet square, single fly, but double lined. Anything better either in workmanship or for packing it would be difficult to find. During our long tramp they served many uses, but I doubt if their walls ever saw a funnier sight than our nightly robing for bed, for the inside must then have looked more like a theatrical dressing-room than anything else.

By the time the caravan began to approach the

southern border of the Kuen Lun, constant exposure, lack of nutrition, and daily marching had had their usual effect upon the animals.

One evening found us descending a low pass 17,450 feet above sea-level. To the west rose a magnificent range, covered with eternal snow, in all the grandeur of untrodden peaks. In the lower valleys the declining sunlight lit up the glacier edges with exquisite ice-green tints. The range ran for eleven miles, bordering the valley we were about to traverse. At the foot of the slope just descended we sought for a spot to camp, but not finding one were forced at last to set up the tents on the bare plain, flat as a board but for the snow, without fuel, grazing, or water, except such as the melted snow afforded. That night we sacrificed the wheel-box in order to provide sufficient fuel to boil water for the tea. The inbred careful habits of our Indian surveyor had so far caused him to treasure the wheel-box; but that night, I think, even his scruples lapsed when the alternative presented itself to his mind.

The following day's march was one of the worst we encountered in North-West Tibet.

For the first eight miles the direction took us across the dead level plain of the night before. Two small frozen lakes alone varied its monotony. About noon we arrived at the foot of a gentle ascent, up which we laboriously picked our way in ever-deepening snow. The ground was full of concealed holes and granite boulders. The slope led up on to a table-land nine miles across, on which the highest point was 18,100 feet above sea-level. The snow was only a foot or two deep, but so full of pitfalls and unseen rocks that it played utter havoc with the caravan. The cold was at times intense.

At its north-east end the plain gradually descends into a deep valley, through which a stream, probably the head waters of the Kiria river, forces its way through a sheer cut gorge in the high range already referred to.

As we quitted the table-land, a northerly storm swept down on us straight from the nearest peaks, adding the final straw to the misery all were enduring. After a march of nearly ten hours we camped for the night, intending, if the valley we were in offered the grazing we hoped for, to give men and animals several days' rest. Miserable day as we had spent, our situation that night was an improvement. Sitting in the comparative comfort of the little tents, we found revenge,—for the unholy upland is handed down to posterity on our Survey map as "The Devil's Plain."

One of the chief charms in life is, we know, its contrasts. And the more suddenly these follow one another the more pleasure do we derive from them. After the experience of the previous weeks, the valley in which we were camped afforded just such a contrast. Though not exactly the vale of Kashmir, it yet contained both grass and water—the former, even so late in the season, better than any our animals had enjoyed since leaving India. The last few marches had also completely worn out the yak, half of whom had been left three days in the rear to follow on more slowly. For these it was absolutely necessary to wait, and when, after three days, they were brought on by the aid of men and ponies sent back to help them, it was equally imperative that they should have time to recover. Late in the season as it now was, our chief fear lay in the fact that winter might be upon us any day. Should such a blow fall, the passage of the dreaded Kuen Lun mountains would have become almost impossible.

During the seven days spent in the valley, which is known to the natives of Polu as Baba Hatan, we were able to make a thorough overhaul of ponies, packs, and camp gear. Daily marching in such a climate affords little chance for the stitch in time, nowhere more necessary. The Survey work also had its obligations. Nor did any member of the caravan more richly deserve the temporary respite from continued motion than Lall Singh, our Indian surveyor. In the daily plotting and measuring connected with a survey such as he was engaged on, no mean task is accomplished. When, in addition, the unusual physical and climatic disabilities are remembered, no praise can be too high for the devotion to duty which prompts such endurance.

From the sheltered spot occupied by our camp the view was like a glimpse of unknown worlds; and inured as we had become to a constant study of a certain type of nature's most exquisite scenery, we never grew tired of that entrancing panorama.

Six miles distant at its upper end the valley was hemmed in by the range of snow-clad mountains previously mentioned. Such a landmark do these

Baba Hatan Valley, N. W. Thibet.

Crossing the Ak-su-la, N. W. Thibet.

form, that though no new discovery was involved, we felt that as a geographical feature they deserve to carry a separate name. We took the liberty of giving them that of the Curzon Range. Opposite to the latter, on the north-east side of our camp, stood another most striking group of rugged ridges, also covered with eternal snows. On either hand both offered as grand and awe-inspiring a view as the human eye could wish for. Here, again, we felt that such a unique mass of peaks deserved recognition and a separate entity, so took the liberty of giving it the name of the Kitchener Group.

Our tents were pitched close to the bank of the stream, which at this point carved a zigzag course through a succession of weird gorges composed of coal-black jagged rock. Through them the water rushes down a succession of rectangular bends. Now and again the stream emerges into the open valley, only once more to be hemmed in and compelled to force a passage through other and equally fantastic cuttings. Above these latter, and near the stream, both sides of the narrow valley are sown with small boulders of the same black rock. In places these are piled into grotesque heaps, which afford, as we afterwards discovered, tempting cover for the hares which inhabit the valley.

After the week's rest we left the Baba Hatan camp, feeling able to face whatever difficulties the crossing of the Kuen Lun mountains might have in store.

Three days later found the caravan climbing from the great central table-land of Tibet towards the southern edge of the mass of mountain ridges which separate it from Chinese Turkestan. The former area, part of which an endeavour has been made to describe in the last chapter, comprises one of the grandest Alpine regions in the world.

The western portion is made up of the more or less fertile valleys of the Indus and Shiok rivers. North of these are the Ling-Zi-Thang and the Aksai-Chin,—vast highlands, like all North-West Tibet uninhabited and uninhabitable. To these uplands the Karakoram mountains form the northern buttress, elevating this unique series of plateaux thousands of feet above the central basin of Chinese Turkestan.

The eastern portion comprises the uninhabited treeless wastes of Northern Tibet, which eventually slope by more gentle gradients to the borders of China proper, increasing somewhat in fertility as the traveller passes east.

Geographically, Tibet itself is divided into two grand portions. One is that whose waters collect to join the Brahmaputra river, the other that drained by the Indus river and its tributaries. The line of separation lies a little to the east of lakes Manasarawar and Rawan-Rud. Western Tibet is again divided by Tibetans into three portions,—Little Tibet or Baltistan, Middle Tibet or Ladak, and Upper Tibet, which is the portion outside the territory of the Maharajah of Kashmir. In the mountain ranges of Western Tibet the average height of the ridges does not exceed 1000 or 2000 feet above the passes, many of which are scarcely at all lower than the highest ridge-crests in which they are situated. The principal ranges average 20,000 feet, the minor ranges from 17,000 to 18,000 feet. Peaks are found in various ranges from 21,000 to 25,000 feet.

Tibet is also classified by Tibetans into two parts—Reng and Chang-Thang. The first signifies a deep valley, low and warm enough for agricultural occupation, and, generally speaking, a country containing such valleys. Chang-Thang means the north plain, but, in common, an elevated plain or wide open valley, too high and too cold for any but pastoral uses. Chang-Thang is the prevailing character in Eastern Ladak and in the north-west of Tibet; Reng of the country nearer Leh and of Western Ladak.

Tibet, as a name for their country, is unknown to the people. Tibet or Tibat, as it is pronounced in Baltistan and Kashmir, is simply called Bod in Ladak. A Tibetan is a Bod-pa to Ladakis.

In Eastern Tibet the words To-Po or Ten-Pen are sometimes used to name the country. Tibet is called by the Chinese Hsi-tsang.

The people of Ladak, like their neighbours in lower Kashmir, do not enjoy any great reputation for courage or manliness. Our experience of them, however, led us to form the opinion that they are considerably better than their reputation. They are a hardy race, and think nothing of physical exposure and privation which few Europeans could stand. During many days and nights, spent at elevations varying between 16,000 and 18,000 feet, the men who formed our caravan lived in the open, their only shelter from the piercing winds and the snow being the nightly zareba they made of the grain sacks, pack-saddles, &c. Their marching powers cannot be excelled; their commissariat is as simple as that of any human being; they do not succumb to sickness, even under unusual trials; and, last but by no means least, the best of them are always cheerful and willing for more work at a pinch. With such characteristics the material cannot be bad. It is probable that in close contact with British officials the Ladaki might earn a higher reputation than he now enjoys.

Of the Tibetans I am unable to speak. In the country traversed by us no human habitation was ever seen, not even a nomad tent. That these districts—that is to say, the country round and south of Aport Tso—are used by the Tibetans for summer grazing is well known. North of a line running east and west through Aport Tso, North-West Tibet is entirely uninhabited throughout the year.

The Changas or Champas are the shepherds of the Chang-Thang, while the inhabitants of the Reng are called Rengpas or Lowlanders.

The climate of this area has one common factor in the dryness of the atmosphere and the rarefaction of the air. The latter condition is more particularly applicable to the higher plateaux and valleys of Tibet, but the symptoms caused by it are felt by some people even at Leh, at a height of only 11,320 feet.

The summer in the Chang-Chenmo valley and North-West Tibet is a very brief one. Round Leh it is not much more extended, though the temperature, as is to be expected, rises higher. The average maximum in August is 78° ; the average minimum in August 46°. The average daily temperature in August 75° ; the barometrical pressure 19.65 inches. On August 24 the temperature in the sun (black bulb) was 130°, and has been as high as 158°.

The passes are, as a rule, not open before the beginning of June. Even then the snow is described by Captain Rawlin, who crossed them in 1903, as "deep and soft" on the Maoemick-la.

At the time we crossed the same pass, on September 9, there was no snow whatever on it, and only a few patches on the east side. We had been warned that snow might fall any day after the beginning of September, but I am of opinion that the winter does not begin in the higher regions as early as is supposed. No snow at all, which lay, fell until September 28, and even then it was not enough to interfere with the progress of a caravan.

On the 16th October we began the crossing of the Kuen Lun main range over the pass called by the natives the Kazil-diwan, 17,000 feet above sea-level, yet all along the route to the south of the pass there was very little snow. On the north side it was 2 and 3 feet deep.

The list of temperatures and weather given in the appendix will enable the reader to form the best idea of the autumn. The winter may be said to last from the end of October or beginning of November until early in May. If there can be said to be a wet season it must be placed in the summer months, for practically there is little spring.

From the point of view of weather, as has already been mentioned, the greatest drawback to travel in North-West Tibet is the west wind, next the changeable nature of the climate from hour to hour. The west wind usually rises between 10 and 12 A.M., continues blowing half a gale until about 4 P.M., then either dies away or continues all day in squalls until late in the evening. More often than not the nights are still. From sunrise until 8 or 9 A.M. is the best part of the day. Even until as late as the middle of October it was much warmer to breakfast outside one's tent in the sun than inside.

Of the variableness of the climate, hardly a day passes without affording some example. I have more than once been sitting basking in the sun shortly after sunrise outside the tent without a skin coat on, and within an hour found myself on the march in blinding snow, wrapped up in all the skins I possessed. It is essential to have always at hand an extra skin coat, also to be able to shed one's garments at any time if necessary.

The resources both of Ladak and North-West Tibet are extremely limited. It may in fact be said that unless minerals are found to exist, the latter place has none. In Ladak, within the area traversed by us, only sufficient agricultural produce is grown in the various valleys to meet the wants of the inhabitants. A small reserve store of grain is maintained at Tankse, and some at Durgo, but with difficulty. What surplus grain accrues to the people is yearly bartered with the Rudok men for salt and *pashm*. The price of the former is prohibitive if brought from India, and it has therefore to be obtained from Western Tibet. The Tibetan prefers grain in exchange to cash, as he cannot eat the latter.

The commerce is confined to the local barter already referred to with the Tibetans, and such as is produced by the passage of the big merchants trading between India and Yarkand.

The labour is to a large extent undertaken by the women, the men seeking employment as coolies or caravan men on the main road from Kashmir.

Nothing is of greater importance to the would-be traveller than the question of transport; and a few additional words on that available throughout the country we traversed on first quitting India may not be out of place.

At such altitudes it is hardly necessary to state that wheeled traffic is out of the question. At the same time, could a light cart be carried over the intermediate high passes, there is scope for the use of them in many parts of North-West Tibet. Some such vehicle as was used by the Japanese in the late war would be the ideal kind.

Before reaching Leh from Simla, I had telegraphed to Captain Patterson, the British Joint Commissioner, asking him to put forward such arrangements as he could for our caravan; at the same time suggesting that mules and donkeys might be collected.

Upon arrival at Leh, in addition to other animals, we found waiting ten mules. These were very fine animals, and had come from Yarkand. They would have suited our wants admirably, but, unfortunately, the price was beyond our means; so with regret we had to confine ourselves to the purchase of ponies.

Six of these mules were at once taken by Captain Patterson for Indian mountain-battery work, at an average price of Rs. 175. They stood 13.1 to 13.3 hands high, and were of great power and bone. The Yarkandi traders put on their own big ponies three maunds (240 lb.) I have myself seen ponies being thus loaded, and the mules would easily carry as much. The only doubt we had as to the superiority of mules is this,—in Tibet, the daily grain ration that can be carried for animals is very limited. As already related, it is useless to suggest that more transport can be taken to do so, for this is not the case. More transport means still more animals to carry food for the first lot, and so on *ad infinitum.*

Every traveller who has entered Tibet finds eventually that a certain number of his animals must be taken simply to be dropped, as the grain they carry is eaten by the rest. After much consideration we decided to take yak for this purpose, and although there are objections to these beasts as means of transport, I should do the same again, but next time send them on in advance of the main caravan.

It has been said that our own ration was 2 lb. per pony, and besides the grain, they picked up what they could. This is never much, and at times, for as long as twenty-four hours, nothing at all. Under such conditions, the point to be weighed is, would a big mule be able to keep his strength, and would he continue to carry as much as a smaller animal who could retain his full vigour upon a lesser daily ration?

For travelling over bad country, for stamina,

The Hill-pony of Northern Kashmir.

for working upon starvation rations, for ease in loading, and for non-liability to stray from camp, the donkey has no equal. A good big donkey will continue to carry almost as much as a pony (150-160 lb.), and he can keep up the ordinary caravan rate of marching—an average of two to two and a-half miles an hour. As an all-round transport animal for Tibet the donkey is very hard to beat, and I have still a tender spot in my heart for one very ancient male who accompanied us,—as game a specimen of his kind as ever lived.

Next in value to the donkey, and only placed below the former in the scale on account of requiring more food, comes the hill-pony of Northern Kashmir. For mountain work, either under saddle or pack, nowhere have I met his equal. Those we constantly rode were little animals under 13.1 hands in height; but they rarely failed us, however impossible the ground we asked them to negotiate. Of the twenty-eight ponies who left Leh in our caravan, only six lived to reach the confines of China proper. Of that number five were altogether worn out, and only one survivor was able, with careful nursing, to complete the journey to Peking. As he had been our daily companion for so many months, I was loth to part with the little fellow, so brought him to England, where he now spends his days running in a field at home, wondering, no doubt, where all the grass he sees comes from.

Of the yak enough has already been said to show that they are more a necessity than an acquisition. Out of the thirty we took with us, seventeen, thanks entirely to our own care, survived up to Baba Hatan. After that the passage of the Kuen Lun killed seven more, leaving ten able to march into Polu, the first village we reached on the northern side of the mountains.

Before leaving the question of transport, a word should be said for sheep as beasts of burden. Their services in the salt trade, carried on between Tibet and Ladak, are in constant request. They are used in hundreds, and their great merit lies in the fact that they can just exist where no larger animal could find enough grazing to live on. Had we realised their value at starting, a drove would certainly have formed part of the caravan, though an amusing incident which happened in the Chang-Chenmo serves to illustrate the risks they run.

Arriving on the banks of a stream, we found it necessary to cross its somewhat swollen waters twice within a mile. On the first occasion, though running strong, the stream was safe for laden beasts, and the caravan got over with difficulty. On the second occasion the river was wider, and we had no means of judging the most likely spot to ford it. Venturing in to try and find a crossing, the little pony I was riding was nearly swept off his legs. The yak, in their usual contrary way, and in spite of our united efforts, chose their own spot, and suffered badly in consequence,—some getting beyond their depth and soaking much of the grain. Five sheep we then had with us fared worse, for they were swept off their legs

Breakfast in Thibet.

Nursing an old companion.

and carried down like corks, swimming, however, to the right bank in the end.

No reference has hitherto been made to the early history of Tibet. To many travellers—more especially in Asia — the early records of any country through which they may journey form, if not the greatest, certainly one of the most lasting pleasures connected with their wanderings.

Until the Younghusband Expedition succeeded in piercing once for all the veil which had for so long screened Lhasa from the world, a halo of mystery hung over Tibet. Nor was this entirely due to the ignorance of the country. Authentic records already existed, and not a few intrepid travellers—such as Bower and Littledale, Welby and Malcolm, Detreuil de Rhins and Sven Hedin, not to mention Sarat Chandra Dass—had crossed the country from various sides. The mystery hung rather on the fact that Lhasa itself was able to remain a forbidden city. In spite of this mystery, the history of Tibet varies in no way from that of all nations in being associated with the history of others whose borders are contiguous.

As early as the year 122 B.C. mention is made in Chinese annals of intercourse with India, then known as Shintu or Thianchu. A century later, in 65 A.D., a certain Chinese emperor, in consequence of a dream, sent ambassadors to Thianchu to obtain instructions in the doctrines of Buddha.

Throughout the greater portion of the third and fourth centuries political intercourse between India and China seems to have been interrupted, although a sea-trade existed at the end of the latter century. Its commencement probably dates from 317-320 A.D., and was at first between Ceylon and China.

During the fifth century various Indian kingdoms repeatedly sent tribute to the Chinese emperors; and in 605 A.D. another Chinese emperor of the Sui dynasty, having formed some ambitious projects, sent to try and induce the kingdoms of Tibet and India to render him homage; but those of India declined to do so, which much enraged the emperor.

About 646 A.D. a Chinese army, assisted by the kings of Tibet and Nepaul, invaded the north-eastern border of India with success, taking many cities, and carrying away one of the Indian kings a prisoner to China.

In 667 A.D., according to the Chinese annals, "the kings of the five Indes"—viz., of Eastern India, Western India, Southern India, Northern India, and Central India—all sent to offer homage to the great Emperor of China.

In 713 A.D. an embassy came to the Emperor Hi-Wang-Tsun from Chandrapida, the then king of Kashmir, acknowledging allegiance. A successor and brother also offered homage, and requested the emperor to send troops into Kashmir, being induced to do so by the rising power of Tibet.

From 713-731 A.D. repeated missions are reported from the different kingdoms of India, one of which begged aid against the Tibetans, asking at the same time that an honorific title might be bestowed upon the Indian monarch's army. The Chinese potentate, after the manner of his countrymen, found this the easiest and most convenient mode of conveying his patronage, so decreed the title of "the Army which cherishes virtue." About this period there is frequent mention in Chinese annals of relations with two kingdoms called Great and Little Poliu, which lay between Kashgar and Kashmir. There is little doubt that the kingdoms in question were Ladak and Baltistan, which were known to a much later date as Great and Little Tibet.

The Tibetans at this time, *circa* 800 A.D., were becoming powerful and troublesome neighbours. After the date mentioned, for a long time no political intercourse is heard of, though there are frequent notices of the visits of Indian Buddhist devotees to the court of China, or of Chinese Buddhists visiting India for religious objects. These pilgrimages, probably more infrequent as the indigenous Buddhism of India gradually perished, had not altogether ceased even in the middle of the fourteenth century.

In the reign of the great Emperor Akbar, the well-known mission of Benedict Goës was despatched from India to China by the advice of Father Jerome Xavier, then at the court of the Emperor Akbar at Delhi, as head of the Mogul Mission. Even at that date merchants were in the habit of trading between India and China, using as the shortest route that from Lahore to Kashmir, thence across the Karakoram pass to Yarkand and Kashgar, and so by the Thian-shan Nanlu to Chia-yu-kuan and China proper. Goës, however, chose the longer and more frequented route by Lahore, Peshawar, Kabul, Badakshan, and the Oxus Valley, thence across the Pamirs to Yarkand.

In later years various conquerors have occupied Kashmir from the fall of the Mogul Empire until the practical absorption of that country into the British Raj in 1846. In 1841 Raja Gulab Singh, after conquering Ladak and Baltistan by the help of Zorawar Singh's troops, turned his attention to Tibet. After making an abortive attempt to occupy the country, he was driven back into Ladak, and Zorawar Singh lost his life. Upon the summit of the Chang-la the remains of a wall are still to be seen. The wall was built by the Tibetans to keep out Zorawar Singh's army,—a childish proceeding repeated by them, as we know, in their endeavour to keep Sir Francis Younghusband out of Lhasa.

CHAPTER IV.

THE PASSAGE OF THE KUEN LUN—A PERILOUS DESCENT—A MISERABLE CAMPING-GROUND — GOLD "POCKETS"— A PLEASANT SURPRISE— THE LUXURY OF EGGS — THE WELCOME SIGHT OF A TREE — A HOSPITABLE BEG—ENTERING POLU IN RAGS.

It is now time to return to the caravan which we left on the borders of the promised land,—that is to say, a land of greater promise than the forsaken wastes we were about to quit.

With such a character as we have given to this latter country, it might be supposed that Nature would have taken little pains to hedge it off from the neighbouring world. But this is far from the case. On the northern side she has planted, in the shape of the dreaded Kuen Lun, such a barrier that even the daring Russian explorers, Kozloff and Roboroffsky, were fain to admit themselves baffled in their attempts to find a feasible route other than the one we made use of.

On October 16 we found ourselves commencing the passage of the Kuen Lun. This occupied us five days, and in that time we covered rather over thirty miles in transit.

Riding ahead of the caravan that morning, Captain Layard, Lall Singh, and myself had by mistake climbed a pass 17,000 feet above sea-level. Our guide being most uncertain about any possible passes, we were obliged to fend for ourselves. As we dragged our ponies up the pass, it seemed impossible for the caravan to ascend, and this proved to be so. They were afterwards unable to negotiate it, finding their way over an easier neck farther to the west. Upon the northern side of the one we crossed fresh snow lay eighteen inches to two feet deep, and a wind raged which was even for Tibet more cruel than usual.

After rejoining the caravan, the view which met our eyes as we gazed through the now falling snow northward into and over the Kuen Lun was one neither my companions nor myself are ever likely to forget. At our feet, and on three sides, stretching apparently without end, lay the wildest and most forbidding jumble of mountain-ranges, peaks, and gorges imaginable. Of all shapes, crossing and recrossing in every direction, needle-pointed or flat, rugged and broken, they had only one common feature, and that lay in their apparently inaccessible nature. To add to this grand but uninviting prospect, snow to the depth of two or three feet covered the northern slopes of all the ranges. In the immediate foreground we stood upon what appeared to be the edge of a sheer *khud*, down which our guide gave us vaguely to understand the route lay.

Owing to the ignorance and stupidity of this man, it was then far too late in the day to attempt such a descent. Had we received any idea of what was before us, it would have been easy to have

In the Kuen Lun Mountains.

The Passage of the Kuen Lun Gorges.

camped upon the southern slope of the pass. As it was, we stood between the devil and the deep sea. Necessity and inclination said advance; prudence whispered be careful how you undertake such a step. To recross the pass was out of the question, so the plunge had to be made. Bidding the caravan remain, Layard and I started the downward climb in hope of finding some possible track. Leading our ponies, we took the slope at the only feasible angle, stumbling all the time into concealed holes, and tripping over boulders covered with frozen snow. At first we followed our guide, but after he had led us down several places, each one more impossible than the other, and from which we were obliged to extricate ourselves and our ponies, he was finally brought up short. A hopeless scramble had landed us on the edge of a waterfall in a small torrent-bed, from which all hope of farther downward progress was barred. Before we had time to consider the next move, our guide, having no pony to lead, and seeing a chance for himself, quietly left us and endeavoured to climb down. From our point of view this did not seem to be altogether playing the game, so in angry tones we hailed him to hold on. Whether it was his anxiety to reach the bottom, or his fears at the tone of our voices, I cannot say. We saw him suddenly lose his hold, then his balance, and finally, to our great amusement, roll headlong down a small cliff into six feet of snow below.

Having disposed of our friend, our own predicament became pressing. To get the ponies and ourselves up again was a dangerous piece of work, but luckily a Ladak pony can climb with any goat; so after a ten minutes' struggle we once more got on comparatively safe ground.

All this time the caravan still remained at the summit of the descent. That they would ever get down that night, if at all, without losing half the loads and ponies, seemed hardly possible. We had, however, made a track of a kind, and it was by following this, with the loss of only one yak, that the caravan eventually reached the bottom. Great was our relief, after waiting an hour and a half, to see the first lot of ponies appear. In a dry watercourse thirty yards across we found sufficient room to pitch the tents badly; and there, huddled together without grass or water save the snow, we passed our first night in the gorges of the Kuen Lun.

While descending from the pass on the previous afternoon we had dropped over 1000 feet on the near side. The first two hours the following morning we descended another 2000 feet, so rapid is the fall from the north to the south side of this gigantic barrier.

Our route at starting led down the gully in which we had camped, and at a point where the former ran into a larger stream-bed we came upon three men, the first human beings met with since leaving Kashmir. Which of the two parties was the more astonished it is hard to say, nor could we obtain anything but a few words from them, owing to the fact that they came from Polu and spoke a Turki dialect only. Our followers managed to ascertain that the men were gold-diggers returning after their summer campaign in the Kuen Lun. Leaving the stream-bed, our guide struck into a side gorge, down which we fought our way all day over going of the most hopeless kind. On either hand rock walls rise hundreds of feet above the stream-bed, the latter being strewn with boulders of all sizes. Never straight for more than a few yards, the bed was only wide enough to hold the half-frozen waters of a little torrent, which descended in pools and small falls, down which the wretched animals slid and fell.

By three o'clock in the afternoon we had been marching for eight hours. Layard and myself had gone on in the apparently hopeless quest of a spot where even one tent might be erected. A more than usually impossible torrent-bed had driven us to climb out on to a small spur overhanging the stream, and there we decided to pass the night. After waiting for three hours in the now fast-falling darkness, we could just make out the leading ponies of the caravan as they appeared a few hundred yards away round the nearest bend in the gorge. They halted, and the headman came on to say that the animals were played out, and that they could come no farther. Mindful of the shelter even a small tent affords, we endeavoured to induce him to alter his opinion, but were soon convinced of the impossibility of the caravan moving even that short distance. Night had fallen, and as the mountain could not come to Mohammed, Mohammed, as we know, had to accommodate the mountain. To climb down into the stream-bed, dragging our ponies after us, was as much as we could manage. Sliding and falling down the slippery rocks to the frozen edge of the stream, we reached the spot where the caravan had halted to find men and animals huddled up miserably among the mass of boulders which here almost obstructed the stream. A few of the yak we knew to have gone ahead earlier in the afternoon, but how or where they had managed to leave the torrent-bed could not in the dark be discovered.

There was nothing for it but to make the best of a bad job, and to help men and animals to be as little uncomfortable as circumstances would allow where they were. Everybody set to work to unload the beasts, and that done all was done that could be.

The men settled themselves under the shelter of the biggest boulders. Each animal either lay down or remained forlornly standing where he had halted, and we ourselves, with Lall Singh, crept into some disused gold "pockets," dug out under the rocky sides of the gorge.

A more weird scene than the latter presented as the moon rose sufficiently high to throw its pale light into the depths of that wild cutting, it has never been my fortune to see. A few facts may perhaps serve to illustrate the uphill task our caravan had that day been obliged to face. The torrent-bed down which they had struggled varied from three or four feet to half as many yards in width Though still running water in the middle, either side was usually frozen some feet out from the boulders which lined it. The depth never exceeded 18 to 20 inches, except in occasional pools,

Our Caravan in the Kuen Lun.

A Camp in the Kuen Lun Gorges.

nor was there a single yard of level bottom throughout its entire length. Thirty-seven times that day had the stream to be forded, generally knee-deep in icy water; and four more yak and one of our biggest ponies was the price we had to pay.

At dawn the following morning we were all astir, every one being anxious to escape from such an inhospitable spot. To become the owner of a gold "pocket" many a man has before now sold himself to the devil. On waking that morning I would willingly have sold his sable majesty all the gold "pockets" to be found in the Kuen Lun for one hour of my own camp-bed.

We began the second day by being forced to carry every item of baggage out of the stream-bed up on to the tiny track we had missed the previous night. Each of the twenty-four ponies in turn had also to be pulled and pushed from the bed of the torrent up on to it. At no time easy, to reload animals on a path whose width prevents any approach to them except "fore and aft," savours more of the doings of the mad hatter in 'Alice in Wonderland' than of serious travellers. When, however, neglect to observe this precaution means a fall over a 60-feet cliff into a torrent-bed, little difficulty is experienced in taking the matter seriously. After some hours, owing to the above causes, as well as to the impracticable nature of the gorge, the caravan had only covered a few hundred yards. By eleven o'clock in the morning men and animals were thoroughly exhausted. We had covered but one mile and a quarter in actual distance, but what with carrying packs, continually lifting fallen ponies and reloading them, lowering the animals down bad bits and hauling them up worse, the men had had enough of it.

To take no thought for the morrow is a maxim often advisable to follow, particularly where a more than usually hard task must be carried through. In our case, however, the morrow was always the bogey. Whatever the day brought forth we usually feared worse for the next, though on this occasion we were wrong. About noon, just before we decided to camp, another party of six men came down the gorge. These also were gold-diggers, on their return to Polu after a summer spent digging for the precious metal in the mountains. The leader of the little band turned out to be the headman of that district, and although our two parties merely passed "the time of day," we had afterwards reason to bless the luck which sent the meeting.

Our camping-ground the third night was upon a narrow spur overhanging the torrent-bed. Upon it the animals found a few mouthfuls of grazing, and we some sand-holes, evidently used as resting-places by the gold-seekers. In these we slept. Just before dark we espied a herd of shapoo far up the cliff-side, and Layard essayed a stalk. The light was failing fast, and every minute counted against him, so it was necessary to take a long and difficult shot. Though unsuccessful this had the effect of starting the herd, and a fine sight it was to watch them dashing down the precipitous hillside into a side ravine to what appeared certain death.

On the fourth day we had hoped to be emerging

from the now hateful gorge, but were doomed to be disappointed. The march commenced by three of the ponies getting together on the goat-track we were endeavouring to follow, with the result that over they went, boxes and all. Having climbed down to pick up what we supposed would be the remains, we were agreeably surprised to find no serious damage. Having righted the loads, we dragged the beasts back on to the track, then the weary daily task recommenced. The torrent-bed was now impassable. In order to advance, it was necessary to climb and descend one spur after another from and to the stream-bed. As these spurs ran up to 300 and 400 feet above the torrent, and as they had almost sheer sides up and down which the 18-inch wide path led at a gradient of about one in four, their frequent recurrence proved killing to laden beasts. Such as the track is, it has been made by the invasion of the gold-diggers. These men usually carry their own packs, though donkeys are sometimes used. So severe is the work of track-making that not one inch more width is added than will suffice to allow of the passage of a donkey, and this was disastrous to us. In more than one place a jutting rock was sufficient to forbid the passage of a laden pony, so off had to come every single *yakdan* in the caravan in order that they might be carried round and reloaded on the far side of the rock. Twice, where the track led over more than usually perpendicular spurs, it became in each case a mere rock-ladder. Here, again, every pony had in turn to be pulled up and lowered down by hand. All day long the track continued thus, at one moment down to the torrent-level, at the end of the next hour winding dizzily up 300 or 400 feet, from whence a sheer slope carried the eye once more to the bottom. At noon, while halting for a short breathing-space, we enjoyed a great surprise. Clambering over the boulders ahead came a party of men the leader of whom at once made known his errand. Having saluted us, he intimated that he had come with his party from Polu, whence our friend the Beg, who had passed the day before, had despatched this little band of fifteen men with twelve donkeys to help us out. Not content with this, the Beg had also sent with the party an abundant and most welcome supply of fresh cakes, fruit, milk, and eggs, which, as the bearer of the good news informed us, was then waiting to be eaten not half a mile ahead. To hear of such luxuries would be enough to revive the spirits of the most hopeless castaways, and our party were by no means in such straits. Somewhat worn out as the caravan was, there was plenty of fight still left in the best of the animals, yet there is no shame in confessing that the complexion of the day changed from that moment. When, after half an hour's further struggle, we emerged into an opening in the gorge and found the reality spread upon the rocks, all our troubles vanished.

To appreciate fully the luxury of eggs it is, perhaps, hardly necessary to visit Tibet, though having done so may somewhat enhance the pleasure felt in once more meeting those simple adornments of the home breakfast-table. Our daily food for two months had consisted mainly of flour and meat, eaten twice in the twenty-four hours—not an enticing cuisine, nor one particularly fattening. May we therefore hope to be forgiven for the human weakness which made possible the sudden change from grave to gay, all on account of a few bodily comforts?

Although it required yet a fifth day's struggle before we were able to win our way through the Kuen Lun mountains, our difficulties were decidedly lessened by the aid of the relief party. The leader, with whom we afterwards became well acquainted at Polu, for it was in his house that the kindness of the Beg lodged us, was a most amiable old gentleman, the proud possessor of the right to wear the green turban, as also to be addressed as Hadji. Under his guidance we gradually approached the northern end of the interminable gorge, up to the last over the same infamous going. As we emerged, the character of the surrounding mountains began to change. The pure rock of the gorge-sides gave place to slaty deposit, while the lower spurs became more soft, the soil resembling loess of a grey dust colour, which the wind carried in clouds, forming a constant haze. We had dropped during the previous thirty miles from 17,700 feet to 9500 feet, and after descending below 10,000 feet the first signs of vegetation began to appear. Though exceedingly scanty, the few dried up rushes and briars to be seen were a relief to the eye, and it is hard even now to repress a smile upon recalling our excitement at meeting a tree. The track at the moment followed the edge of a narrow strip of cultivation which, although already harvested, savoured of vegetation. Below ran the same torrent we had followed for days, but, like its mountain cousins, so tamed here as to have lost all semblance of its former wild self. At the end of the cultivation the ground rose, and there at some distance from the ridge stood a solitary tree: great was the enthusiasm when it came into view, for it was the first we had seen since quitting India.

Clear of the main gorge, the character of the country undergoes a startling and rapid transformation. Instead of the rock cuttings and perpendicular cliffs, the track descends into rolling dust-coloured hills and open downs, at a height of 8400 feet. The latter are covered with a close-growing vetch, which in the spring probably affords excellent grazing. Not a vestige of trees, grass, or other vegetation is to be seen except the vetch. At some distance away from the mountains and entrance to the gorge, the sudden geological change is still more apparent. The last jagged range to the south, snow-clad throughout most of its length, gives way as though in one step to dust-coloured hills 2000 feet lower in height.

Pushing on to reach Polu that afternoon, we crossed the downs, to drop by steep sandy tracks hedged by coarse reed-grass into the valley in which the village itself stands. A mile out we were met by our friend the Beg, accompanied by a mounted cavalcade, who, as is the custom in such out-of-the-way spots, was anxious to do honour to the approaching guest.

It was naturally a great pleasure to find ourselves once more among fellow-men. At the same time, we rather wished that our reception had taken place in the dusk.

The Beg and his company, when they had passed us in the gorge, were birds of the same feather. Neither party had enjoyed the advantages civilisation is supposed to confer for many weeks; certainly neither Captain Layard nor myself had had our clothes off since crossing the Chang-la.

Now all was different, Riding fat good-looking ponies, our host's cavalcade appeared quite imposing, especially as he and his men were also well dressed in clean clothes and embroidered coats. We, on the other hand, must have presented a deplorable appearance. Exposure to wind and weather and, be it whispered, lack of soap and water, had tended to make us nearly as dark of skin as a clean Turki; besides which the cutting wind of Tibet had cracked and chapped both hands and faces somewhat badly. Manners, we know, maketh man, but what of clothes! The fur coats and boots which "Mr Cook" had provided us with in Srinagar had, at their first appearance, cast upon their possessors the air of respectability a well-made coat always imparts: now, alas! the reverse was the case. Like a ready-made suit which in a shop window looks the perfection of shape and fit, what more depressing garment can be conceived than the same suit after six months' wear? To much the same state had our skin coats descended. Alternately soaked by the snow and dried up by the sun, slept in, buttonless and torn, they hung together, and that was all that could be said in their favour.

From the above description it may easily be imagined that our personal appearance cannot have impressed the good people of Polu; but luckily in the East a traveller is mainly judged by the size of his following, and from that point of view our caravan was sufficiently extensive still to make up for its somewhat forlorn appearance.

CHAPTER V.

AN IDEAL PLACE FOR A REST-CURE—A HOUSE IN POLU—FLESH-POTS AND LUXURY—THE TURKIS OF POLU—HAWKS AND HAWKING—A DIPLOMATIC "DEAL" IN DONKEYS—THE KIRIA RIVER—TWO SELFISH *AKSAKALS*—THE OASIS OF KOOKHIA—KIRIA—A FRIENDLY AMBAN—CHINESE TURKESTAN—THE EASTERN TURKISH DIALECT—THE ANDIJANIS AS TRADERS.

To any highly-strung inhabitant of the West, worn out with the effort to keep pace with present-day social requirements, Polu is strongly recommended as a delightful spot in which to make a rest-cure. Hidden away at the foot of the Kuen Lun mountains, whose snowy peaks present a magnificent study of the grandest winter scenery, the village is equally unapproachable on its northern side. Between Polu and Kiria a belt of sandy desert must be crossed which occupies three marches. Only after this is effected can the jaded and neurotic traveller hope to enjoy perfect peace, where motor omnibuses are still unknown, and where street traffic is yet in its infancy.

It was with such feeling as an invalid might be expected to entertain that we woke under a roof on the morning after our arrival at Polu. Peaceful indeed were the half dreamy thoughts which floated through one's mind, once the first shock of not having to rise and move on had been got over. Thanks to the kindness of our host, we were lodged in the home of our friend the Hadji, he who had so unexpectedly met and delivered us from the unpleasant gorges of the previous week. The home stood in a little side lane abutting on the main street; the latter is itself only a few feet wide, tree-bordered, with a runnel of clear water flowing down one side.

The village of Polu resembles the type found throughout Chinese Turkestan and the East generally. It is a collection of flat-roofed, mud-brick houses, huddled together to form a regular warren. Round the houses are enclosed yards, outer yards, and cattle pens. Beyond these again, on the outskirts, more enclosures, surrounded by the same mud walls, in which are grown the vegetables to supply the home consumption.

The peculiarity at once noticed in any village in Chinese Turkestan is the unusual construction of the roofs. In the well-to-do houses these are supported upon heavy wooden beams, ornamented with some effort at carving, having a square in the centre of the roof raised some three feet above the level of the remaining roof-space. The sides of the raised portion are made of open woodwork, without parchment or paper such as is used by the Chinese for windows, so that there is nothing to prevent their being sealed up with felt or straw when the cold season approaches.

By this simple arrangement, increased facilities for admitting both light and fresh air are more or less forced upon the occupants,—a tribute this to the knowledge of the habits of his *confrères*, which stamps the inventor as a man of no mean resource. With regard to sanitation the Turki is perhaps less of an Asiatic than usual; and certainly, so far as concerns the cleanliness of his water-supply, he is far ahead of his Chinese masters.

The home of our host was typical of those of the better class. Furnished as it was for us with a profusion of bright-coloured Khotan rugs and felts, it afforded, comparatively speaking, a high degree of comfort. From the street the visitor enters a central courtyard through a door in the mud wall. More than half the courtyard is usually roofed over, but the front side is open to the air. All round the court is a wide lounge, made of mud bricks smoothly plastered over, resembling a Chinese *kang*. Here, when the traveller arrives, baggage is unpacked and stacked, visits are received, and tea is taken. In fact, during the summer season, the dais becomes the regular living-place of the family. Off this central court the rooms open each with its own door, fireplace, and humble set of furniture. Spotless cleanliness was our usual experience, and the grey smooth floor and walls, in which small niches act as cupboards, formed a most pleasing colour contrast when the bright rugs were exposed.

At the season of the year we reached Polu, the autumn, the inner rooms were just beginning to be occupied. After the experience of the previous weeks it is unnecessary to say how we revelled in the luxury of wood fires, warmth, fresh eggs, and milk, not to mention honey. Under such conditions "the flesh-pots of Egypt" became a reality never before so perfectly understood, and had some Turki Moses suggested to us a return over the bleak plateaux we had successfully crossed, I am afraid that our murmurings would have been both deep and loud.

The appearance of the people of Polu gives the idea that they are well off, nor do their surroundings in any way detract from the impression. Well dressed, and possessing large herds of sheep, cattle, and ponies, with ample water, that most priceless boon throughout the East, a cultivated area some miles in length, the standard of living is a high one. Eminently so if we compare it with that of the Indian ryot.

In addition to the comforts mentioned above, the people have also the gold industry to fall back on, which we in the West would in many cases consider of sufficient interest to engage all our spare time.

In temperament the Turkis of Polu are decidedly sociable, being also healthy-looking and handsome; their women-folk are allowed a considerable freedom of intercourse. Respectable women of the higher class are often to be met journeying alone to market, and always riding astride, as all good Turkis do. Their costume is a picturesque one. The round or conical fur cap and long boots are the usual equipment of both men, women, and children, the loose trousers or semi-skirt being the only difference in the sexes. It was customary to see the women pull the white veil they wear over their faces upon passing us, but of their own menkind very little notice is taken.

No description of Polu would be complete which omitted to make mention of the hawks and the hawking, which appears to form the chief amusement of all classes. It is unusual to enter the courtyard of any but the poorest houses and not find one or more hawks fastened to a perch. Nowhere in the East have I seen such beautiful specimens nor birds of such a size.

From the little kestrel to eagles, which are so huge as to appear impossible for a man to carry, and which, if unhooded, one was afraid to approach, all sizes are represented. When it is added that the quarry hunted ranges from chickor to shapoo and bara-sing, some idea may be gained of the wide range of game pursued by these enthusiastic sportsmen.

After two days' rest, with complete forgetfulness of aught but the present, it was necessary to think of a fresh start. The first thing to be done was to dismiss the yak men, who had served us so badly throughout, and whose three months' contract had expired. This was soon accomplished, all the more quickly that, in spite of protestations and entreaties, our hearts were hardened to all cries for extra *baksheish.* The next necessity was to dispose of the most feeble of our remaining ponies, instead of which we decided to take on a drove of donkeys. Against the number of donkeys we required we suggested exchanging so many ponies, the value of both, strong and well, being in the ratio of three or four donkeys to one pony. Here, as usual, difficulties at once arose. Our ponies, we were told, were worthless, worn out, and of no use to any one. In vain we pointed out that after three months' rest a pony who had gone through what our ponies had would never die. Our hosts were well aware that we must move on, also that some of our animals were incapable of doing so, and the chances of a deal did not look rosy. Once more experience came to our aid and enabled us finally to bring our friends to see reason.

Before commencing the journey we had decided to leave no animal behind to die by inches. The friendly bullet was invariably to be their destiny. Although it may sound somewhat of an Irishism, adherence to this rule had more than once temporarily saved the lives of both yak and ponies. Knowing that we should carry out our intention, and disliking, as most Mohammedans do, to see an animal killed in cold blood, our drivers often made renewed efforts to bring along those which they would not otherwise have troubled about, no matter under what circumstances one was left behind. Now again we made it known that under no conditions whatever would any animal of ours remain at Polu alive unless confided to the care of some individual; and further, that for this to happen it was necessary that we should receive a *quid pro quo* in the shape of donkey flesh at a fair rate of exchange. Few things are more difficult in mental calisthenics than to convince an Asiatic mind that what is said is intended to be understood literally. In this connection the previous experience of our caravan men of a rigid adherence to the spoken word by us, on all occasions, was a very strong card. To see five ponies who were merely temporarily disabled led forth to be shot was not at all to the liking of our friends at Polu. The knowing ones were well aware that they could become owners of these ponies on decidedly advantageous terms. So it only required a few hours' more haggling before the charm worked and we won our point. By the afternoon of the third day we had got the donkeys; and all the necessary exchanges having been effected, we were once more prepared to take the road.

Quitting Polu, amid the respectful good-byes of our kindly hosts, we followed the course of the Kiria river under the guidance of two *aksakals* (literally greybeards), sent by the Chinese Amban at Kiria to escort the caravan. The track very soon struck into rolling sand-hills, where we experienced the first intimation of the proximity of the Takla Makan desert. This was conveyed in an everlasting haze, caused by the action of the wind carrying the minute particles of sand. Apart from the inability to see farther than two or three miles, the haze is not sufficiently thick to be objectionable. The limitation of view was, however, no small handicap to our survey work. It was felt the more that on certain days distant ranges and peaks could be seen and their bearings taken, but on others, when it was most necessary for the sake of cross-bearings that the same landmarks should be again sighted, the haze would remain impenetrable.

The channel of the Kiria river, alongside which our direction lay, is here of curious construction.

In the soft sand, below which is a substratum of gravel, the stream has carved a canal-like course some two hundred feet in depth. The sides are perpendicular, and though within a few yards of the river-bank throughout the first day's march, not a drop of water could we obtain. After pushing on for nineteen miles, every minute in hopes that the banks of the stream would let us down to the water, we were forced to halt. Darkness found us still without it, both grass and grazing being also conspicuous by their absence. For boiling water a few dried up bushes alone afforded the necessary fuel. By the aid of ropes and a bucket we were able to secure enough water for the men and ourselves, but the animals were forced to go without. So suddenly had we been overtaken that there was not time to wait for the tents or to pitch them. We therefore bivouacked in the soft sand where we had halted, arranging our valises in a hollow under the shelter of the scrub. The following morning at dawn we watered the animals with a few mouthfuls apiece, drawn from the river. This accomplished, the caravan was soon under weigh, only to find to our annoyance that the precipitous banks almost immediately did slope away, giving easy access to the river-bed in under a mile from the previous night's camp. Such are the little accidents which prevent monotony in the daily march, and to them we were always ready to bow. What did cause a feeling of resentment was the fact that our two *aksakals* had quietly left us in the lurch the previous evening, and, being themselves well mounted, had pushed on for the much-desired water.

After the climatic experiences we had encountered in Tibet, the first two months of our stay in Chinese Turkestan were a delightful change.

From being obliged to wear skin coats, so thick as almost to stand alone, to appearing in one's shirt-sleeves, is a somewhat sudden transformation. But seldom was one so welcome.

A drop of 13,000 feet has its attendant advantages, and never did an oasis so entirely fulfil its *métier* as the first we entered before reaching Kiria. As the name implies, the physical resources of such spots invite contrast with their surroundings, but fully to appreciate the mere human delight in that contrast, it is necessary to come direct, as it were, downstairs from the roof into a splendid winter garden.

In more senses than one do the Tibetan plateaux represent a roof, and as a winter garden we had no fault to find with our oases. Emerging from the desert sands across a line almost as marked as a park fence, we suddenly found ourselves surrounded by walled farmsteads, buried in fruit and other tall trees, the foliage of the latter just turning into a bright golden yellow. The dusty track down which we rode had on either side a double row of weeping willows, at the back of which stretched stacks of Indian corn lately harvested. Buried in small vineyards, interlaced with water-cuts, we passed one snug farm after another. From the doors old crones stare, and favour us with voluble, and perhaps luckily unintelligible, comments, chattering at the same time to cheery little mites of children; while the younger women shyly hid themselves behind the boundary walls wherever an opening gave a chance of a glimpse at the passing strangers. For nearly an hour we rode thus, until a more than usually tempting garden invited us to halt, and there we set about pitching the tents.

Kookhia, the not unpleasing name of our Garden of Eden, turned out to be closer to Kiria than we had imagined. The following day a ride of a few miles through tree-bordered lanes, past well-to-do homesteads, brought us into its immediate vicinity. Entering the town itself, the traveller suddenly finds himself in a long street converted into a covered bazar, a mild imitation of those found in Bokhara, Samarcand, and other big Asiatic towns. Though the headmen had been sent out to meet us with the usual presents of fruit, dried raisins, and other condiments, the Amban himself did not appear. We were escorted to the house prepared for us, which stood on the outskirts of the town, with a large courtyard in front and a pretty little garden behind. From one corner of the latter we enjoyed a lovely view southwards across the Kiria river. Below the house, between the garden and the river, stretched a wide belt of trees, through whose autumn foliage ran every tint of red, orange, and yellow. Beyond this mass of colour the ribbon-like strip of river wound below a high bank of brown mud, while in the far distance the yellow sands formed an apparently limitless background.

Kiria has been the subject of considerable discussion among the few European travellers who have visited the place, owing mainly to the difficulty of reconciling the present site with the itinerary of Marco Polo after that famous traveller left Khotan. Like other historically interesting points concerning this region, it has, in late years, been solved by the industry of Dr Stein, the eminent archæologist, who is even now prosecuting further researches in this fascinating district. The present Kiria, as Dr Stein has already demonstrated, is not the site of Pimo (the Pein of Marco Polo) which it has been thought by other travellers to be.

The ruins of the latter city were discovered and traced by Dr Stein some distance to the north of the Khotan - Nia route, where the site is locally known as Uzun-Tati. The present town of Kiria is divided into two portions—the so-called old city containing about one thousand mud-brick houses, and the new city nearly double the number. The covered bazar forms the chief street, which is entered by a small wooden gateway. There are six or seven *serai* or inns, and ninety to a hundred small shops. The population is chiefly Mohammedan, but there are also eighty to one hundred Chinese residents. Cloths, knives, and some common Chinese leather-work are the chief goods sold; most of the minor native luxuries come from Khotan and the West.

While at Kiria our reception by the Amban was most cordial. He called upon us, and we of course returned his visit. He insisted upon supplying our caravan with fodder and forage during our stay, and utterly declined to take any payment. To him also we were indebted for the comfortable house we occupied; and though prepared to accept, to that extent, the hospitality so freely offered in the East, it was somewhat embarrassing to be beholden for all our wants, simple though they were. The Amban was a young-looking man of thirty-seven, a native of Honan province. He gave us to understand that he was the son of an official occupying a high position in Chinese Turkestan, where he had himself been for twelve years. Of a jovial disposition, fond of good living and cheerful company, he invited us to stay for a week, and to accept his hospitality. Finding that we were firm, and intended to continue the journey with as little delay as possible, he pressed us to honour him with our company at least at one feast, promising, if we would only consent, to show us round the town, and metaphorically to "paint Kiria red." Charmed as we were by his evident friendliness, and careful as we intended to be always to smooth the path for other European travellers who might follow in our steps, we were reluctantly obliged to decline. Previous experience of Chinese dinners had taught us both to look with respect, not untinged with awe, upon such banquets; besides which, the simple habits of the last few months, and abstention from all liquor, had unfitted us to uphold the honour of our countrymen.

Before following the fortunes of the caravan farther into the interior of Chinese Turkestan, it is necessary that my readers should be made acquainted with the previous history and present conditions of this great dependency of China.

Chinese Turkestan is known to have been under the jurisdiction of that country as early as 150 B.C.

In the time of the great Han dynasty not only did their power extend to the present western boundary of the Hsing Chiang, but even as far west as the Caspian their suzerainty was acknowledged. The first expedition of which Chinese annals speak is one sent by an emperor of the same Han dynasty, under an officer called Chang-kian. The expedition was sent to open up, if possible, communication with Indo-Scythian tribes, known to the Chinese as Uei-Chi, who, having been driven out of their original kingdom somewhere between Khotan and China, had settled themselves in Bactriana, in their turn ejecting from thence a Greek dynasty. About the same period the Chinese began to take vigorous measures against the Huns, Tartar tribes who had settled in Chinese Turkestan, and by 50 B.C. their power was firmly established throughout the whole dominion.

During the early part of the first century their power decayed, but towards the end of that period a famous Chinese general, Panchao by name, appeared in the field, and in a few years reconquered the whole territory, including Kashgar, pushing his victories again as far as the Caspian across the whole of what is now Russian Turkestan. From this date until about 600 A.D., when the Sui dynasty was in power, Chinese dominion over their frontier provinces would appear to have almost lapsed. But by 627 A.D. a new ruler, Taitsung of the Tang dynasty, had once more consolidated

Chinese authority, and had carried the empire as far west as Samarcand. About the end of the seventh century the Chinese power in the Far West had reached its zenith.

From this time till the commencement of the Mongol conquest of China, which began about 950 A.D., little is heard of the central Asiatic portion of the empire. It is known to have been occupied even as far north as the Tien Shan Nan-lu by an invasion from Tibet, and to have been held by Tibetans.

When Chingis Khan, the Mongol emperor, gradually asserted his power over the then Chinese Empire, he captured, in 1205, the kingdom of Tangut, which occupied the extreme north-west, probably a portion of it lying within what is now the Hsing Chiang. Okkodai, the son of Chingis, carried his Mongol hordes, as is well known, as far west as the confines of Poland, embracing in these conquests the whole of Central Asia. Under Kublai Khan, a successor to Okkodai, Chinese Turkestan was included in what was then known as the Chagatai Khanate or middle empire of the Tartars. It is of interest to remember that this empire also included most of Russian Turkestan and Afghanistan.

During the years succeeding the gradual decay and fall of the Mongol dynasty, which passed away about 1368 A.D., the history of Chinese Turkestan is that common to the larger part of Asia at that period.

One ephemeral kingdom succeeded another, as Khan after Khan endeavoured either to extend his dominions or to consolidate what he possessed. During this time Kashgar and Khotan figure prominently as capitals, sometimes of a kingdom extending as far north as Aksu and Turfan, sometimes, in the case of Khotan, of a princedom not stretching far beyond its own immediate limits.

The rulers of Eastern Turkestan have nearly always been Mohammedans, from the time of Tughlak Tinur, who was the first Mohammedan sovereign of Kashgar, of the lineage of Chingis.

In 1757 Zungaria was conquered by the Chinese, and the following year, by sowing discord among the local rulers, they succeeded in bringing Turkestan also under their rule. From that date until the present time Chinese administration has continued to be enforced. Frequent risings, such as those instigated by Mohammed Ali, the Khan of Khokhand, in 1812, and more than one rebellion, have marked the course of their rule, but though severely shaken it survived even the outbreak of 1866, which gave rise to Yakub Beg.

The geographical area commonly known as Chinese Turkestan is a somewhat vague one. By some geographers it is considered to embrace the larger portion of the western extra-mural Chinese Empire. By others the area so described is confined to the basins drained by the streams which run into Lopnor, as well as by those which lose themselves in the great central desert, the Takla Makan.

From the Chinese point of view the latter are more nearly correct, the territory being always known to the people of that vast empire as the

Hsing Chiang or new frontier. The general boundaries are as follows: On the north the Tian Shan and the Altai Mountains; on the west the Tian Shan, the Kizil Art, and the Pamirs; on the south the main range of the giant Kuen Lun forms an almost impregnable barrier, whilst on the east no such natural boundary exists. Although the desert of Gobi stretches as far as the Khingan range, situated in longitude 120 E., that portion of it included in Chinese Turkestan may be said to end at the main track which leads from Ansi-Chou in Kansu province to Hami in the Hsing Chiang. For the greater part of its length the frontier of Chinese Turkestan is coterminous with that of Russia. From the Taghdumbash Pamir and Fort Murgabi, as far north-east as Kuldja and Tarbogutai, the frontiers actually touch. Continuing north and east, China is approached through and hemmed in by Russian territory the whole way to the border of Manchuria, a distance of nearly 3000 miles.

The inhabitants of the Hsing Chiang are for the most part Mohammedans of Turki descent. They are a branch of the so-called Eastern Turks which includes the Uzbegs of Russian Turkestan. The home of the original Turks was in the vicinity of the Altai mountains, whence they migrated in large numbers at an early period of history towards China and towards Turkestan. It was in the latter direction that they encountered the line of least resistance, and thither they therefore wandered in the greatest numbers. The Western Turks comprise the Osmanli or Ottoman branch and the

Turcomans,—in fact, they represent what is commonly understood in Europe by the word Turk. The language in use among these people is known as the Chagatai dialect. It is the oldest form of Turkish which has come down to us in the Arab character, and it is still spoken throughout Trans-Oxiana, Turkestan, and Kashgar.

In Yarkand and Kashgar this language is known as Turki, while in Samarcand and Bokhara it is called Uzbegi. We know that many of the masterpieces of Arabic literature owe their origin to Mohammedans of Central Asia, as, during the flourishing literary period of the Timur dynasty, the capital of which was at Samarcand, all theological and didactic works were written—as they still are—in Arabic: their authors rarely employed in their compositions the principal vernacular of their countries—viz., Eastern Turkish.

In addition to the native Turkis, the population of Chinese Turkestan, especially in the vicinity of Kashgar, includes a large number of aliens. Attracted to the country in the first instance as traders and afterwards in many cases remaining as settlers, these outsiders soon adopt, at any rate, the outward character of the ordinary population. Among them are Indian traders of various races: Pathans, Kashmiris, Baluchis, Cabulis, as well as the ubiquitous Andijanis, the latter subjects of the Czar of Russia. There are, too, a fairly large proportion of Chinese and Turki half-breeds, also some Tibetans. Of Chinese, the southern part of the Hsing Chiang holds very few. Here and there poor traders, in many cases opium-sodden specimens of the worst type, may be met with in the bazars of Kiria, Nia, Cherchen, or Chakalik. As a rule, the Amban or district magistrate is himself the only representative of the respectable class of Chinese. The underlings attached to the various magistrates,—*yamen*-runners, interpreters, and such like minor hangers-on, — though dressed as Chinese, are, in almost every case, Turkis or half-breeds.

Of the physical aspects of the Turkis of this area it is difficult to speak. To look at, both men and women are decidedly a fine race, nor is sickness common in the country districts. If, however, we accept their character, as history has exposed it, even during the last half-century, we find unmistakable evidence that they are lacking in almost every quality which a really martial race possesses.

To make another comparison. The natives of Chinese Turkestan are not so fine a looking race as the Turkomans and Uzbegs, both of Turkish descent, who are met with in Bokhara and other parts of Russian Turkestan. Yet again, the character of both branches may be deduced from the fact that the Bokhariots, as soldiers, are looked upon with as much contempt by the Russians as are the inhabitants of Eastern Turkestan by the Chinese.

Environment, it is well known, has a good deal to do with forming the character of any race, and the peaceful habits—not to use a stronger expression—of these dwellers in the oases on the southern side of the Takla Makan desert may partly be due to their agricultural and pastoral pursuits.

Unharried by war, for the rebellion initiated by Yakub Beg is the only instance in the last half-

Turki Women at Kiria.

Ready for Hawking.

century, and supplied by nature with sufficient for their wants in the shape of good harvests, the existence of these tribesmen is indeed simple to a degree. Among the crops which flourish in most of the oases are wheat, cotton, hemp (*charras*), opium, tobacco, and Indian corn; while vegetables and fruit of the best quality grow freely. The methods of agriculture in force are naturally those of the uninstructed East; nor is high farming or the use of iron instruments necessary in a soil both light and so fertile. The pasturing of flocks and herds is chiefly confined to the shepherds who dwell along the lower slopes of the Kuen Lun range. Here are to be found the necessary requisites of grass and water, the latter supplied by the numerous torrential streams which serve to carry off the melting snows, only eventually to perish in their turn, absorbed by the remorseless sands of the central desert.

From reference made to the peaceful character of the Turki population, it might be assumed that the possession of such traits would lead to a busy commercial life. The opposite is, however, the case.

For the most part the commerce of Chinese Turkestan is at present in the hands of Russian subjects, though in some of the larger towns, to the north of the Takla Makan, the Chinese have of late years shown more intention to compete. The trading class, *par excellence*, is composed of Andijanis, inhabitants of Western Turkestan, who may fairly be described as the Jews of Central Asia. In almost every small oasis along the inhabited strip which borders the Kuen Lun, as well as over the northern trades routes, the Andijanis are found. Even in

China proper, in the province of Kansu, their shops are to be seen competing and holding their own with those of the industrious Chinese.

The chief articles of import they sell are Russian ironware, leather-work, coloured cottons, candles, matches, and lump sugar. Of superior goods, there is a kind of black cloth for best clothes, like alpaca, and, in addition, they have introduced embroidery for those able to afford such a luxury.

The Indian traders are naturally in greatest force at Kashgar and in the neighbourhood of Yarkand, though they have also settled at Kuchar. At Cherchen we fell in with a small company, to whom reference is made in a later chapter.

CHAPTER VI.

INTRODUCTION OF BUDDHISM INTO CHINA—A GARDEN ENCAMPMENT —A CHINESE *OCTROI*—NIYA AND ITS BURIED RUINS—A SPORTING BEG—A VARIETY PACK OF HOUNDS—PRIMITIVE SPEARS—HAWKING —A PIG HUNT—A PICTURESQUE BEAT—AN IMPROMPTU HORSE-RACE—ONE OF NATURE'S GENTLEMEN.

UPON leaving Kiria a choice of routes is open to the traveller proceeding east. Mention has already been made of the ancient main track which centuries past formed the connecting link between China and India. Fifteen hundred years ago this route was as well known, at any rate to the Chinese who controlled it, as it is to-day, and for this reason. At the commencement of our era, Buddhism first began to find its way to China from India. Ancient Chinese records prove that it was chiefly by the passage to and fro along this very route of many devotees, priests, and pilgrims, that the transformation took place. Although as early as 126 B.C. the first reports of "the great renunciation" had reached China, it was not for some little while that the religion Prince Siddartha founded was adopted in that country. The story of the return of the envoy Chang C'hien, who was the first to tell of Buddhism, is worthy of being remembered. In the present day we are apt to consider we live in an era of travel, but what would be said now of such a journey as that made by Chang C'hien? Leaving China about 140 B.C., this intrepid man began his wanderings by being kept a prisoner by the Huns in Chinese Turkestan for ten years. Escaping from their clutches, he eventually reached his destination, the capital of an Indo-Scythian race, situated on the north bank of the Oxus river. Returning through Bactriana, he again ventured into the country of the Huns, but on attempting to pass by the Khotan-Lopnor route, that which we were now traversing, was captured a second time. How long he was detained is not clear, but whatever the period it was only after thirteen years' absence that he was able again to reach China. The actual adoption of Buddhism by the Chinese occurred about the year 67 A.D., and following the example of most of the great religions of the world, the introduction of it is ascribed in Chinese annals to a miraculous agency.

In the reign of the Emperor Mingti, one of the eastern Han dynasty, that potentate dreamed a dream. In his sleep, it is related, he imagined that he saw a golden figure floating in a halo of light across the room. Unable, like Pharaoh, to conceive what meaning to place upon his dream, Mingti assembled his wise men and astrologers, and from them invited suggestions as to its interpretation. Unpleasant as such a call upon their inventive faculties must have been, it is probable that these wiseacres were sufficiently in touch with the thoughts and hopes of their noble master to be able to judge with some certainty what was expected of them. They hinted in reply that the figure seen by the emperor was probably that of Buddha,—for with the new religion it must be remembered they were already familiar, and the result of this explanation was the despatch of a special envoy to India to investigate the truth. After a considerable period of absence the envoys returned, having obtained not only the necessary sacred books, pictures, and insignia of the new religion, but having also been fortunate enough to persuade some Indian priests to accompany them to the home of their ruler. It was after this manner that a faith as pure as any the world has known was introduced to China,—a country and people by whom for nearly two thousand years it has since been neglected and debased.

As long ago as the fifth century, two of the best known of Chinese pilgrims, Fa Hien and Hiuen Tsang, have given us the results of separate journeys made over the route we now intended to follow. Both Fa Hien and Hiuen Tsang were born travellers, and both have left records as interesting as they are authentic. From their writings, and particularly those of the latter, we are indebted for mention of many places and towns whose very sites are now unknown. In spite of what has already been done in the way of exploration, it is more than possible that we are only beginning to unravel many of the archæological and historical mysteries connected with a former and far more flourishing state in the western half of Chinese Turkestan. Few as fascinating scenes for such work are to be found in the present day. Unfortunately China itself, which from its past history and — in spite of Western criticism — its present wonderful state of general civilisation, ought to be a subject of interest, especially to our countrymen, is even now a sealed book to the great majority. Why this should be so it is difficult to imagine. One reason lies perhaps in the difficulty—nay, almost impossibility, to dwellers in Europe—of becoming acquainted with either its past or present records. Intimately connected as these have been shown to be with the middle East, even as early as the first century of our era, we in Europe have little knowledge of them, and until it is more widely realised how close this connection was with our own great Indian empire, and that almost entirely by means of the ancient route referred to, interest in the early civilisation of China, and in its later history, will, it is to be feared, be confined to a very limited number of inquirers.

Some eighty miles east of Kiria stands the town of Niya, though such places cannot be called towns in the European sense of the word. It is at Niya that the choice of tracks to Cherchen is offered. Three marches suffice to cover the distance from Kiria to Niya, and throughout these we again made the curiously rapid transit from the rich vegetation of the oases to the desert sands. At times as much as thirty feet high, these sand-ridges continue on occasions for two hundred yards in length. The depressions between the ridges are sometimes only twenty to thirty feet across, and the main ridges are irregularly connected by other subsidiary ones of shorter length. At intervals patches are found four hundred yards square where the surface is more or less level, small sand-heaps being dotted over it. The desert track is well marked by local traffic over and round the sand-dunes, but it would be impossible to follow it at night,—the usual thick haze limited the view to a distance of under a mile. Time is luckily of no object in the East, and for the sake of the pack animals it is as well that it should be so. Very trying are the heavy sands, and the constant surmounting of the loose ridges is most wearying to anything but camels. For ourselves, it was still a source of pleasure to feel warm and to bask in the sun. To add to our happiness, we had obtained a fresh supply of tobacco at Kiria, and though it bore more resemblance to dried sawdust than the plant it was sold to us as representing, we were in no condition to be fastidious.

One of the most pleasing camping-grounds we had yet enjoyed fell to our lot between Kiria and Niya. The tents had been pitched in a pretty garden, surrounded by what are locally known as *jigda* trees, a species of date, which is universally eaten throughout the oases. The garden belonged to an old widow who, by the look of the farmstead, should have been comfortably blessed with this world's goods. She was eager that we should accept her hospitality, so far as the use of her garden was concerned, and, but for the sake of *les convenances*, we would have invited her to join us round the glorious camp-fire our men prepared. Sitting toasting ourselves that night by the blazing logs, sheltered from every breath of wind, we compared our present condition with that through which we had lately passed. Coming from the all-day trek in the desert, the garden filled with its trees and Indian corn seemed all the prettier, and as we lay watching the myriads of stars which lit the darkness above our heads, the fulness of the wanderer's joy at not being under a roof was ours.

Before starting in the morning we bade good-bye to the old lady, nor did she forget to tell us, and that most volubly, what a lot she had given for the piece of silver she had received. For the sake of her widowhood we doubled the value of the silver, though she had given us little but shelter, which in the East one does not usually pay for.

Traversing one of the smaller oases next day, we were amused to find a typical example of Chinese procedure and habits of thought. The tiny village of which the oasis consisted was composed of one narrow lane, at the end of which stood an *octroi* hut built of mud-and-wattle. Across the end of the lane was a light though imposing gateway of wood, some eighteen feet high, on each side of which had been erected twenty yards of high fencing, no more nor less. All round the village and on each side of the fence the endless sands represented the wide, wide world, nor was there any conceivable reason why this official-looking barrier should have been erected, for assuredly no occupant of the village need ever enter its portals. To the European mind it was ludicrous in the extreme, which only served to remind us how far apart is the Oriental from the Occidental train of thought. Observing in jest to one of our own caravan men that some villager might accidentally ride his donkey round the paling instead of through the gate, the remark was literally accepted and replied to with a solemnity befitting the occasion. No doubt, had we been aware of it, we left in that village a reputation for dense stupidity in not knowing what a gate was intended for.

As the track approaches Niya the character of the surrounding country changes. In the last few miles the sandy ridges give place to rocks and stones, among which may be traced the shallow overflow channels of the Niya river when in flood. Outside the village the caravan was met as usual by the local Beg. A comfortable *serai* had been already prepared for our arrival, so it was unnecessary to camp. It had been our intention to follow local custom and to make a pilgrimage from Niya to a well-known tomb, that of Imam Jafar Sadik, but we were unable to do so. The shrine is situated four days' march to the north, and is reached by following the Niya river down its course towards the desert. It was here that Dr Stein made some of his most valuable finds four years previously. Among them the ancient tablets inscribed with Kharoshti characters take the chief place, and are fully described by him in his interesting book, 'The Sand-buried Ruins of Khotan.' Being unable to devote ourselves, much to our regret, to the study of buried cities, we decided instead to accept the offer made by the Beg to hawk and hunt boar with him on the following day. The name Niya covers the surrounding district as well as the village, and in the country adjacent to the river to the north the Beg has as fine a domain to pursue the sport he loves as any one could desire. On either side of the river the country is thick jungle, with open well-watered patches, which, besides affording excellent pasturage, are the haunt of hares, wild boar, and quantities of geese and duck. Beyond the strips of vegetation bordering the stream lie the sands of the desert, the change from the one to the other being, as already remarked, as abrupt as though a boundary fence was there. One advantage in this is that in beating for game it is only necessary to follow the river, for sooner or later the quarry will be unearthed. After the evening meal we discussed the question of the morrow's hunt with the Beg, who, we soon discovered, was as fond of sport as ourselves.

His sentiments might have been summed up in the well-known lines attributed by Whyte-Melville to the owner of "the good grey mare":—

> "I have lived my life—I am nearly done,—
> I have played the game all round;
> But I freely admit that the best of my fun
> I owe it to horse and hound."

Could he but have enjoyed the privilege of reading his own thoughts so delightfully put, he would have been the first to appreciate the truth expressed in these lines. Having listened for some time to the accounts the Beg gave of his hawks, we asked whether there was any other form of sport to be had. To our delight he replied that there were pig which we could shoot, but which he hunted with dogs and spears. We could hardly credit our hearing at the latter words, but a string of questions from both of us soon showed that we had made no mistake, and that there was every chance of our tasting once more the finest sport that the world holds. After another hour's discussion of details—of spears, dogs, beaters, ponies, &c.,—all was satisfactorily arranged. The Beg possessed only two spears, but promised that another should be locally made and ready by the morning. The dogs he ordered there and then to be caught and shut up for the night; and the necessary arrangements for beaters and ponies appeared to require no preliminary preparation. Bidding each other good-night the Beg departed, leaving us with the most pleasant anticipation for the morrow we had enjoyed since quitting India.

Waking at dawn, we found our host to be indeed a man of his word. In the half-light of morning in the village street were collected the ponies, men, and dogs, and a more mixed or quainter group it is difficult to imagine. The animals which the Beg was kind enough to provide were useful beasts, though small. My own was a young four-year-old, 13.1 hands high, but good-looking, and as game as could be. The Beg and his men were also on useful animals, both tough and wiry, though good looks were not their strong point. Of the followers no description could hope to give a true idea. A local meet of the hounds in the west of Ireland would perhaps produce some few types representing what we found—that is, as nearly as anything European could. But that the Beg's men knew their job and were eager to do it we very soon discovered. Of the hounds, too, it is useless to hope to give much idea.

There were only four of them, but once seen they could never be forgotten. Had it been necessary to classify the whole pack in the quite impossible supposition that they were to figure at a local dog show, they could have found a corner upon only one set of benches, those usually devoted to the heterogeneous mixture known as the Variety Class. No sooner did one discover some resemblance to a terrier's head in one of them than it became equally evident that the rest of his body was that of a bob-tailed sheep-dog. Another old lady was a perfect Borzois, so far as her head and body could be named, but, unfortunately, Nature in a thoughtless moment had given her the legs of a spaniel. Of the other two no description need be attempted. Both were evidently reluctant to exchange the comforts of loafing in the village for the danger of routing out boar. And to reach the scene of our sport they had to be dragged out at the end of a long rope by one of the followers, who did his best to hang them whenever a stray bush happened to get between him and the dogs.

While I had been looking over the *personnel*, my companion had busied himself in finding what were to us the most important things, the spears. Turning to speak to him, I found him in doubtful admiration of the weightiest and largest specimen we had ever seen. Some 2 inches in diameter, there was about 10 feet length of shaft. At the end, tacked on by two local-looking nails, was 18 inches of old iron shaped at the point. The shaft was both new and rough,—balance it had none; on a 13-hand pony it was no easy matter to keep any of it off the ground: but who could look a gift-horse in the mouth? The Beg had promised to do his best, and had done it for our benefit; so we gladly accepted the will for the deed, warning ourselves, however, to be careful when the time came to use the spear.

Quitting the village, an hour's smart jog through the dusty outskirts, where one well-to-do farm after another was passed, brought our party into wilder country. We were now back on the banks of the river, which are here flat but covered with low scrub and jheels,—a paradise for the countless flocks of duck, geese, and teal which dwell there. As he took his favourite hawk from his own attendant, a hint from the Beg gave us to understand that business was about to commence. One of the curiosities of local sport is the manner in which these men appear able to keep their hawks on wrist while galloping over very rough ground. Spreading ourselves to look for the necessary duck, it was not long before we came upon a flock in a low-lying bit of wet ground. The Beg at once cantered forward, and when still a few hundred yards distant from the now rising duck, threw his hawk, and away she sped. Going like the proverbial arrow, she made straight for the flock, but, wheeling abruptly just short of them, swung suddenly round to fly back and re-perch gracefully on the outstretched arm of the Beg. Here was a bad beginning, but the next effort was more successful. Crossing an open bit of ground, a few duck suddenly rose from a concealed pond some distance to our right. Without a moment's hesitation the Beg again galloped forward, loosing his hawk with one throw, and on this occasion with great success. The duck were not three hundred yards distant, had hardly even risen, when like a flash the hawk was upon them. This time there was no hesitation, and, almost quicker than the eye could follow, she struck, and down went hawk and duck, locked together, into the scrub.

Cantering up, we offered our congratulations in dumb show to the now smiling Beg, and requested his permission to take a photograph. This he very readily accorded, and the result may be seen in the pictures on another page. For the next few hours we amused ourselves with various flights—both successful and unsuccessful. Sometimes the hawks appeared unwilling to strike though able, and at other times, of course, luck was against them. Occasionally a hawk not only would not attempt to chase but declined to return. It then would perch on the nearest tree, and much blandishment was required on the part of its master to regain possession of the handsome creature. By mid-day the duck were mostly gone, so it was decided to give up the hawking and try for a boar. To reach the best ground required a ride of another ten miles in the direction of the desert, but still through the scrub, which gradually thickened and grew higher as we drew near the favourite ground.

It was not long before the tracks of fresh pig were discovered, and though at first we attempted to initiate a methodical effort at beating, very soon each man was hunting on his own account. Through the scrub ran some clear brooks where the ground sometimes opened out, and alongside which the pig evidently wallowed. In vain we followed what appeared to be fresh tracks. These usually led either into impenetrable jungle or were lost among the other marks which here ran in all directions. After an hour of this disappointing work we were all relieved to hear that a boar had been harboured by one of the native hunters in a large shallow jheel. The jheel was so thickly covered with tall reeds, fifteen to sixteen feet high, that only with the greatest difficulty could the trackers penetrate. Sitting on the edge of the scrub, we were watching their slow advance when suddenly a rustle, followed by a quick parting of the reeds just ahead of them, told us the boar was there. In another minute loud shouts and holloas — and the Turki can holloa — proclaimed that he had broke on the far side of the jheel. For the moment we were prepared to face the muddy water in the endeavour to follow in his track, but the Beg, with one yell, turned his pony, and digging both heels in, galloped wildly up the jheel-side. Breaking from the fairly open scrub into a narrow cattle-track, he quickened his pace, evidently riding to cut off the boar at the head of the jheel. Nothing loath, as soon as we understood the situation, we followed in his wake. The path was barely wide enough for a calf, and as full of holes and as poached as a jungle track usually is. On either side the scrub at times nearly met overhead, and the track occasionally wound almost at right angles to avoid some particularly dense piece of growth. Forgetful of such trifles, and only intent upon retaining possession of our unwieldy spears, we still followed our leader, whom we could see at intervals disappearing at full gallop round one corner after another. Ten minutes of this work brought us nearly to the top end of the jheel where the track forked. One branch ran on, the other turned short, crossing the shallow end through the now thinning reeds. Following the latter path, I succeeded in forcing a way through, just in time to see the Beg clear the scrub and swing away left-handed in the direction he evidently imagined the boar had taken. Hesitating for a moment, I was wondering whether the beast had yet emerged, when a crash on my right put all doubts at rest.

Not twenty yards away a great grey boar trotted slowly up the side of the sandy hillock, pursued by one dog, and at the same moment became aware of my presence. There was no time to think, not even to remember the caution we had vowed to observe when called upon to make use of the ill-balanced old spear. Down went mine, and shaking up my little pony I made for the boar. Whether the unusual sight of a white man or the shouts of the natives caused the brute to change his mind, I do not know; suffice it to say that he checked his charge in mid-career, and swung off up the sand-hill just as my pony jinked violently, ingloriously turning his tail upon the boar. "Well for him," I can hear the experienced pig-sticker remark, "that the boar had two minds," and perhaps it was; but the sight of as fine a specimen of the old grey pig as the heart could desire had fairly set our blood boiling. Throwing caution to the winds, and forgetful alike of doubtful spears, infernal ground, even, I am sorry to say, of the old dog, whom we mercilessly over-rode, away went my companion and myself in full pursuit, followed at some little distance by the Beg, who had now come up, and two of the best mounted of his men. For a quarter of an hour we enjoyed the feeling of bliss which only those can realise who have been hard at the heels of either boar or fox at their best pace for that time; but gradually we began to lose ground. The line our quarry took led us deeper and deeper into the jungle, and in spite of the efforts of our gallant little ponies, it was evident that utter grief must soon follow the attempt to continue. The scrub was up to the ponies' necks, there was no possibility of seeing the boar, and we had long ago distanced the Beg and his men. Sadly we allowed our streaming animals to slow down, and though we pushed on into a thick patch where another of the dogs appeared to be busy, we had evidently lost our boar. Returning somewhat disconsolate at the disappointment, we made for a reed hut, or *satma* as they are called, to eat the sandwiches we had brought with us. Having soon disposed of these, the whole party moved off once more for a second draw. The jheel had provided such sport in the morning that the Beg suggested trying there again.

Stripping off their long boots, the men waded in, and in a short time another boar was reported roused. After beating the reeds, as far as the men dared to wade in, with little result, the Beg ordered them to be fired. This was no easy matter, nor could the men get the fire to spread, although the reeds were set alight in three or four places. While this was going on we sat on the edge of the water thoroughly enjoying the picture before us.

The jheel was situated under rising sand-hills which ran along one side of it. Upon the hillocks the Beg had placed what might be called his "whips," in order to view the boar should he break that side. Not content with their elevated position, both these men were to be seen at intervals standing upright on their ponies' backs. A strange sight it was to see them balanced at full height on their ungainly saddles. Each man held his bridle in one hand, while with the other each shaded his eyes as he peered on all sides over the surrounding country. In the immediate foreground heavy coils of grey smoke hung over the yellow reed-tops, while the roaring fire made blotches of flaming red against the muddy water below. In the immediate foreground, wading nearly up to their waists, wild figures pushed their way back and forwards among the reeds, directed by the Beg, who had now dismounted from his pony, and was shouting directions from the bank.

The whole scene combined a wonderful mixture of life and colour to which no photograph could attempt to do justice. Nothing but the brush of an artist could have caught the spirit of such a picture, and unfortunately the occasions are rare when a combination of painter and such a scene are both ready to hand. In spite of all the efforts made to cause the boar to break, he declined to do so, unless, indeed, as we began to think, he had slipped away earlier in the afternoon, avoiding the keen eyes of both look-out men. As the day was drawing on, and we were some fifteen miles from home, a move was now made in the direction of Niya. Though we had all been in the saddle since dawn, our host seemed to consider there was yet time for more hawking, and on the way home he treated us to several flights. Whether it was that the hawks were weary or were disinclined to fly so late in the day, I cannot pretend to say, knowing little of the sport of hawking. Whatever the reason may have been, the only result of the Beg's efforts was one failure after another, until at last, angered at the apparent disinclination of his favourite hawk, he began to throw it indiscriminately at crows, larks, or anything that flew by. After one final failure at some duck which had settled in an open pool on the river, the Beg desisted. The hawk had missed the duck and had settled on the far bank of the stream, from which it was with difficulty retrieved. We were then some five miles from Niya, and expected to be allowed to jog home in well-contented peace, but were soon undeceived.

Rejoining us where we had waited for him while he had made his last unsuccessful flight, the Beg set his pony going towards home at a good pace, and we followed suit. Not content with this, he drove his animal ahead with one of his men, evidently wishing us to take part in an extempore race.

Now the blood of few Englishmen can withstand such a challenge, even though they have been ten hours on the back of the same pony, and that a little beast such as those we rode. Away flew the Beg and his man, and after him went we *ventre à terre.*

The track to Niya was a sandy strip of soft going, and down this, as we drew near the outskirts of the village, the weary natives were placidly making their way home; nor did they seem to consider there was anything unusual in the method we chose of returning. I was beginning to wonder how we could be expected to avoid upsetting half the respectable townsfolk in Niya, when our abrupt arrival at a bend of the river put a stop to our headlong course.

Slowly we forded the shallow stream, and as if touched by a spell the whole company became suddenly solemn Asiatics once more. We had left Niya, as has been said, at dawn; we returned at dusk. It was the last day of Ramazan, and not a morsel of food had the Beg or any of his followers touched for many hours. All honour to them that they could show themselves such whole-hearted children under such a strain.

Mindful of the feast, and anxious that our host should be able to reach his house as soon as possible, for the moon would shortly rise, we tried in vain to dissuade him from accompanying us home. True to the courteous instinct which seems to have its origin in the East, the Beg insisted upon seeing us to the gate of our *serai*. There, in receipt of our grateful thanks, he left us, but I can see his tall upright figure now. Built in a larger mould than is usual among his compatriots, he was a man of silent reserved character. Possessing in addition a tireless frame, a keen love of the open, and a very warm heart, our friend was as good a specimen of one of nature's gentlemen as could be found.

CHAPTER VII.

THE MOUNTAIN ROUTE TO CHERCHEN—THE GORGES OF THE NIYA RIVER—SORGHACK—GOLD-DIGGINGS—DOWN THE MINE—PRE-HISTORIC METHODS—VARIABLE MEASURES OF DISTANCE—THE SHEPHERDS OF THE KUEN LUN—KOPA—THE MYSTERY OF A SOUP-TIN—THE MARCH TO CHERCHEN—A RUSH FOR WATER—AN UN-FRIENDLY *AKSAKAL*—THE AMBAN OF CHERCHEN—THE VERACITY OF MARCO POLO—CHINESE AND INDIAN TRADERS—THE AMBAN'S CIGAR.

It is at Niya that the choice of routes to Cherchen and Lopnor must be made. In view of the desert crossing we intended to make from Lopnor to the Chinese frontier, it was our present aim as far as possible to spare the animals. Time, within limits, was a secondary consideration.

By taking what is known as the desert route to Cherchen, the chance is afforded the traveller of further acquaintance with the buried cities of the past. He must, however, be prepared for greater difficulties in the matter of supplies and water than is met with on the southern route which we intended to follow. It was at Endere on the desert route, half-way between Cherchen and Niya, that another of Dr Stein's important finds was made. In the excavations carried out by him there, Tibetan paper leaves of a date *circa* 750 A.D. were brought to light, which add valuable evidence to that already afforded by Chinese annals of an invasion of Chinese Turkestan by those wild people about that date.

Having decided to take the mountain track, we left Niya on the morning of 3rd November. It was not without some misgiving that we turned our steps south again, for there facing us, when the haze allowed, rose the rugged peaks of the Kuen Lun mountains, and to renew acquaintance with them was the last thing we wished for.

Hidden away on their northern slopes lies Sorghack. And it was for this spot, the centre of the local gold industry, that we were now bound.

Between Sorghack and Niya lies a stretch of waste land some thirty miles wide. Upon it nothing grows, nor is there vegetation of any kind. A rock-strewn glacis to the lower Kuen Lun hills, this lifeless strip completely cuts off Sorghack from the more fertile oases to the north. Midway a family of enterprising Turkis have started a half-way camp, represented by two or three miserable hovels, to which water, wood, and grass had all to be sent to enable us to cross. Rising from the midst of the bare plain, the little encampment has all the appearance of a small island. Though close to the right bank of the Niya river, this proximity is of no value. The river-bank is fifty feet deep and a cliff, preventing access to the bed of the stream. The latter, though 200 to 250 yards across at this point, was quite waterless.

In preparation for facing the eighteen miles into Sorghack, we rose the next morning by starlight to find a large convoy of men and donkeys, 250 in number, had come down from that place in the night. They had been engaged in taking up stores from Niya, whence every bit of food and fodder for the gold-diggers has to be fetched. Sorghack has no supplies of its own. Continuing across the rock-hewn waste, we followed the right bank of the stream. Its cliff-like sides are still more rugged and broken, and at times as much as 200 feet high, with a sheer drop into the stream-bed. The stratum through which the mountain torrents have carved a way is composed of soft gravelly soil, in which stones of all sizes are embedded.

The track followed one of the gravelly terraces which may be seen on both banks. These show signs of having formed an earlier bed, being arranged like successive steps from the present level of the plain down to the edge of the gorge now constituting the channel. On the terraces the big stones are water-worn and smooth, relics of a previous time when they lay in the bed of the stream. Some have circular holes hollowed smooth by the well-known action of water grinding a small pebble in a cup where the latter has lodged.

Approaching closer to Sorghack, the rocky plain as it gradually rises gives way to broken dusty hills of loess formation, equally devoid of vegetation. Over the hills and deep ravines leads a good track, ten feet broad. Skilfully engineered at very steep gradients, it crosses the ridges mainly at right angles. On both sides of it numerous old gold-pockets were to be seen, as they had also been for the last two or three miles in the river-bed. Mounting one of the steepest gradients of all by a good zigzag track, we reached a ridge from which a view is obtained over a cup in the bare hills. In the bottom of this cup lies the present gold centre, and a more arid uninviting spot could not easily be found. Though marked upon European maps as of the same size as Liverpool or Philadelphia, Sorghack is merely a collection of wattle-built semi-underground huts and regular caves. It has all the appearance of the early mining camp with which Bret Harte once made us familiar. Lack of water and an all-enveloping dust are its two main characteristics. The Niya river runs past the village on the west and southern sides at the distance of one mile. The flood water has carved its way through the soft loess soil, forming a precipitous and picturesque gorge some hundred feet deep. So cliff-like are the sides of the gorge, that in order to obtain access to the bottom, the inhabitants have been driven to make use of the bed of one of the numerous subsidiary gullies which have been cut into the main gorge by the overflow of the surface-water during the rains, or at the time of the snow melting. This subsidiary gully starts from the general level at some distance from the edge of the main gorge, but so pliable and easily worn is the loess soil that the water, instead of cutting its way to the gorge above ground, has actually worn a channel more rapidly by tunnelling, with the result that the gully debouches into the bed of the main gorge in this curious manner. Down this freak pathway alone, to use an Americanism, is any access to the precious water obtainable. And it is only by making use of it that the inhabitants of Sorghack can drive their donkeys, or go themselves to fetch water. A strange sight it was to see the animals and the poorer inhabitants painfully struggling up this winding tunnel, the gradient of which forbids one to ride. Nothing could better exemplify the difficulties of water-supply, or the character of the inhabitants, who make no effort to relieve themselves by attempting to create artificial storage.

The only respectable buildings at Sorghack stand in a walled enclosure, eighty yards square. These are the official offices and gold stores, and do not represent anything more extravagant in the building line than a better kind of mud-built abode, fitted with Chinese lattice and paper windows. Here we were lodged. Sŏrrăck, as the name is locally pronounced, contains about two thousand inhabitants, all of whom are registered gold-diggers who work for the Chinese authorities.

According to our information the Beg buys all the gold that is produced, and sends it to the Amban at Kiria. The people working at the diggings are, if necessary, supplied by the Beg with money for food as each market-day comes round, but this is only necessary when they have had ill-luck and have not struck gold. When found, as has been said, the Beg buys, though according to what we were told, takes would be a more correct description of the deal. The people

Working the Gold Mines at Sorghack.

Winnowing Gold at Sorghack.

come to Sorghack of their own free will,—and there is said to be no lack of workers,—but once arrived no one can go away so long as they are to any extent in debt to the Beg for food money. Though not exactly a *corvée* system, the difference between what exists and the former is a somewhat fine one.

Sorghack was first worked about one hundred years ago by Mongol Kalmucks, who discovered the gold. There are acres of ground covered with old pockets, most of which are now disused. Not more than sixty to seventy are at present being worked in the immediate vicinity.

Unlike the exploiting carried on in the mountains farther west, the mining at Sorghack is worked by means of deep shafts, locally known as *kan.* The take from these of course varies year by year. Some months, when small nuggets are not scarce, the find, according to the figures we were able to obtain, is of no inconsiderable value, and that in spite of the prehistoric methods still in vogue.

Each shaft is in charge of six to eight men, women, and children. At the top of the hole is a rickety windlass, worked by two men. To the windlass two ancient-looking frayed ropes, the one of hair the other of hide, were attached. Both were liberally knotted and re-joined. At the mouth the hole is some five feet square, and for the first seven or eight feet of the descent the sides are strutted with rough logs, and are indifferently riveted with brushwood. Below this the hole narrows rapidly, having neither boarding nor brushwood. For three-quarters of the descent the shaft is perpendicular, the last quarter is at a slight angle. The depth is about ninety feet, which it took us four perilous moments to discover. At the start it is necessary to attach oneself as best may be to the two ancient ropes. No cradle of any kind is thought of; so after making one or two loops through which the legs are thrust, the nervous foreigner swings down into space and utter darkness. After having been scraped and jerked until he begins to curse the bump of inquisitiveness which induced him to undertake such a mad enterprise, the bottom of the shaft is reached. Knees and elbows have suffered severely, the hide-thong loop has scored the tender part of one's back, the knots and joins of the ropes have blistered the palm of one's hands, but what matter! Do you not stand at the bottom of a gold-mine shaft, within touch of gold, perhaps upon gold? What more can the heart of covetous man desire?

From the bottom of this particular shaft a low tunnel, one hundred and three paces in length, has been excavated. It is from three to four feet in height, and from one-and-a-half to two feet in width. The stratum through which the tunnel is bored is composed of shaly sand and gravel, with an occasional outcrop of rock. Four men work below, one of whom continues tunnelling and excavating the earth. Another puts the soil into small skin bags, with which the third creeps back and forwards to the bottom of the shaft. The fourth sees to the hoisting. Greater labour for the time expended on it could not be imagined. The sole tools in use consisted of one wooden club, into the head of which a short iron spike five inches long had been fixed, and a rude iron-headed hammer with which the soil is loosened before being put into the skin bags by hand. There is neither shovel nor trolley, and the only light available is from two tiny *chiraghs* A closer imitation of primeval man at work one is not likely to see again.

Arrived at the top, each skin bag is emptied of its contents on to the heap of soil from the hole. A man or woman then dips into the heap a rough wooden bowl, and holding it in both hands high above his or her head, shakes out all the contents on to a five-foot square felt, thus winnowing the soil in the way threshed grain is invariably treated in the East. More than once is this process repeated; then, if no nuggets are found, attention is turned to the residue now left upon the felt—a layer of very fine gravel. On the knee is the order of the day, and handful after handful of the gravel is taken from the felt and blown upon to separate the soil from any specks of gold-dust which it may contain. To repeat that the method looked primitive, conveys but in the faintest manner the impression we gained from watching such an extraordinary performance. It appeared as though any number of tiny nuggets might be passed by, and as though most of the gold-dust must be blown away; but the wise man knows that the East has its immemorial customs, and any one conversant with it is aware that they are as unchangeable as all the laws of the Medes and Persians put together.

The mining industry at Sorghack is said not to be what it was, though whether this piece of information was thrown in for our benefit or not I am unable to say.

Another good working had been in use for some little time. This is situated to the south, one march farther into the mountains, and rejoices in the euphonious name of Choongsai-shamalluck.

After quitting Sorghack, we turned east along the lower slopes of the Kuen Lun. The general character of the country alternates between rolling sandy downs and open moorland covered with a kind of wild thyme, which the animals eat greedily. A considerable number of shepherds live a more or less wandering existence, having the care of hundreds of sheep, the property of well-to-do men at Kiria, Niya, or Cherchen. To the south of the track we followed, at a distance of only two or three miles, the snow-capped ridges of the lower main ranges could be seen. From the Kuen Lun descend at frequent intervals numerous mountain streams and small rivers. These afford one of the most striking physical features of this district.

The ten days' march from Sorghack to Kopa was by no means the least pleasant part of our journey. Although villages are not to be found along the track, there are a few hamlets of which Kara-sai, on a small stream of the same name, is the most important.

At the time of the year we found ourselves traversing this district no climate could have been more pleasant. In Eastern Turkestan one of the chief physical features is the dryness of the atmosphere, and how exhilarating this feeling is travellers to Egypt know well. Though we sometimes made use of mud huts, or even the cave-dwellings of the shepherds, our nights were for the most part spent in camp. Water being as always the difficulty, our tents were almost invariably pitched in the bed of one of the torrent gorges previously described. The general elevation of the route followed is between 7000 and 9000 feet above sea-level; but after the previous weeks spent on the Tibetan plateaux, the temperature never troubled us. Far more minor inconvenience was caused by the difficulty experienced in arriving at any approximate English equivalent in distance for that in use among the Turkis. A *potai* is the common unit of road measurement in these parts, and, as usual in the East, it varies according to the nature of the country over which the traveller is passing. For purposes of calculation it may be reckoned at between two-and-a-quarter and two-and-a-half miles; but we found yet another factor of variation, and that lay in whether the number of *potai* was given for mounted men riding ponies, or for the slow-moving ass or camel. Though it is true that no self-respecting Turki ever walks if it can possibly be avoided, not many of the country folk can afford ponies. The use of these is confined more or less to the comparatively wealthy, such as the headmen or Begs, but it is a very poor household which cannot produce one or more donkeys.

Along the base of the Kuen Lun range animal life, so far as game is concerned, is conspicuous by its absence. A few small hares represented all that we saw, nor are birds any more common.

The shepherd's life is no easy one, though to these hardy specimens it has probably a charm of its own. As an example of the value of money in such out-of-the-way parts, it may be mentioned that the daily wage for which a man will do some work for another is four pice (Indian money) a-day. That of the shepherds is not very much more handsome. On account of a year's work they receive thirty *tengeh* (wages, about Rs. 7), also a sheepskin coat, which they probably renew as often as they require from the flocks under their charge.

From the sources of the various streams which drain the snow-water from the Kuen Lun, there are one or two possible passes into Tibet. At what seasons these are available only the local shepherds know; and, like the man in the story, they are not always anxious to tell.

As the caravan approached Kopa, the track followed ran into broken rugged hills and gullies of a very wild character. Old gold-pockets, all worked out, line the so-called path. Immediately before reaching Kopa, the latter crosses a desolate rocky stretch of ground which no self-respecting pack animal would negotiate for choice, but this is the only approach from the west. Kopa itself is a more sordid edition of Sorghack, and consists of some fifty to sixty underground hovels, built of stones and mud, with a few of slightly more civilised calibre. We were offered and accepted the guest-house, a somewhat high-sounding title for a mud-hut, which is occupied by any minor Chinese official when ill-fate compels him to include Kopa in a tour of inspection from Cherchen.

The gold industry here we were informed was not doing well, and if appearances go for anything in this world, I can readily believe it. The previous Beg was said to have driven many people away owing to his bad treatment. Not only would he not pay them fairly for their gold, but his greed for "pickings" prevented his ever providing sufficient food for those whose luck at the mining was out.

From Kopa there are again two tracks to Cherchen. The most direct one traverses a practically waterless strip of desert, and can only be used by camels or by mounted men able to carry what little they require, and capable of riding through in from forty-eight to fifty-six hours. Even then it is necessary to ride by night as well as by day, and such a journey was out of the question with as large a caravan as we still owned.

The night after leaving Kopa an amusing incident happened by which we lost our evening meal, and that on a night too when it was particularly required. A long and tiring march of twenty-one miles had occupied the caravan from 7 A.M. to 5 P.M. The usual difficulty of reaching water had somewhat lengthened the day. At last we spied a few shepherds' hovels, and the long promised water appeared in the shape of a small torrent bed. Overlooking the latter were two caves dug out of the hillside, and to save pitching the tents we settled to sleep in them. It was too late on arrival, and the men too tired, to do much cooking, so we gave them a sheep and contented ourselves with a cold meal, save for an army ration which we put in front of the fire to warm. On the sandy floor of the low cave we spread our valises and began to make preparations for a snug night. Fuel in unusual quantity had been collected for us, which, with a good fireplace and a natural chimney, made a roaring fire inside the cave. This perhaps accounted for the mishap which followed. Reclining as near the crackling heap of red-hot roots as a continual shower of sparks would allow, we were lazily speculating upon the contents of the ration tin, whether lentils, pea, or other variety of condensed soup, when a loud explosion sent us both rolling over backwards. In the first moment it was difficult to collect one's thoughts, and visions of a cartridge having accidentally dropped into the fire flashed through my mind as I shouted to my companion to ask if he was hurt. An answer in the negative was reassuring, and as soon as we recovered our wits sufficiently to laugh we began to look first for the tin, then for its contents. Strange as it may sound, not a vestige of either could be found; and to this day it remains a mystery why the lentils or baked beans, not to mention the tin, did not plaster us from head to foot.

Our explosion occurred at Tak Bai, by which name the few cave-dwellings are known to the natives. They have chosen a picturesque spot of which, unfortunately, no photograph was taken. We were fated to have many less comfortable camps than the shepherds' caves.

Getting away as usual by starlight in the morning, a view of some exquisite colouring just before the sun rose was our reward. On two sides the lower hills wore a greyish tinge. Behind them, clear cut and black in the coming light, rose the higher snow-clad ranges. To the north stretched the *sai*, only half visible owing to the haze, and even its bare ugliness softened by a purple glow the reflection of the rising sun. Eastwards, above what at such a distance appeared to be a low ridge, every shade of rose colour, saffron, and pale orange, formed a feast of delicate colour from the midst of which rose the sun itself. A march of twenty-six miles, which our caravan took just over twelve hours to accomplish, brought us to Achen, from whence a waterless stretch of desert and *sai*, seventy miles across, has to be faced to reach Cherchen. Achen consists of only three or four shepherds' hovels, although honoured with a place on European maps. We had hoped to make some preparations there to help to cross the strip of waterless country referred to. But all that could be done was to arrange to send a mounted man ahead to Cherchen, asking that fodder and water should be sent out from there to meet us. This done, we made our own plans accordingly, congratulating ourselves upon having been able to secure a native who would undertake the task. It was arranged to make a short march of ten or twelve miles the first day, and to carry ice for that night's supply. At the end of the second day's march, which it was intended should be double the distance if the animals would stand it, we hoped to find the Cherchen supplies. With them there would be no question but that the town itself could be reached on the third day.

It was not without some misgivings that we had drawn up our plans, owing to the fact that our caravan *bashi* had long proved himself useless where any "bundobust" had to be made. At the same time we were obliged to trust him to some extent, as he was our only means of communication with the native Turkis. Himself an Arghun, or half-breed, he was acquainted with the local dialect, while between him and ourselves Hindustani was the only medium of conversation.

Arrived at the end of the first day's march over a sandy scrub country, the ice we had brought sufficed to give each of the animals a few mouthfuls of water. Mindful of the chance that our Cherchen envoy might not be so certain to carry out our arrangements as Rahim, our caravan *bashi*, assured us he would be, a little of the ice was held in reserve.

Up at 3 A.M. for the second day's march our route continued over the same sandy waste, diversified only by low ridges and what appeared to be dry water-courses. After twenty miles of this, the heavy going began to tell upon the animals, and it was time, we thought, to discover some traces of the Cherchen people, who, as we supposed, were waiting our approach. About 2 P.M., after nearly twelve hours' marching, Rahim was sent forward in hopes of finding them. After another two hours it became evident that if we did not call a halt, nature would very soon do so, for some of the weaker ponies were played out. We struggled slowly forward, however, until thirty miles had been accomplished, when, as there were no signs of any

A Dug-out near Achen, where we slept a night.

The Amban of Cherchen.

supplies, we were forced to camp. Without water, save for about one quart apiece from the reserve, fuel, or food, the ponies that night were in a bad way. Besides the ice, we had kept a few handfuls of *bhoosa* in case of what did occur happening, so that they got enough to keep them on their legs. Our local guide insisted that we could reach Cherchen by 2 P.M. the following day, and that being so we knew that we could always rest a day and recoup the animals for the extra exertion.

The third day's march began somewhat badly, for the pack ponies were mostly disinclined to move, and evidently seriously in want of water. To make matters worse, our track led at first over a waste of sand-dunes devoid of any sign of vegetation, across which we ploughed through loose sand over the animals' fetlocks, rising and falling over sand waves of equally loose foundation, fifteen to twenty feet in height. Fortunately this strip only lasted a few miles, giving way to a more open and firmer plain where gravel began to take the place of the heavy sand.

After covering fifteen miles, we saw what in the distance looked like a running stream, and knowing that we must be somewhere in the vicinity of the Cherchen river, our spirits rose. Another mile enabled us to make out the stream to be a reality, and on the banks of it we could see through our glasses both men and ponies. Here at last were the long-wished-for supplies, and once again the load of suspense and apprehension was lifted from our minds. Trotting ahead of the caravan, I soon approached the stream, which turned out to be a brook, known locally as the Yelgun river. Beside it the Beg of Cherchen and some Indian traders, who were then passing through Cherchen, and had heard of our approach, were waiting to welcome us, having brought with them the usual offering of fruit, tea, and other delicacies. Having greeted the Beg and the merchants with whom I could converse, I inquired if our mounted forerunner had ever reached Cherchen, and was informed that he had, but that our request had not been understood. I was about to ask the chief merchant for some explanation, and to endeavour to arrive at the reason for such unusual neglect of the laws of hospitality in the East, when the approach of the caravan prevented any further inquiry. Not half an hour previously I had left a miserable train of animals, tired of life, and unable to take the slightest interest in the day's proceedings. Approaching, I saw a very different sight. At a distance of some hundreds of yards the ponies smelt the water, and before we could stop them, regardless of *yakdans*, loads, or tent-poles, they made for it at a run. It was useless to attempt to control a score of loose animals, so we made no effort to do so, and into the stream they dashed, sousing their muzzles over their nostrils to drink again and again.

While our animals were quenching their three days' thirst, we were not sorry to attack the luscious fruit our hosts had provided. The whole caravan was once more on good terms with itself, so cheerfully we rode the last five miles into Cherchen, improving the opportunity by conversation with the leader of the merchants. After enlightening us as to his own affairs and those of the company—eight in all—who travelled with him, he accounted to us for the non-arrival of our supplies from Cherchen. From the story he told it appeared that our messenger had arrived, and that the Amban had been made acquainted with our wants. No reproach could be attached to this Chinese official, who in the course of the usual routine gave orders to one of the *aksakals*, or headmen, to make the necessary arrangements to meet our request, also those required to prepare for our arrival. Now the *aksakal* happened, unfortunately, and as is not often the case, to be an Andijani, a Russian subject, who was unlikely to bestir himself on behalf of those who did not owe allegiance to his master the Czar, more especially when they appeared to drop from the clouds, and those clouds which hovered on the Tibet border. Whatever the *aksakal's* reasons may have been, the trader's story afterwards received confirmation. When on reaching Cherchen we had been shown the farmstead set aside for our accommodation, our men found that no preparations whatever had been made to collect food or fodder for the ponies. In every oasis so far, nothing had been left undone that could tend to increase the comfort of either the men, our animals, or ourselves, and although, except at Kiria, we invariably paid well, the attention was none the less acceptable.

Great was the disgust of our following at the reception now accorded, so a messenger was forthwith despatched to report the *aksakal* to the

Amban. The latter himself soon appeared, and roundly abusing the *aksakal* before the assembled crowd for his want of manners, soon restored to our own followers their temporary loss of "face."

The house itself was of the same type as those already described at Polu. It had a spacious courtyard, half open, some forty feet square, which, furnished by the Amban's orders with felts and rugs, was most comfortable. The Amban himself, whose photograph adorns one of our pages, was a cheerful old gentleman, a native of Hunan province. In addition to the felts and rugs, he sent us two camp-stools, which made a most agreeable change from always sitting on the ground; he also ordered for us a native *pillau* for the evening meal. One of the chief pleasures we enjoyed on reaching any of the oases was that it offered the chance for a real good bath and a complete change. The sand and dust anywhere in the vicinity of the desert is all-embracing, and in a few days thickly covers one's hair, beard, and clothes.

Cherchen is the Charchan of Marco Polo, and is described by that wonderful traveller as "a province of Great Turkey, lying between northwest and east. The people worship Mahommet. There are numerous towns and villages, and the chief city of the kingdom bears its name, Charchan." It was towards the end of the thirteenth century that the Venetian had visited Cherchen, in the course of the memorable journey throughout which as a young man he accompanied his uncles from Europe to the Court of Kublai Khan near Peking. Starting from Acre in Palestine, the trio passed through Persia to the Gulf. Whatever the original intention of the travellers had been, at Hormuz, in the Gulf, they changed their plans. Retracing their steps, they passed north through Persia once more to Khorassan, and from there to Balkh in Afghanistan. From Balkh they made their way along the present northern border of Afghanistan to Badakshan and the Pamirs, whence they struck down on Chinese Turkestan at Kashgar. After quitting that even then important trade centre, Marco Polo and his two companions threaded their way through the series of oases I have endeavoured to describe, passing Khotan, Kiria—though probably north of the present site,—Niya, and Cherchen, to reach Chakalik in the vicinity of Lopnor.

In the present century, just six hundred years later, we are now beginning to inquire where all these "numerous towns and villages" are, for Marco Polo has long been proved to be a truthful man: and we find, as Dr Stein and others have shown, and are even now continuing to prove, that they have almost all succumbed to the slow but remorseless attacks of the desert sands. Whether these latter will be found to cover the buried treasures Egypt and Persia have yielded remains to be seen, and is unlikely, but it may with confidence be said that they have yet to disgorge a wealth of historical and perhaps ethnological remains to the intelligent explorer with time, energy, and the means to give to such an enticing task.

The Cherchen of to-day is a mean place of one rambling street, 180 yards in length, on either side of which are a few wretched shops which represent the usual Asiatic bazar. The bazar is not roofed, and the inhabitants look poorer and more unkempt than those of any of the oases we had traversed. In extent the Cherchen oasis is the largest yet seen, having an area some six miles from north to south by two-and-a-half from east to west.

The town is situated close to the left bank of the Cherchen Darya, which is the most considerable stream met with since we quitted India. At the point where it passes the town it has a bed about 160 yards in width, with a swift stream 30 feet across, and in places 3 to 4 feet deep. When crossed by us, on leaving Cherchen, immediately above the town the river ran in five channels. The average width of these was 20 to 25 feet, and their depth 18 inches. In the spring the river usually overflows, filling some low-lying land north of the village. Some doubt appears to exist as to the exact site of old Cherchen. We were informed locally that it once stood at a distance of seven miles to the north-east, but there are numerous remains close to the town on the west, under two miles away.

It may be of some interest in enabling the reader to form an idea of the size and importance, or the reverse, of such a place as Cherchen, if a few details are given concerning its taxable revenue and its supplies. And although in doing so reference must be made to the typically Chinese habits of our friend the Amban, he will no doubt bear no ill-feeling.

Included in the oasis of Cherchen are 150 farms

and houses of a kind. The inhabitants of these own collectively some 100 ponies and 3000 sheep and goats. Eight thousand *tengeh* (4 *tengeh* roughly =1 rupee) is the amount of annual tax on the Cherchen land revenue. Four thousand *tengeh* in addition are paid by the wandering shepherds of the district. In addition to both the above taxes, two *tengeh* out of every ten *tengeh's* worth of goods sold in the market on bazar days is taken as extra squeeze. Incredible as such a tax may sound, there is, I regret to say, no doubt whatever as to its being a fact. That it was the private perquisite of our friend of the camp-stools may, I am afraid, be taken for granted. After all, even a Chinese magistrate in far Turkestan must live.

At Cherchen the presence of the Indian traders already mentioned enabled us to increase considerably our knowledge of local ways and customs.

The Indian traders are naturally in greatest force at Kashgar and in the neighbourhood of Yarkand, though they have also settled at Kuchar. The party we met had been for ten or twelve years in the habit of visiting the chief centres of Chinese Turkestan, spending alternate years there and in India. From their appearance and the information they gave they appeared to be men of substance and responsible merchants ; at the same time they complained of the drawbacks incidental to the attempt to trade in a country where Russian influence has hitherto been predominant. Supported by the position rightly allowed by Russia to the Consul-General who ably represents his country's interests at Kashgar, the Andijani traders are not afraid to place whatever obstacle they can, legitimate or otherwise, in the path of their Indian opponents. From the complaints made by the chief of the Pathan merchants, I gathered that one of the chief difficulties they had to contend with was lack of transport. He affirmed that to hire it anywhere was almost an impossibility. The merchants are therefore obliged to own and maintain an expensive caravan of good animals, which, so long as things go well, he allowed, is no hindrance to the profit of their venture. When, however, luck is against them, and the hardships of the road are too much for their animals, to hire is out of the question, so serious delay and consequent money loss are the inevitable result.

Whether Chinese influence is against Indian traders is a question not easily answered. On the particular portion of the route these men use, which we followed, they are probably welcome. The goods they supply, such as cloth of a superior class, turbans, Indian tea, pepper, and embroidery for the well-to-do Turki families, constitute luxuries, and are not obtainable by the officials and richer inhabitants except from the Indian traders. At other centres, when the goods they offer come into competition with those of the Chinese vendors, there is little doubt of the result. Any one acquainted with the latter class is fully aware that they would not scruple to make free use of local influence to the undoing of the Indian trader.

One other point of interest concerning British (Indian) trade with Central Asia is worthy of mention, and it refers to the question of passports.

It was said by the chief of the Indian traders that they either did not or could not obtain from the British authorities passports which were of equal use to those supplied to the Russian subjects. The impression I gathered was that the fault was rather their own, but of this I cannot speak positively, though the matter is not without interest. The Andijani colony at Cherchen is a fairly large one, consisting of seven families who came from the neighbourhood of Bokhara, all, of course, being Russian subjects. Ostensibly these Andijanis are farmers, though some, as is more usually the case with them, deal in merchandise. One or two are said to return each year to Russian Turkestan in order to purchase fresh goods. It was probably only a coincidence which caused them to put about the usual story of the intended return of two of their number as soon as our arrival was known of at Cherchen. It may also have been mere coincidence that the two should have left Cherchen before we did, but exactly in the opposite direction. It is hardly necessary to remark that the intelligence arrangements must be very complete which enable the Consul-General of a Power—and that not Chinese—at Kashgar to obtain in so short a time after their arrival, at such an out-of-the-way spot as is Cherchen, full particulars of European travellers at first hand.

Interest in the latter town might at first seem inexplicable, but not when it is stated that one of the very few known accessible routes which lead from Chinese Turkestan into Tibet is approached up the Cherchen river.

Before quitting the town we had the pleasure of receiving another visit from the Amban. This time closer acquaintance with us caused him to be much more at his ease. He had previously sent a welcome present of a duck, two chickens, and a sheep, with some vegetables, to which he now added the camp-stools. Not wishing to be outdone, yet somewhat put to it to produce anything unfamiliar to him from our scanty stores, we finally fell back upon the old plan dear to London cabmen, and "left it to him." Having inspected most of our belongings, he appeared much pleased with some wax matches; also, when their use had been explained, with some Indian cigars which we were treasuring for Christmas. Here, then, was a cue, so we hastened to seize it, laying both matches and a cigar figuratively at his feet. In addition to these treasures, we added a folding camp-chair which had been bought in an extravagant moment at Srinagar; and though this was about the first time we had ever succeeded in putting it together, chiefly owing to what the advertisement of its sale described as its capacity for shutting up,—especially when not required to,—it quite won the Amban's heart.

CHAPTER VIII.

LOU-LAN—TWO DESCRIPTIONS OF 77 B.C. AND 1900 A.D.—THE LOPNOR CONTROVERSY — MARCO POLO'S DESCRIPTION OF THE DESERT — SVEN HEDIN'S DISCOVERIES — A BEWILDERING JUNGLE TRACK — GIGANTIC TREES—CHANGING WATERWAYS—AN OCEAN OF SAND—THE CONQUEST OF TORRENTS BY SAND—THE VALUE OF A DEAD PONY—A PONY IN A CORN PIT—A WANDERING SPORTSMAN—BRITISH BOOTS IN FASHION AT LHASA—THE OASIS OF CHAKALIK—AN AGED AMBAN—A PRESENT OF DOVER POWDERS.

BEFORE proceeding with the details of our march after leaving Cherchen, such historical facts as are available of the region about to be traversed are due to the reader. Without some slight knowledge of the past it might seem, from the description which follows, to have been a mere waste of time to penetrate such a country. But enough has already been said to account for the wish to do so. Early Chinese records furnish conclusive proof of a flourishing state of civilisation in the Lop district as far back as the commencement of the Christian era, and these records are continued, through the accounts of various Buddhist pilgrims and later travellers, up to about the seventh century. At the beginning of the eighth century the Mohammedan invasion swept into Eastern Turkestan, submerging temporarily the Chinese power. Until Marco Polo, 1295 A.D., so to speak, refound the southern route to China—*i.e.*, that *viâ* Khotan, Kiria, and Lopnor—little is known of it from European sources. Two centuries later we have more authentic records in the story of the well-known embassy which Shah Rukh sent from his capital, Herat, in 1419 A.D., to the court of China. Though the embassy reached that country by the northern route, through Eastern Turkestan, passing from Tash-kendt in Russian Turkestan *viâ* the Ili river to the town now called Hami, it was obliged, owing to local disturbances, to make the return journey by the southern or Lopnor route to Khotan, Kashgar, and Herat. Even before this period, owing to the lawless character of such inhabitants as there were, as well as to the steady advance of the dreaded sands, which were gradually reducing the whole district to one vast desert, the southern route had ceased to be a highway.

Such evidence as we can now produce enables us to believe these past records, which otherwise the evidence of one's own eyes would most unhesitatingly discredit.

A most interesting account of Lou-lan, which is marked on the map as lying north-east of the Lop country and south of the Kuruk-tag, has been given from Chinese translations by Mr George Macartney, the British representative at Kashgar. The site of this ancient kingdom, known to the Chinese as Shen-shen, was explored by Sven Hedin during the course of his last journey to Lopnor. A comparison of the account of that district in 77 B.C., given by Mr Macartney, and of that given by Sven Hedin of the sand-swept desert he explored, under which the same district lay in 1900, is full of interest to any inquirer into the past of this wonderful country.

"At the epoch these chronicles were written," says Mr Macartney, "about the birth of Christ, the kingdom of Shen-shen, we are told, contained 1570 families, forming a population of 14,100 people, with 2192 trained troops.

"The land is sandy and salt, and there are few cultivated fields. The country relies on the neighbouring kingdom for cereals and agricultural products. The country produces jade, abundance of rushes, the tamaria, the Cloecocca vermicifera, and white grass. The people remove their cattle for pasturage whenever they can find sufficiency of water and herbage. They have asses, horses, and camels. They can fabricate military weapons."

And now let us compare Sven Hedin's description of Lou-lan, standing on the same spot some 2000 years later:—

"The view was broad and open, and altogether *sui generis*. The desert presented a uniform dreary aspect, with its sharp-edged broken terraces and 'tables'—*yardangs* of yellow clay. At intervals stood a house, more or less mutilated by time: but the entire region was uninhabited except for myself and my dog."

I have said that the site of Lou-lan lies north-east of Lopnor, and have unintentionally introduced what is known as the Lopnor controversy. The actual site of the lake has, for years past, been a matter of discussion between such well-known explorers as the late Colonel Prjevalsky, Sven Hedin,

Baron Richthofen, Pievtsoff, and Kozloff, to mention only the chief authorities.

The point at issue is whether the spot now marked in most European maps as Lopnor is the rightful position, or whether the true site was not a more northerly one, as marked in Sven Hedin's map, close to Lou-lan. Scientifically the question is of no small importance: to readers of this chapter it is only so on account of a seemingly curious omission on the part of Marco Polo, the earliest European authority upon this region, to make any mention of the lake at all. Of a town he calls Lop he speaks in the following terms:—

"Lop is a large town at the edge of the desert, which is called the desert of Lop, and is situated between east and north-east. It belongs to the great Khan, and the people worship Mahomet. Now such persons as propose to cross the desert take a week's rest in this town to refresh themselves and their cattle; and then they make ready for the journey, taking with them a month's supply for man and best. On quitting this city they enter the desert. The length of this desert is so great that, 'tis said, it would take a year and more to ride from one end of it to the other. And here, where its breadth is least, it takes a month to cross it. 'Tis all composed of hills and valleys of sand, and not a thing to eat is to be found on it. . . . Beasts there are none, for there is nought for them to eat. But there is a marvellous thing related of this desert, which is, that when travellers are on the move by night, and one of them chances to lag behind or to fall asleep or the like, when he tries to gain his company again he will hear spirits talking, and will suppose them to be his comrades. Sometimes the spirits will call him by name: and thus shall a traveller ofttimes be led astray, so that he never finds his party. And in this way many have perished. Sometimes the stray travellers will hear, as it were, the tramp and hum of a great cavalcade of people away from the real line of the road, and, taking this to be their own company, they will follow the sound; and when day breaks they find that a cheat has been put on them, and that they are in an ill plight. . . . And sometimes you shall hear the sound of a variety of musical instruments, and still more commonly the sound of drums." "So thus it is," he ends, "that the desert is crossed."

The desert referred to by Marco Polo was known to the Chinese of ancient days as Liu-sha = shifting sands. The explanation of his omission to mention the lake of Lop is the simple one, that he never saw it. M. Henri Cordier, in his very interesting revision of Sir Henry Yule's book of Sieur Marco Polo, has pointed this out. "From Cherchen," writes M. Cordier, referring to Marco Polo, "he followed, I believe, neither Prjevalsky's nor Pievtsoff's route, but the old route from Khotan to Si-ngan-fu, in the old bed of the Cherchen Daria, above and almost parallel to the new bed, to the Tarim, then between Sven Hedin's and Prjevalsky's lakes (Lopnor), and across the desert to Sachu to join the ancient Chinese road of the Han dynasty, partly explored by M. Bonin from Sachu." Here, then, is the natural and, in this light, simple explanation why Marco Polo omitted any reference to the lake. I may add that it was our good fortune to see this ancient bed of the Cherchen Darya, near the town of that name, and later on to find, and for some distance to follow, the eastern end of the ancient desert highway. This was when we had nearly succeeded in crossing the Kum Tag, the present name of the desert on European maps, but to this reference will be made hereafter.

Having endeavoured to indicate briefly the chief facts connected with the history of the Lop country, let us now return to follow the fortunes of our own slender caravan as it commenced, not without some trepidation, to enter that desolate stretch of country abhorred of Marco Polo.

From Cherchen we decided to follow the right bank of the river: first, because Sven Hedin, one of the few Europeans who had attempted to pass that way, had there discovered some graves of a type other than Mohammedan; and secondly, because local information stated it was the best track for ponies.

Of the graves, or any knowledge of them, our local guides pretended ignorance. The interest connected with these remains lies in the fact that, according to Sven Hedin, the coffins contained the mummified bodies of non-Chinese or Mongolian people. He assumes that they were probably the remains of a set who went by the name of "Raskolnikis," or Nonconformists, a few of whom are said by him to have migrated from Siberia to this far country, perhaps in search of religious freedom.

After crossing the Cherchen river to the right bank, we turned our footsteps north-east to follow its course half-way to Chakalik; and the entire change in the character of the country through which we marched was not unwelcome.

The track itself was a mere jungle path eighteen inches wide, and ran alternately through high reeds, belts of scrub jungle, with *tograck* forest, mostly dead, or over flat open marshland.

To us the chief delight was in the unlimited fuel and the freedom from any care as to the presence of water or grazing. The latter was furnished by a small dried reed, not unlike bamboo grass, which the animals eat readily.

We had been assured by local sportsmen at Cherchen that ample game was to be found between that place and Chakalik. On the strength of their stories we had engaged two shikarris, but, except as guides, found them of little use. Had our Cherchen friends told of numerous tracks of game, they would have been well within the truth, for those of both pig and deer ran all through the jungle, but of game itself we saw very little. A few specimens of Prjevalsky's gazelle rewarded us for a good deal of rough riding, but pig or *marol* we were never able to bag. Alongside the river in many parts it was only possible to push through the dried reeds, mounted, by following the tracks the wild boar had made. The reeds were frequently as high as the head of a mounted man, and the track just sufficiently broad and winding to allow of our advancing in single file. Much as we wished for the sight of a boar, the thought has more than once occurred since, that perhaps the reality of the meeting might not have been all that fancy painted it at the time. To attempt to leave the track, or even to turn round in many places, was an impossibility, owing to the dense growth; to see five yards ahead was quite out of the question. Under such conditions, to attempt to dispute the right-of-way with an old boar, armed too with only a sporting .303, and mounted, appears on reflection to be too great odds on the boar.

During this part of its course the Cherchen river winds considerably. At times during the day the track would run along the top of its low bank; at others we found ourselves cut off from the river by a mile or two of almost impenetrable jungle.

The nightly camp was usually made as near the river as possible, and sometimes it was our good fortune to hit on very pleasant and pretty spots. It was always our custom to halt one day in the seven in order that men and animals should enjoy a well-earned rest; and as luck would have it we found ourselves amid pleasant surroundings the day the weekly halt was due. Kolalenger was the name of our camp, though how a name is always forthcoming when asked for, at no matter what spot in the midst of the jungle, I could never ascertain. No doubt certain districts have regular names given by the shepherds who there graze their flocks at different times of the year. Of these, most are obtained from natural causes, or from some incident long remembered in local lore. In the former category was the

Trying the ice near Chakalik.

Yak leaving Camp.

name of another of our camps a few nights back. Kengleika means, in local dialect, "the broad inundated track," and the reason for the name was obvious, though we found the district fairly dry. Near Kola-lenger the Cherchen has a bed of sixty yards width, but the running water narrows to twenty-five to thirty feet, which here flows under the right bank. On November 27 the stream was full of floating ice, and quite a small block would have sufficed to cause a jam and the consequent freezing over of the river. On the left bank of the river the sand-hills of the desert approach close to the water, and rise to a height of some thirty feet in places. One of the features of the forest belts is the extraordinary size of some of the dead trees. Veritable giants they must once have been; and nothing so clearly indicates the direction and presence of ancient river-beds as do these heroes of bygone days. Local tradition pretends that the life of one of these trees denotes the flight of time in a ratio of a thousand years to grow, a thousand to live, and a thousand more to die; and without subscribing fully to this somewhat oriental description of the life of a *tograck*, no doubt they should help to determine when the channels which once gave them life ceased to hold water. I measured one of the largest trees and found it to be 211 inches in circumference (17 feet 7 inches). Some idea of the size was gathered from the relatively diminutive appearance of the shikarri and pony. A most weird effect these ancient giants have in the moonlight, and sitting round the camp-fire one could not help pondering upon the past centuries through which they had blossomed and lived, and of the strange hordes they may have sheltered,—Huns, Tartars, Mongols, all long ago vanished.

Another feature of the right bank of the Cherchen river was the number of ancient river-beds we crossed. One we camped in had a depth of from fifteen to twenty feet, and a width of from ninety to a hundred and twenty feet. That the Cherchen, which continues to flow, had in times past so often changed its channel is a point of great interest, for after-experience proved to us that the marshes and lake-beds of the whole of this region have undoubtedly done, and are doing, the same. The interest connected with this fact is chiefly based on the effect it may have in throwing additional light upon the yet unsettled problem of the situation of Lopnor itself.

In view of the scientific interest involved in the question of the inconstancy of all water-channels in this vast basin, I will quote another case. About latitude 94° E. on the Chinese side of the Kum Tag desert, we explored a wide expanse of lagoon and lake, known on our maps as Kara Nor. Here all the signs necessary to substantiate the inconstancy of such areas are very clearly marked. No two people who have examined Kara Nor and its ramifications would disagree in saying that both in area, depth, and actual position, it never, for any length of time, remains constant. I venture to think no one who has seen that district, and is acquainted with the minute proofs to which Sven Hedin has put his theory, will again deny that not only Lopnor, but the whole Kara Koshun basin, wherever small lagoons and depressions exist, is in the same state.

Here and there on the banks of the Cherchen reed huts or *satma* are found, which are made use of by the shepherds during the spring and autumn. From May to September insects render life unbearable near the river, and then both men and beasts are driven away from its vicinity. The shepherds remain in this district until the snow falls in December, when they move nearer to Cherchen. We sometimes came upon open spaces alongside the river where the reeds had been burnt. This is done for the grazing, not for cultivation. As we moved up the river it was not always possible to camp on the banks of it. It was then necessary to use the water in the ponds, which was usually more or less tainted, sometimes salt, but more frequently brackish, with an unpleasant smell from the decaying reed-roots.

On the eighth day after leaving Cherchen we turned our backs to the river, and struck a course slightly south of east, in order to reach Chakalik. As soon as the vicinity of the river was left behind, the surrounding country again became heavy sand. It was here that we first became acquainted with the curious root-heaps, which afterwards form a familiar figure in the landscape. On the edge of the forest-belts huge sandy mounds eighteen to twenty feet high are to be seen, which contain dead roots and decayed branches of trees. How the roots come to be laid bare and the mounds erected, it is not easy to say. Erected, strictly speaking, they are not, for their extraordinary appearance can only be the result of denudation by the action of the wind. Round these gigantic heaps the track wound, to emerge at intervals on to undulating sand-hills, where the dunes were the highest yet met with. Sometimes skirting, sometimes climbing these, rising and falling every few score yards, our animals soon began to feel the change for the worse. The biggest dunes are miniature cliffs, occasionally as much as forty feet high. Very striking, indeed, is the appearance of these larger conformations. Another sample of this sand country had to be crossed the same afternoon, which only differed from the last in being even more trying to the caravan.

Having traversed one of the many belts of decayed forest, the track emerged by a gentle ascent of 100 feet on to what had all the appearance of a sea of loose sand. The effect was that of the ocean in a calm, but with a heavy swell on. The dunes and miniature cliffs now gave place to smooth glacis-like slopes, half to three-quarters of a mile in extent. Except on the exposed ridges, where the sand was partially frozen, the going was very heavy. During the daytime, at this season, the prevailing wind was from the north-east. It rose with gentle regularity about 9.30 A.M., but gradually increased in force, until it died away with equal punctuality about 5 P.M. As a rule the nights were calm and very clear.

We passed, this day, a curious reminder of the sovereign power, in the shape of a small well-kept wattle hut. It stands empty, apropos to nothing at all, and is surrounded by a neat moat. Inside the hut is a wooden board on two stout posts, with an inscription graven on it in both Chinese and Turki characters. This states that the hut is the boundary between the Cherchen and Chakalik administrative districts, though to whom, except to the wild animals, the subject can be of any interest, only those who pay for the upkeep of the hut know. In a way, too, it is characteristic of the Chinese love for outward effect, for to maintain even this sign of external power in such an out-of-the-way spot, serves to remind the few Turki who pass that Chinese administration is a fact as well as a name.

Half-way between the river and Chakalik we camped on the banks of a small stream, then quite dry, which suffices to afford a few acres of cultivation to some wild-looking natives. The miserable collection of huts rejoices in the name of Vash Shar.

The river-bed varies from fifty to one hundred and twenty yards in breadth, and so far as could be judged in its then state it never succeeds in reaching the Cherchen river.

Although a respectable volume of water at certain seasons of the year, the Vash Shar struggles past the hamlet, only to meet the fate of all these snow-fed streams. Nothing in the shape of running water seems able to withstand the dreaded sands. For although the former leave the mountains, as we saw earlier, foaming torrents with every appearance of being able to sweep anything from their course, the passive resistance of the latter invariably conquers in the end.

At Vash Shar we had to regret the loss of two more caravan ponies, besides which, thanks to the stupidity of one of the village boys, I nearly lost my riding animal. One of the caravan animals altogether broke down, so was put out of his misery. Our shikarri at once pounced on him, and proceeded to cut off all four feet. Upon being asked the reason for his haste, he remarked —"Has he not four shoes, and in the shoes are there not nails?"

Such is the value of the smallest piece of iron in a country where wood entirely takes its place. We also added another item of information to our stock over the death of the pony. When the shikarri had finished his work, a second man at once commenced to skin both hind legs: this, he informed us, was the choicest part of the animal for leather, and as his boots often required patching, was it not wrong to waste it?

The accident to my own pony occurred as we arrived at Vash Shar. After dismounting I handed the reins to a village urchin, with signs to walk the animal round while I went to select a spot for the camp. I had got off the pony in one corner of a walled enclosure where the corn is threshed, and where, according to local custom, it is also stored in deep circular pits, a few feet in diameter. Before I had crossed the enclosure I heard the sound of a scuffle, then a shriek from the lad, and upon turning round, what was my astonishment to see no pony, and the lad wildly gesticulating on the edge of one of the pits. Without any idea of what had happened, I ran to the pit and there saw the wretched animal curled up at the bottom, quite unable to move. As he lay with the front of his head jammed against his tail, he looked for all the world like a whiting ready trussed to be cooked. How he got into such a position or how he managed to fall into so narrow a pit at all, I never understood. However, we set to work to dig him out, and after twenty minutes were able to pull him on to his legs. Making a ramp at one end of the now enlarged pit, out he walked, neither himself nor my European saddle any the worse. Before reaching Chakalik one other small stream was crossed. This is locally called the Jhilijk river, and was the only stream, since leaving the Cherchen, which held any water.

Between Cherchen and Chakalik we had met very few local travellers, and only one of any interest. This was a cheery fellow, half sportsman by profession, wholly a wanderer by nature. He carried with him an ancient and prehistoric blunderbuss, and appeared to be immensely taken with our rifles. Of his own movements he talked freely, and, as is the custom of the road in the East to which all honest travellers must conform, we, with slight reservation, were equally communicative. Our friend informed us that he had only twelve days previously returned from Lhasa, where he had been as guide to a Lama who had been making the pilgrimage. The latter had commenced his journey in far-away Semipalatinsk, whence, after crossing into Chinese Turkestan, he made his way by the Ili river to Chakalik. From such vast distances do devout

Buddhists come. Having fingered most of our clothing, and inquired the price of the rest of it, our cheerful friend expressed much admiration for our boots. For want of anything to say to keep the conversation going, I inquired if he had ever seen any like them before. "Oh yes," he replied without hesitation; "since the white soldiers were at Lhasa everybody there wears boots like yours"!

That Sir Francis Younghusband had left an indelible impression of British strength and justice we were fully aware, but that he had also set the fashion in "ammunition" boots, the world has not hitherto been informed.

Our arrival at Chakalik was signalised by a heavy snow-storm, and we were now face to face with winter, which previous experience in North China had taught us not to regard lightly. Immediately before entering the town, though it is only by courtesy that it can be so described, the Chakalik-su is crossed. The stream runs in two channels, each about a hundred yards across, and they enclose a small island. Both were dry, having, we were informed, run out twelve days previously. In this condition they remain for six or eight weeks, when the snow in the channels may begin to melt.

The oasis which the name Chakalik covers is a small one, having a length from east to west of four-and-a-half miles. From north to south it is narrower, being only a strip one-and-a-half miles at widest. The village is the headquarters of the last administrative district towards China, and boasts an Amban. Chakalik has an importance quite beyond its size, as being the centre upon which four important native routes converge. Though the traffic on any one of the four is insignificant, as we count it in Europe, it is none the less steady, and each track serves, as all in the East do, as a means of disseminating information slowly but surely over very wide distances. Of these tracks by far the most important is the one which connects in thirty-three marches to the north, *viâ* Korla, with Urumtsi, the capital city of Chinese Turkestan, and to the south across the Altyn Tag with Lhasa. The latter place is a three months' journey from Chakalik for ordinary native travellers, but the distance can be covered in two months by well-mounted men to whom time is an object. The third most important route is that connecting Chakalik with Yarkand, the one by which we had come. A fourth leads south and east, following for some distance the northern base of the Altyn Tag. It then turns north to Sa-chu, on the borders of China proper.

The position of Chakalik is a peculiar one, and but for being on the highroad to Tibet it would be of no importance. Hitherto, at each oasis and town, such as Kiria and Niya, according to local opinion we appeared to be widening the distance between ourselves and the centre of civilisation, which to them meant first Khotan and then Yarkand. At Chakalik, on the contrary, the Amban's thoughts and conversation were always of Urumtsi and the north, or of China. He appeared to take little or no interest in the parts through which we had come, and when he did speak of Cherchen or Niya, it was much as a confirmed Londoner might of Manchester or Birmingham.

Chakalik itself consists of one mean street, partly covered in, and under a quarter of a mile long. Throughout a considerable portion of its length both sides are lined by poor shops; but except once in eight days, when the local market is going on, only the butchers and bakers give themselves the trouble of opening. The population of the village is between four and five hundred souls, and though the general air is not one of wealth, the level of comfort is fairly high. At the north-west corner of the village stands a temple of pure Chinese pattern. Following the usual custom in that country this is half guest-house, half-temple. The offices of the Amban, though not the *yamen*, stand on the north side of the main street. These are surrounded by a crenellated mud wall sixteen feet high, which would offer no serious defence, except to a Turki mob not over anxious to get in. At the east end of the one street stands, in miniature, a ludicrous copy of a Chinese city gateway. It could never have been imposing, except possibly to the smallest of the Turki ragamuffins who play hide-and-seek up its tumbled-down stairway; but as we viewed it nothing could have been less like the gates of Peking. As usual in the East, and especially in China, outward show was the first consideration, and so long as the smooth plaster lasted, the gateway may perhaps have fulfilled that object. Unfortunately for the one architectural *chef-d'œuvre* of Chakalik, the late snow-storm had fairly given it away, for underneath one layer of bricks all the rest was brushwood.

The Amban lives in a country house, built like

a *yamèn*, three-quarters of a mile outside this gateway. His reception of us, as well as our treatment by him during the week we were compelled to spend at Chakalik, have left only the kindliest memories. He was a handsome old gentleman of nearly seventy, who took proper pride in his personal appearance and position. A Hupeh man, his own home was at Hankow, and upon the delights of that now most important town he was never weary of talking. At the time of our visit he had been two years at Chakalik, having spent the greater part of his official career in Turkestan. During our stay he paid us daily visits, or we him, and talked with a freedom upon any subject unusual in Chinese officials.

His first call was made in state in a Peking cart, with a proper escort, though a rather quaint assortment. Some of these may be seen on another page in the photograph taken in the courtyard of our *serai*. For over an hour the old gentleman sat and talked, much of his time being, as usual, taken up with a minute examination of our camp kit, guns, and stores. My camp-bed of the "X" pattern was an entire novelty, and when popped into its bag for his benefit, his admiration was boundless. Coffee and prunes helped to while away the time; and so much did he enjoy the latter that we were forced to present him with one of the last of the bottles from our store cupboard. Having got the Amban into the right humour, we thought it politic to unfold our plan for attempting to explore the desert between Chakalik and the Chinese border. It was necessary that his goodwill should be secured, as, without it, we were well aware neither animals nor men would be forthcoming.

At Leh the contract with our men and the caravan *bashi* had been made for Chakalik, and here they were about to leave us to return to India. To lose the services of these men, who had served us faithfully and for the most part well, was a blow. However good the new lot might turn out to be, we were strangers to one another, neither was there the same tie between us as usually exists in India between master and man. In addition to purchasing or hiring camels, we had also to refit the entire caravan. Tents, saddlery, clothing, and boots were all in need of repair; and it was through the good offices of our present guest that we hoped to make everything smooth. His reception of our suggested plan was at first decidedly doubtful, nor was it only the opinion of the official he expressed when he begged us not to make the attempt. "The road by Urumtsi and Hami is much the best," he said; "if you go the other way you will die and never get there."

Accepting this opinion as entirely one of personal regard for our safety, we made light of the matter, but were relieved when, after a little time, the Amban promised his official support. Having done so, to his credit be it said, he more than fulfilled his word. Our object temporarily gained, we refrained for the moment from pushing the matter any farther, preferring to hear our host relate his experiences of life as they appear to a

Chinese official in Central Asia. There was no lack of conversation, for the Amban was evidently pleased at the opportunity of meeting his fellow-men, foreigners though they might be. Before the visit was concluded he began to complain of a cough, besides detailing the symptoms from which a brother who lived with him, he said, was suffering. A few minutes previously we had been unwise enough to allow him to see the small medicine case we carried, which we ought to have known would be quite sufficient to inoculate him with all the diseases it was designed to cure. Luckily the particular ill he announced himself a victim to did not require much diagnosing. We promptly recommended, and handed to his head factotum for the old gentleman's use, four Dover powder tabloids. When it came to prescribing for the absent brother our knowledge of pharmacy was hardly equal to the task of recognising the symptoms from which he had been said to suffer. As a harmless general remedy I suggested phenacetin, but this we decided not to try, as my companion remarked that it was only used for sea-sickness. Dover powders, our own favourite medicine, we did not like to prescribe, as in the East etiquette forbids an inferior even to suffer from the same form of malady as a superior, and the Amban was already booked for Dover powders. There seemed nothing for it but to strike out a new line and hope for the best; so to ensure the absent brother receiving every chance, we fell back on that ever popular remedy, quinine. With half a dozen of these tabloids in one hand and as many

Dover powder ones in the other, with minute instructions as to the time they were to be taken and the quantity, we eventually helped the Amban into his Peking cart, triumphantly bidding him what, in spite of our prescriptions, we hoped was only a temporary farewell.

The next few days were fully occupied in attending to such matters as the hiring of the new men and camels, as well as by the attempt to discover a guide. The purchase of sufficient grain was another item of importance.

In the intervals of leisure we renewed our acquaintance with hawking, and that under the wing of another good sportsman who traded in skins. We also endeavoured to ascertain if the site of the present town is an old one; but in the East such inquiries are usually not fruitful of information. Immediately to the north-east of the present main street there are the ruins of an ancient fort. These are only just traceable, and with no means of verification it would be pure guesswork to hazard an opinion as to their age. A modern, and for local requirements suffficently solid, fort stands south of the east-end of the town. It is barely a quarter of a mile from the gate previously mentioned, and commands the village. In shape the fort is square, with crenellated walls of mud-brick 100 yards long. The trace has a double enceinte, with moat and corner towers. Inside are barrack huts and stables for the usual non-existent garrison. At the time of our visit the latter was represented by a bright-looking active Turki youth, who was practising the lance exercise with no small skill, for the edification of two other youngsters. Though at first abashed by our presence, he soon regained confidence enough to give another performance; but how or from whom he had learnt the drill we were unable to ascertain. Inquiring from a respectable Chinaman, the only other occupant of the fort, what had become of its garrison, we received the answer we had expected. As happens with such curious frequency to garrisons in China, the whole five hundred had been sent away "into the country" the day before our arrival.

Later on the commander of the fort honoured us with a call. He was a pleasant fellow of about thirty-eight years of age—a Honan man—and left the impression that he was quite wasted in his present position, as well as utterly sick of life at Chakalik.

The only other building of any note is a small mosque which stands in a courtyard adjacent to the bazar. The building is of the plainest and simplest kind, hardly rising above the mud-brick standard. As a Mohammedan the Turki takes his religion, as he does most mundane affairs, lightly. While "doing" the bazar one market-day, when it was supposed to be in full swing, we found that it was also the fashionable day for attending the mosque. The swing was entirely absent from the proceedings in the bazar, which, perhaps, accounted for my being able to pick up a fine pair of leather embroidered saddle-bags for the price of what is commonly known at home as a hold-all. These saddle-bags are heirlooms, and form part of the invariable equipment of any well-to-do Turki when on the road.

After a week, of which the last days passed somewhat impatiently, the long-delayed camels ordered by the Amban appeared. He had already selected the men he intended should accompany us, as well as fixed the wages they were to receive.

The last day we proceeded in all the state we could muster to make our adieux at the Amban's country residence. We were by this time on most friendly terms, and the daily passage of one party to call on the other had become one of the events to which the bazar loafers looked forward. Having repeated our polite speeches, according to Chinese custom, and having also relieved our feelings by expressing our most grateful thanks for all the old gentleman had been kind enough to do for us, we rose to take our departure. In the courtyard of the *yamen* building a score or so of the inhabitants, and the usual retinue, were drawn up. Not content with this, the Amban also insisted upon firing three pop-guns which stood in the yard. The only result of this honour was to make it utterly impossible for us to get anywhere near our frightened ponies. When the firing began I had just put out my hand to say good-bye in the European fashion, which the Amban had adopted from us, and this he promptly seized and retained, much to Layard's amusement, until the saluting was over.

CHAPTER IX.

TEARFUL FAREWELLS—AN ANCIENT SEA-SHORE—ABDAL—MARCO POLO AND THE DESERT SOUNDS—ROOT-HEAPS—A CHRISTMAS EVE DINNER IN THE DESERT—THE FINDING OF A BAG OF CORN—A DESERT TRAGEDY—THE CHINESE *TORLA* OR WATCH-TOWERS—A WIND-STORM IN THE DESERT—KARA NOR—A DEVOTED SURVEYOR—SACHU.

NOT until we had left Chakalik was it possible to realise the full force of the description given by Marco Polo of the Lop country. A first instalment of what might be expected was suggested by the behaviour of the wives and mothers of the new caravan men as we marched out of Chakalik. Sven Hedin has remarked, in one of his journeys, upon the callousness with which a certain follower left his home and family at a moment's notice to accompany him on a year's absence. Our experience was, unfortunately, quite the reverse. For the first mile out of Chakalik our progress resembled, in miniature, the march of a regiment at home about to embark for foreign service. Most tearful were the farewells, and again and again were final embraces exchanged between the men and their families. By the time Abdal was reached matters had somewhat improved, but either the new lot were a lugubrious set or visions of the desert-crossing lay heavy upon their minds. From Chakalik to Abdal is a matter of four days' march. Snow lay widely spread, though not deep, and as the south-western end of the Kara Koshun marshes was approached, the surrounding country presented a most gloomy picture. On all sides a dreary waste of marsh stretches to the horizon. Occasional belts of decayed jungle and dried reeds do but add to the mournful aspect of the general surroundings. It is well known that the whole of the vast basin of Central Asia, with which European maps are familiar under the name of the Gobi desert, and which occupies the centre of that continent, was once a great ocean. Pumpelly and other authorities are of opinion that this ocean, which at a comparatively recent geological date extended from the Caspian to the Khinghan mountains in Manchuria, was drained by a volcanic upheaval. That this ocean theory is correct no one who has visited the central portion of the basin, which includes Lopnor, the Kara Koshun marshes, and the Kum Tag desert, could doubt. From the point of view of physical geography, the eastern end of the Lopnor basin also offers most interesting and convincing evidence of the truth of this theory. Every day spent by our caravan in the Kum Tag desert, east of Lopnor, confirms the impression which the configuration of the land suggests—viz., that one is travelling along an ancient sea-shore. So strong is the impression that it is impossible to describe this portion of the desert in other language than would be used were this still the case.

In a paper read by Prince Krapotkin at a meeting

The Amban of Chakalik and Retinue.

Camels on the march in the Kum Tag Desert.

of the Royal Geographical Society in March 1903, the whole situation is stated most succinctly, and no more exact appreciation of the true situation can be gained than by quoting a brief portion of the opinion there expressed. "With regard to Lopnor," says Prince Krapotkin, "I will permit myself to remark that I do not think that the lake Kara Koshun—that is, the Lopnor of Prjevalsky—can be considered as anything else but the present remainder from the great lake Lopnor. But what appears to me quite certain, after Sven Hedin's surveys, levellings, and discoveries, is that there was first a time when Lopnor covered the whole of the triangular space which is limited, on the west by the southward course of the Tarim, on the south-east by the lake Kara Koshun, and on the north-east by the escarpment of the Kurruk-tag, which runs in a north-west to south-east direction. The place of the sixty springs, Altimish Bulak, which has been visited previously by the Russian explorers, and lies, according to their determinations, at an altitude of 3600 feet, stands on the border of the escarpment and the triangular space between the escarpment; the Tarim river, and the plains which spread at the foot of the Altyn Tag, must have been occupied some time by a large basin, upon the shores of which stood that spot of the Lou-lan region in which Sven Hedin found such interesting manuscripts. Later on the lake occupied the eastern part only of that triangular basin, and now the lake Kara Koshun, or the Lopnor of Prjevalsky, represents the southern trough of that depression which continues still to be occupied by what has survived of the Lopnor. At any rate, when the full reports and the levellings of Sven Hedin are published and the whole district is better explored, it will certainly appear that within this triangular depression, the Lopnor desert in Stieler's atlas map, the lake was changing its position in proportion as it decreased, and it may change it several times more before the general desiccation of Central Asia, which is going on at great speed, will finally move the Tarim lake farther south-westwards to meet the Cherchen, and finally reduce what will remain of the Lopnor to the little lake Kara-buran which we see at the junction of the Yarkand Darya with the Cherchen river."

The last few miles before the traveller reaches Abdal presents the most depressing stretch of landscape since Chakalik. Crossing the snow-covered *sai* the action of the wind was most marked, not only upon the sand, but upon the fine gravel of which the *sai* is partly composed. Through the snow the tops of small ridges of gravel rise to a height of from twelve to eighteen inches. As regular as, and resembling the tops of, small waves breaking upon a sea-shore, these ridges run at right angles to the prevailing winds, north-east to south-west. Each "wavelet" is from six to forty feet in length. They are slightly convex towards the prevailing north-east wind, and the general formation extends for miles.

Abdal itself is a collection of reed *satma*, among which are a few mud hovels belonging to the headmen. The settlement contains some fifteen families, who exist mainly by the fishing in the spring and

A Reed Hut and one of our Tents near Abdal.

Crushed Ice for the Ponies.

summer. The huts lie for three-quarters of a mile along the right bank of the Cherchen Darya, which here empties itself into the marshes. While we were at Abdal the river was hard frozen some six inches down, and had been so for eighteen days. To the natives the river is known as the Cherchen, but, according to the story told by an old man, the Cherchen is considered by them to be composed of three other streams—the Yarkand river, the Kucha river, and the Karasha river. Our reception, even at this miserable spot, was as cordial as the inhabitants could make it. The Lop men are of the same type as the Turkis, and the existence led by these hardy marshmen is indeed a trying one. At the time of our visit the thermometer had begun to register 40° to 50° of frost during the night, and the north-east wind, though somewhat less cruel than the west wind of Tibet, was sufficiently trying. Exposed to such biting cold during the winter months, the contrast of the heat of summer is, according to Sven Hedin, no less trying. Worst of all, the insect plague of mosquitoes and gadflies is such that during the summer not even the shepherds nor their flocks dare remain near the marsh district. At Abdal we were joined by the guide who was to escort us across the desert. He had been procured by our friend the Amban of Chakalik, and turned out to be a faithful servant.

Upon 17th December our party left Abdal to attempt the passage of the desert. It was our intention at first to make direct for Sachu or, as it is always known locally, Tung-huang, but we eventually changed our plans owing to suggestions from the guide. After leaving Abdal the general direction ran north-east and east-north-east for the next month. Skirting the southern edge of the Kara Koshun marshes, we camped the first night beside its frozen border. Here we were reminded of the quaint description given by Marco Polo of this district, and more especially of his remarks as to the sounds of musical instruments and drums said to be heard by travellers. That these legends have some foundation in fact we discovered for ourselves, especially when the Oriental language Marco Polo would use in describing them is allowed for. In the East slight exaggeration is considered an art, not, as in the West, a fault. To our camp that evening on the edge of the ice weird sounds came floating. These were nothing but the groaning and booming of the ice, re-echoing from and over the distant marshes as the temperature dropped and it froze harder. Not being an Asiatic, I should describe it as the far-off sound of trumpeting elephants, but of the two descriptions that of Marco Polo is certainly the more poetical.

It was not until three days after quitting Abdal that we found ourselves approaching the first series of sandy cliffs which so obviously denote the shores of a former ancient sea. So far our track had run over rough frozen mud, locally known as *shor*, or through reed jungle in which are dotted the sand root-heaps previously mentioned. The *shor* is a mixture of salt deposit, dust, and lime, and has the appearance of a clay field newly steam-ploughed, then frozen solid. For miles our track ran over ground of this nature, and the effect on both the ponies and camels was to knock their feet to pieces. Though never found on the *shor*, the sand root-heaps which exist in the desert are a real blessing to the traveller, for without them fuel would be unobtainable. Many a good bonfire we owed to their presence, nor were they to be despised as wind-screens under which to camp at night. In order to give some idea of the size of these mounds, it may be mentioned that one, which we tried to set light to, measured fifteen feet in height, and was forty paces round the base. As a display our effort was a failure, but as a magnified camp-fire it sent us all to bed happy that night.

It is difficult to account satisfactorily in detail for the presence of these root-heaps, which vary so greatly in size. That they are caused by the invasion of the sand there is of course no doubt, and where the largest still remain they are in all probability the graves of bygone forests which edged this inland sea. The heaps found in the desert are on a very much smaller scale than these near Abdal. They exist for the most part where marshy spots or springs are or have once been. Each bush when alive naturally dropped its fronds in the autumn directly into its own roots. This continued year after year, and each sand-storm, or even the ordinary high winds which prevail, blew the sand more and more into and on to the bushes. As the sand covers the fronds heaped at the roots and mixes with them, it so gradually turns them into the sand-heaps which, while the bush still lived, had the top showing. Now that the bushes are dead, and the ceaseless struggle with the overwhelming sand is finished, the latter has spread all over the bush.

The first line of cliffs met with rose at a point where the bed of the desert was 2300 feet above sea-level. The cliffs themselves averaged thirty-five feet in height, were covered on top with fine gravel, and had buttress-like faces to the north. Along the base of the cliffs ran a strip of reed-grass some twenty to forty yards wide, in which at intervals were marshy springs of very saline water. Once having struck the cliffs, our guide pursued his way along the reed-strip until we camped for the night. The water which oozed from the wet spots was here unfit for use, so the ponies had to be fed on crushed ice. It was our custom to melt as much of the ice we carried as would suffice for the evening wants of men and ponies; but it not unfrequently happened that the fuel wherewith to melt the ice was as scarce as the water itself. One night our guide informed us that for three days neither water nor fuel was to be found, so at starting next morning sufficient roots were piled on the camels to last that time. The following day the guide struck away from the foot of the cliffs out into the bare desert. Throughout this march no sign of vegetation was to be seen, the surface being of the nature already alluded to as *shor*. The cliffs appeared to run on east as far as the eye could see. After a poor camp on the *shor*, with, luckily for us, a windless night, we resumed the march. Continuing north-east, it was not long before sandhills appeared in the distance, rising like a group of islands from the desert. These were forty to fifty feet high, and the surface of the ground adjacent either gravelly sand or a hard lagoon-like bottom. A few miles farther on more hillocks and sand-ridges appeared, and at nine miles from the last camp we found ourselves at the foot of another line of cliffs almost identical with the first. The direction of the new shore was from east-north-east to west-south-west, and the cliffs ran as high in places as sixty feet. Below them again was the strip of dried reed-grass, thirty yards broad, with the same marshy spots at intervals. Through the face of the cliffs a running stream of shallow water, a few feet wide and frozen solid, had carved a way. When running it must waste itself in the reed-strip or, when the ice was broken, farther on in the desert. The frozen pools round the spot where it emerged from the cliffs were found to be very salt. An interesting point is raised by the question how long the little stream had taken to carve the miniature gorge in the cliffs. The latter was fifty to sixty feet deep, and at the top had a breadth of thirty feet. During the passage of the Kum Tag we were, as for most of our journey, dependent upon our rifles for meat. The local name for the small gazelle is *juggran* and these pretty little animals were found at intervals all through the desert. This particular camp seemed to be a favourite retreat, and though the satisfaction of stalking and bagging a buck at 300 yards was ours, we felt that it was taking an unfair advantage to wait for them at their own water-holes. Of the wild camel we did not obtain a specimen, although in certain portions of the desert their tracks, rolling spots, and "runs," are as common as are those of hares at home.

Throughout part of another day's march we followed the base of the cliffs until in the afternoon they became less regular. Isolated hillocks thrust themselves in front of the main line, but the general nature of the cliffs remained the same. Once more our guide intimated his intention to quit the cliffs, so we struck away north-north-east. As before, the line of cliffs continued east as far as the eye was able to follow them. Within five miles we had reached yet a third line of cliffs, identical with the other two. This last we approached, as it were, from behind, turning to march along the top of the escarpment. Continuing along the cliffs for the next five miles, we crossed what correspond to regular bays and inlets on the sea-shore. At the foot of the cliffs ran the usual strip of reed-grass, with some marshy spots. Three small springs of somewhat saline character afforded the best water we had tasted since leaving Abdal; and that evening, as there was some doubt about any for the next few days, and as it was Christmas Eve, we decided to give the animals and ourselves a day's rest, and to spend as merry a Christmas as possible under the circumstances. The next day was spent in making a detailed section of the face of the cliff, which may be found in the Appendix, also in celebrating the day. For a dinner in the middle of the Kum Tag desert we were rather proud of our menu. Should it tempt any *blasé* diner-out to travel so far in search of the local condiments, I can assure him that he will also find there an appetite he has long been a stranger to.

CHRISTMAS EVE DINNER. KUM TAG DESERT.

Latitude by stars, 40° 22′ 25″

Pôtage à la désert.
Poisson à Lopnor glacé.
Rôti Venaison Juggran.
Gâteau de Riz.
Abricots à sec à la Turkestan.
Miel glacé.
Finest Hankow tea à la Mandarin Chakalik.
Liqueurs: Cognac with salt water.
Une demi tasse without, to correct the first.
Cigars: the last two of the finest Leh bazar brand.

Boxing-Day found the caravan traversing a terrace of hard gravel half-way up the cliff face, but still continuing along the old sea-shore. Having crossed a large promontory, we descended into a big bay which runs back two miles to the south. In the bay stood some curious flat-topped islands eighty to ninety feet high. The bed of the bay is covered with reed-grass and clay mud, the fine gravel which is found on the tops of the cliffs being conspicuous by its absence. The next afternoon we turned away from the cliffs, and for the first time found ourselves in the vicinity of some of the curious terrace formations or clay *yardangs* which Sven Hedin alludes to. Scored and eroded by the action of wind and water, the shapes assumed by this formation are of the quaintest kind. The first we saw displayed the most perfect natural imitation of a ruined city imaginable, and such I took it to be. Riding over towards it, even closer inspection did not dispel the illusion, for after climbing the outer *débris* one still retained the impression of ruined walls from which towers, gateways, and buttresses had gradually fallen away.

Although we had finally quitted the line of cliffs, these could be seen four or five miles distant to the south. In the open desert stony ridges, upon which rock outcropped, began to appear. The sub-formation of all these ridges, as well as of the hillocks which intervened, is the same as that of the cliffs. The sand is not loose and soft, but hard pressed, clean and clay-like, as if built up. Passing one of these ridges we received undoubted evidence that the desert route is used at times, for entirely by accident one of the followers discovered a piece of sacking, portion of a bag, buried at the foot of one of the terraces, which turned out to contain Indian corn.

I had climbed to the top of the highest ridge in order to try and get a view over the surrounding country for survey work, while Lall Singh was plotting at its foot. One of the men holding the ponies noticed the corner of the bag sticking out from the base of the ridge. Such an extraordinary find naturally excited his curiosity, and, shouting to me, the man at once began to dig away the soil as best he could. A few minutes' work rewarded us by the find of the above-mentioned treasure-trove, and although further search was made in every direction nothing more was seen.

To make this unlooked-for gift more valuable still, we had found the previous evening that our grain was being used up quicker than we had anticipated—at least, our progress so far had been slower; so there and then the famished ponies had one good meal in addition to their miserable ration of a pound a-day.

While at Chakalik the Amban, in a fit of confidence, had told us that he was expecting a second wife, whom, he added with Chinese naïveté, he had purchased at Sachu. He then proceeded to state that she would probably come by the desert track, adding, "That is, if they can come before the winter is over." The latter portion of his remark may sound strange, as winter, it might be assumed, was a season to be avoided. It is, however, the only time the crossing of the desert can be attempted, owing to the fact that ice for water can then be carried. The Amban also stated that only three or four camels would constitute the caravan of his second wife, in order that they might use the utmost haste. The difficulty of the task assigned to the escort he fully allowed, but consoled himself by saying that it was easy enough to buy wives in China.

It was not until our bag of corn had been discovered that we even gave a second thought to the story the old gentleman had related, but, trying to account for such an extraordinary find, we began to wonder if it could have any connection with his love-affair. That it had, and a very sad one, other and later finds of quite a different kind proved almost conclusively; and the story may as well be told now, though it was some time before we realised the whole truth. A few days after the discovery of the corn I was attracted by the antics of the caravan dog, who had accompanied us from Abdal, and riding over to see what interested him, I found the remains of two camels and a pack-saddle.

It is necessary here to interpolate somewhat, in order to make clear the sequence of subsequent events. Our own caravan had by this time suffered from lack of water and short commons, several of the ponies had had to be shot, one of the camels had given up altogether, and a second was very lame. In order not to drop any of the baggage it was imperative, owing to the loss of ponies, to increase the loads all round, and this was just what the animals could not stand.

One evening the camels, who usually marched separately owing to their slow pace, had kept ahead of the caravan and had gone on too far. The main body were forced to camp, and so the camels had to be recalled or left out. It was decided to send a man to try and find them, although there was no small risk of his temporarily losing both parties.

Where we had halted the desert was as bare as the palm of one's hand, the surface still composed of the unyielding *shor*. With the camels was the supply of both ice and roots for fuel, so it was imperative that they should rejoin the caravan that night. Long after dark we heard in the distance the well-known "Hoi Hoich!" the high-pitched cry with which the Turki driver urges on his patient camels; and right glad we were, not only at the prospect of food, but also that our messenger had been successful. To get back our animals in safety was sufficient to put every one into good-humour, but there was still greater cause for rejoicing when our headman came to report that the camel-drivers had brought in a strange camel they had found. Had he said, created by a miracle, our astonishment could hardly have been greater.

The wild camel, according to the natives, can wind a man ten miles off, and a tame specimen was just as likely to be found wandering in the desert as it would be in Piccadilly. The captured animal was saddleless, but without doubt a tame one. Where, then, could he have come from? At the moment our sense of relief at the extraordinary piece of good fortune overrode every other feeling, for here was the very help we would yesterday have paid almost any sum for. That night our men set to work to make a temporary pack-saddle for the new-comer, and in the morning we were able to transfer the loads of four ponies on to his broad back.

But it is necessary to finish the story of the Amban's caravan first. In the latest capture, when we had had time to think, we found confirmation of our worst fears. Already two of the total number of animals which the Amban had stated would convey his young wife, had been found dead. Here undoubtedly was a third, probably the only one left alive. What, then, had happened to the travellers who accompanied them?

What was the fate of the poor little girl? It is better perhaps not to inquire, not even to think. Unable at best to do more than hobble a few yards on her own feet, what chance of escape had she, even if the escort would be burdened with her in the attempt they probably made to regain their starting-point? If her camels did die, to us knowing the desert there was little doubt as to her end. Let us hope that it came quickly.

By the end of December we had begun to find the question of water a difficulty. In the strips of vegetation, which ran along the base of the lines of cliff, water of a kind, or ice, was usually forthcoming. Once the cliffs had been left behind, the question became one of digging. As a rule a depth of from five to six feet produced a few inches of liquid, half mud half water, for which when it came we were thankful. Occasionally it was necessary to go deeper. Some of the sweetest water tasted in the desert was the result of a ten-foot excavation. The last day of the year found the caravan camped by a good water-hole, and, as the weekly rest was about due, we decided to see the old year out with a sufficiency of that priceless liquid.

Shortly before the New Year camp, for the first time since Abdal, the boundless horizon to the north was broken in the distance by an indistinct line of hills. After the rest to the ponies on New-Year's Day I was able temporarily to quit the caravan to explore the northern range. Strange as it may sound to suggest any difficulty in such a simple transaction, the condition of our ponies and caravan at this time must not be forgotten. In the half-starved state the majority were in, it was as much as each could do to carry his pair of *yakdans* through the day. Only the strongest could be ridden, and even these not out of a walk. Under such circumstances, to venture to leave the caravan, even to ride on a magnetic bearing at right angles to it, had all the excitement of novelty. New-Year's Day was a beautiful specimen of the Central Asian climate at its best, and to those who are acquainted with its dry exhilarating character, this is no mean praise. A two hours' ride over heavy sand-dunes, frozen *shor*, and lagoon bottoms, brought me to the edge of the *sai*, which, as usual, led up to the base of the hills. Having crossed this gravelly glacis for about a mile, clay *yardangs* were met with until the last 400 feet, when the range rises precipitously to a narrow rugged ridge 800 to 1000 feet high. This ridge is composed of hard clay-like mud, below which there is possibly sand. No vegetation whatever is to be seen on the range. The general direction is from east-north-east to west-south-west, the ridge curving towards the east and lessening in height as it does so. In the only European map of these regions in our possession, the southern ranges of the Kurruk-tag were not shown nearly so far south. But that the range visited was one of these there can be little doubt.

The evening of the day I rejoined the caravan was the same on which the camel was brought into camp. It has already been mentioned that no pack-saddle was with him, but our men soon made up one. By this extraordinary piece of good fortune our present fears of having to leave any baggage behind were ended.

On January 2nd we reached a good water-hole which, on account of the three tiny trees it possesses, boasts the name Tograck-kuduck. It was beside the same hole that Sven Hedin camped in 1901 when he left the Anan Baruin-ula in the Sartang district of Tibet, to cross the Kum Tag desert from south to north. And in this connection an interesting point arose. After leaving Tograck-kuduck, Sven Hedin struck due north. In the description of the next few days' journey, he writes:[1] "Now, according to the existing maps of the centre of Asia, there ought to have been a considerable mountain-range across our path; but such elevations as we saw were so insignificant as scarcely to deserve the name of mountains at all."

The appearance during our journey, for the first time since Abdal, of any mountain-ranges to the north, has already been recorded. And that this should have happened only thirty-five miles west of the spot where Sven Hedin, from the better maps he probably had, expected to find them, speaks well for the accuracy of these latter. That Sven Hedin should have happened to cross the eastern end of the range where it evidently dwindles to a mere succession of ridges, serves to show how easily wrong impressions may arise, even

[1] 'Central Asia and Tibet,' by Sven Hedin. Vol. ii. p. 89.

in the case of such a highly-trained and accurate observer as the great Swedish traveller. Had he crossed what we have called the Tograck-kuduck valley, thirty-five miles farther to the west, he would have been confronted by the mountain-range which his maps led him to expect.

After leaving the water-hole of Tograck-kuduck the traveller continues in the region of clay-terraces, and the single towers of the same formation. The surface of the desert varies between heavy sand and firmer ground, with clumps of thin reed bushes, the latter only occupying the lagoon-like depressions which are now a common feature. Between the depressions are bare open plains, whose surface is fine hard gravel. On them not a blade of vegetation is to be seen.

Twenty days from Abdal we camped one evening by a good water-hole in one of these depressions, finding, much to our surprise, a clearly-marked river-bed, in which were a quantity of growing reeds and some undergrowth. The stream flows from east to west down a ravine 400 yards wide, and has itself a bed-breadth of twenty to twenty-five yards. We found it frozen solid, having the banks thickly covered with reeds and the familiar root-heaps. On one bank of the stream among the reeds was a water-hole containing the sweetest water we had yet found. Five miles to the north of the stream-bed a range of mountains about 1000 feet in height obscures the horizon. This spot formed the most comfortable camp we had enjoyed in the desert, and, but for the fact of losing my riding pony there, would have left nothing but pleasant memories. How he met his death we could never ascertain. Upon going to break the ice on the water-hole at dawn, the pony was found stone dead, with his head hanging over the hole. Whether he had been attempting to get down to the water during the night and had slipped and dislocated his spinal cord, it was impossible to tell. The loss was a heavy one, as by it we were almost reduced to daily walking during the rest of the desert passage. The death of this pony made the sixth which had succumbed since leaving Abdal.

It was near the eastern side of this stream-bed that the first of the *torla* or watch-towers, which marked the ancient Chinese highway referred to in an earlier chapter, was discovered. Not far from the *torla* we came on a fairly well-marked track leading north-west. This, I believe, was the one made use of by M. Bonin on his adventurous journey from Sachu to the ancient site of Lou-lan, thence on to the Tarim river. There is from this spot also a broad *araba* track made by the people of Sachu, who, our guide said, were in the habit of venturing so far into the desert during the summer in order to obtain wood from the old belts of *tograck.* The same evening we reached the western end of a long and almost dry lagoon, where ramifications extend east as far as Kara Nor.

After a long and hard march of eighteen miles, made on foot, we camped under shelter of a small rise—luckily for us, as it turned out. The usual meal and pipe saw us under the rugs; but before there was time to drop off to sleep a furious storm broke over the camp: anything like the force of the wind we had never experienced before. Luckily the tents were under a gentle rise, and made fast fore and aft to some small trees; the pegs also, as was our custom, were anchored down by the *yakdans* placed on top of them. For five hours the tents swayed and rocked like boats at sea, threatening every moment to be blown clean away; and all that could be done was to cling tightly to the front pole, hoping that the additional weight might prevent the final catastrophe. The storm broke in mad gusts about 9 P.M., blew its hardest about 10 P.M., and, as we foolishly imagined, appeared to be subsiding at 11 P.M. Feeling the wind going down, we ventured to quit the tent-poles and to exchange confidences as to the damage, so far as we could make ourselves heard. Hardly had we crept back into our rugs and gone off to sleep, when we were once more awoke by the same terrific gusts and wild shaking of the tents. There was nothing to be done but to jump out into 25° of frost and again hang with all one's weight on to the tent-pole. For another two-and-a-half hours the gale raged, until we almost began to despair of keeping the wind out. Had the door-fastenings given, or one gust managed to get in, the whole tent would have gone. Luckily neither of these things happened, and by half-past 2 A.M. it was safe to creep back once more into one's rugs,—and this time for what was left of the night. Waking in the morning there was no sign of wind or storm; and but for layer upon layer of fine sand which had penetrated everywhere, the whole Kara-buran might have been a nightmare.

In the morning we explored the lagoon, finding along its southern border the remains of another ancient watch-tower—one of a series of four visible from this point, including the one already mentioned. The watch-towers are some two miles apart, well placed to be seen, and on a line nearly west and east. The first watch-tower is built of mud- or clay-bricks, between which are layers of reeds. It had a base some thirty feet square at the bottom and fifteen feet at the top. The entrance must have been by ladder, or, as is still seen on the watch-towers in north-west Kansu, by a very slender stairway outside up one wall. This stairway is also of mud-brick; but one can be destroyed in a few minutes once the defenders have mounted.

Five miles to the north of the lagoon the spurs of the nearest Kurruk-tag can be seen. During the following day, having crossed an undulating wind-swept plateau covered with fine gravel, we dropped as usual into a depression in which there has been, and is now at times, a lagoon. At the south-east end we came upon the ruins of an ancient fortified post or *kurgan*. The walls are built of small clay- or mud-bricks, and are still fourteen to sixteen feet thick. It had two entrances—one to the west, another to the north,—and was roofless. The walls are twenty to twenty-five feet high, and were once probably higher. The post is of wonderful solidity, and in its day must have been impregnable.

Later on the same day another *kurgan* was discovered; but this was of larger dimensions, and probably held a permanent garrison. The remains of the double walls are eighty yards long by fifty wide outside, the inner walls being some thirty feet above ground-level. The site overlooks a wide-spreading lagoon eight to ten miles in extent, the bed of which held little water, being filled for the most part with reed-jungle and clay mounds. In the lagoon bed we found the first signs of the presence of human beings at no great distance, in the shape of a herd of ponies. These are turned out by the Sachu people to fend for themselves during the winter, and proved a great find to us. Three more of our ponies were on their last legs, so it did not take us very long to round up and catch three of the herd. On to these we speedily transferred our pack-saddle and *yakdans*, leaving our own beasts—not without a pang, for they had served us faithfully and well through much hardship for nearly six months. The same day the first men seen since Abdal were met in the shape of three Chinamen with two *araba* in search of wood. They were driving cattle in the *araba*, and, for Chinamen, displayed no little interest at meeting us.

Our camp this night was on the south-west shore of Kara Nor, which we spent the following day in exploring. The first sight of it had been obtained the previous afternoon when, just before deciding to camp, we were rejoiced to see a wide expanse of what looked like water, but turned out to be ice. The longest axis of the lake is from west to east, on a bearing drawn at 270° to 70°. The breadth of the present frozen water is one and a quarter miles from north to south. The lake-bed is bounded on the north by a ridge of hills whose lower clay terraces form its boundary, though the lake does not at present reach them. To the south is a wide sweep of clay cliffs thirty-five feet at their highest point. A portion of the southern boundary of the lake is without cliffs, being only a gentle slope from the higher ground. The actual breadth of the lake-bed across the middle does not exceed five miles, two-thirds of which is now reeds four to five feet high, where are patches of frozen water varying from small ponds to sheets of ten acres in extent. To the west the lake has all the appearance of flooding out at times for miles, filling all the channels and receiving the water from many side nullahs and depressions. These floods may reach from fifteen to eighteen miles' distance at certain seasons, though never one unbroken sheet of water. The main lake-bed, as we saw it, was nowhere more than six feet deep. The breadth of the bed at its present western end is two miles one furlong. The ice on the lake was too solid to attempt to break it. Opposite our camp it was cracked right across, though re-frozen over into a line of small hummocks eighteen inches high. This was probably due to the action of the wind and the shallowness of the western end at the time the lake was first frozen. The dust has so discoloured the ice that at a few yards' distance it has the appearance of a mud bottom.

The following hypsometer observations were taken on the southern shore of the lake. Water boils at 207°; air shade temperature, 3 P.M., 21½° Fahr; aneroid height 3000 feet; aneroid pressure 26.60 inches.

Close to the edge of the lake were the ruins of a *torla*, in which some fragments of pottery were the only indications of its earlier occupation.

A quaint incident which happened at this camp illustrates the character of our surveyor, Lall Singh, better than any written description. A man more absorbed in his work than he was it would be impossible to find. Reference has already been made to the pluck and determination he showed in Tibet, nor did he ever deviate by a hair's-breadth from the highest ideal of duty. To a personal character, which made our intercourse invariably most cordial, he added a sublime modesty which no amount of patting on the back could do away with. His first thoughts in the morning and his last at night were of his plane table, and, as the following little incident shows, during the day it was his one care.

We had returned from a long day's survey of the lake, and Layard and myself were seated round the camp-fire taking a meal and congratulating ourselves upon a useful day's work. Lall Singh was putting the finishing touches to the map a few yards away. We suddenly heard him make some remark, but as he continued sketching we did not trouble to turn round. Again he spoke, and this time we caught his words, "Shikar arghir, sahib" ("something to shoot approaches"). Jumping up, we ran for the little .303, seeing at the same time three gazelle advancing apparently quite unconscious of us or the camp.

Taking up a position behind Lall Singh's tent, I took the buck standing and knocked him over, then had a second barrel at the other beast as they cantered away, but missed. All this and more occurred within 100 yards of his tent, but I hardly think Lall Singh raised his eyes from his plane table. As he was when he so solemnly reported the arrival of the *shikar*, so he remained ten minutes later when Layard returned from bagging the one I had missed.

On the third day after quitting the shores of Kara Nor we reached Sachu. The first indication of civilisation is conveyed by the appearance of a line of trees stretching north and south but still six miles distant. In three hours we had reached the edge of the cultivated oasis which surrounds the town, and another hour and a half of slow riding through well-to-do farms and bare fields brought us to the really imposing gates.

Outside the west wall of Sachu runs a fair-sized stream, the overflow of which forms a wide frozen lake. A rickety wood bridge spans the former, but we crossed the ice by a muddy track made by the farmers' carts. The view of most Chinese walled towns is a picturesque one, and coming, as we did, from the heart of the desert, both the aspect of the town and the bustle of its immediate surroundings fairly took away our breath.

We had taken the precaution to send on one of our men in the early morning to announce our arrival. With him went the letters of introduction which our friend, the Amban of Chakalik, had been kind enough to provide, also my Chinese visiting-card. Armed with the former, our messenger's reception was assured, and we were promptly met outside the walls by a *yamen* runner, who conducted us at once to a house prepared for our reception off a quiet side-street inside the walls.

CHAPTER X.

THE BOUNDARIES OF CHINESE TURKESTAN—INTERIOR ROUTES—THE FIVE ROUTES OF ENTRANCE AND EGRESS—ANCIENT CONNECTION WITH INDIA—BUDDHISM AS A POWER—CHINESE ADMINISTRATION—CURRENCY AND TAXATION—MINING—MILITARY ORGANISATION—THE COURIER POST—RUSSIAN DOMINATION—SIGNS OF A NEW ERA IN ASIA.

ONE of the chief characteristics of those who live in this strenuous century is a distinct impatience with the older nations of the world in that they are not more modern. Whether we are watching the adoption of an up-to-date constitution, as in Persia, by a nation whose political organisation has hardly changed in the course of some two thousand years, or the final disruption of a corrupt and worthless bureaucracy, as in Russia, the uppermost thought in the minds of most onlookers is that the change does not come as rapidly as they would desire. In the present day not many of these ancient and interesting countries have been left to be studied, but among them—itself a dependency of the hoariest among nations—is the area through which our journey had led us. It is of the present and future condition of Chinese Turkestan that I propose to speak in this chapter, in hopes that the long and close connection it once bore to India may cause some more permanent interest to be extended to a country in which singularly little is at present taken.

Invariably known to the Chinese as the Hsing Chiang or new frontier, the name given to this area on European maps is a somewhat vague one. For present purposes the general boundaries of Chinese Turkestan may be defined thus: on the south it is bordered by an almost impassable wall formed by the Kuen Lun mountains; on the north by the Tian Shan mountains and their eastern offshoots; on the west by the Alai mountains, the Kizil Art, and the great Pamirs; on the east no natural boundary exists, but an artificial one is found in the main north-west road leading from Peking to Kashgar, which here crosses the desert at its narrowest point from An-si-chou to Hami.

More interesting than the geographical boundaries are the political areas which surround Chinese Turkestan. Throughout the greater part of its length the position of Northern China marches with that of Russia. From the Taghdumbash Pamir for some 3000 miles north and east, Chinese territory is coterminous with that of Russia, its ever-expanding neighbour. In the south-west corner lies one of the most debatable lands in Asia, which is commonly called the Roof of the World, where three empires meet. To the south lie Kashmir, otherwise British India, and Tibet, whose suzerain is China. On its eastern side Chinese Turkestan is physically open all round, but actually the only approach to it is through a thin strip of semi-cultivated territory in North-West Kansu.

Before finally quitting the subject, some reference should be made to the political and military points of interest connected with this area. In addition it may be of value to sum up briefly the possibilities of economic expansion. Like all countries which have remained until the beginning of the twentieth century cut off by lack of communication from the trade of the outside world, Chinese Turkestan is starved for want of railway connection.

Whether the present apparent enthusiasm in China for the advent of such modern aids to trade is genuine or not, the writer cannot undertake to decide. That many Chinese officials who wield authority in these far-away portions of the empire are prepared to welcome railways, he can vouch for from personal knowledge.

The subject is one which not only concerns the trade of Chinese Turkestan, but possibly the ultimate retention by the Imperial Power of its far-distant dependency. Before considering the question of linking up Urumtsi with Peking by rail, it will be necessary for those responsible for its construction to decide upon the track between the latter city and the capital of Kansu province. And here again the problem is by no means simple. Though Lan-chou as the capital deserves first consideration from the administrative point of view, technical and engineering considerations make it more than likely that Liang-chou, a town second only to the provincial capital in importance, will be the first to welcome the arrival of the Huo-lun-chê (fire-wheel-cart), the quaint designation by which the railway train is known to Celestials. As this question is fully discussed in a later chapter, it is unnecessary to dwell upon it here.

One of the main points to be studied in examining the future of any country, whether from the commercial, military, or administrative point of view, is that of its communication. The subject of roads cannot but lead to that of influence and privilege.

The area under discussion is traversed by three main routes—two of major and one of minor importance. All thre start from An-si-chou on the Kansu border, and run west to the Russian frontier. As far as Hami the two northern tracks have together formed the great north-west road from Peking. At Hami, which town stands ten stages' distance across the desert from An-si-chou, they bifurcate. After dividing, the northern branch is known as the Tian Shan Pei-zu, or north road. This runs from Hami *viâ* Urumtsi, the capital of Chinese Turkestan, to Kuldja, close to the Russian frontier. Urumtsi is always known to the Chinese as Hoong Miaotzu, or the Red Temple, from the fact that there is a notable temple there.

Kuldja was well known in Europe at the time of the Yakub Beg rising, being then occupied, as was the whole of Ili, by Russian troops. On account of its geographical situation it may not improbably be heard of again, though whether as once more containing a Russian garrison, or as one of the new defensive outposts of a regenerated China, time alone will show.

The other branch of the two main routes is called

the Tian Shan Nan-lu, or south road. This runs west from Hami along the northern border of the central desert to Kashgar, passing through towns and oases of varying importance, the chief of which are Karasha, Ak-su, and Marah Bashi.

The third and little used of the main routes, after quitting An-si-chou, runs south of the Takla Makan desert along the lower spurs of the Kuen Lun main range, at a height of between 4000 and 8000 feet above sea-level. This track also divides into two at Cherchen, a well-to-do oasis 200 miles west of Lopnor. From Cherchèn, one branch runs direct through the desert to Kiria, and the other to the same town, but along the northern base of the Kuen Lun. After uniting at Kiria these two tracks lead on as one to Yarkand, Kashgar, and the Russian frontier.

So much for the lateral communications which traverse the Hsing Chiang, but we must not omit to notice that these three routes are also connected across the desert from north to south by lesser cross tracks. The most important of these is a caravan track between Urumtsi and Chakalik, which runs *viâ* Karasha and Korla down the Taria river past Lopnor.

The second cross communication is maintained between Khotan and Ak-su, where a track follows the Khotan river in about twenty-three marches to the latter place.

Having dealt with the interior routes traversing Chinese Turkestan, a few words may be said of some of the most important roads which lead out of, or into, that country.

1. The first, though perhaps the least important, except to us as a nation, is that from India *viâ* Leh and the Karakoram pass, by which most of the communication, and all such trade as there is, passes to India. An alternative route to this, but one seldom used, is that *viâ* Gilgit, Hunza, and Tashkurgan.

2. The second is the main road connecting Eastern or Chinese with Western or Russian Turkestan, which from Kashgar follows the Kizil-su over the Terek pass across the frontier to Osh.

3. The third is a caravan route from Ak-su up the river of the same name over the Tian Shan mountains, thence across the Russian frontier *viâ* Issikul, to join the present post-road, and future railway line, at Pish Pek.

4. The fourth is the continuation, west, of the Tian Shan north road, which leads up the Ili river over the Russian frontier, on to the post-road between Vernoe and Kopal. It may be of interest to state that in the course of a journey through Central Asia, made in 1902, I passed through Pish Pek and Vernoe. The country surrounding the latter place is as rich an agricultural district as could be desired. No finer country for colonisation exists than some that will be traversed by the new Tash-Kent-Omsk railway; yet why do we hear of new and extended schemes for settling such inhospitable and far-away regions as East Siberia or the Amur country?

5. The fifth of the exterior main routes leading into Chinese Turkestan is in some ways the most

important, for it connects Chakalik, near Lopnor, with Lhasa.

From Lhasa to Chakalik the journey can be made in two months by well-mounted travellers,—the usual time occupied by the many pilgrims who pass that way is three months.

Between Urumtsi, the capital of Chinese Turkestan, and Peking on the east is a space of some 2000 miles. Of this distance, at the present moment, not one mile is linked by rail, although it is hoped that Si-an Fu in Lhemi may soon be thus connected with Peking. The great highway connecting Chinese Turkestan with the capital is throughout most of its length a mere track, which passes over a succession of rugged passes as high, in the case of the Wu-shi-ling, the best known, as 10,000 feet. A road, in the European sense of the word, it is not. For hundreds of miles it is merely a track, worn throughout twenty centuries by the wheels of countless Chinese carts, untouched from year to year, unless rendered actually impassable, owing to climatic disturbances: such is the only communication uniting this far dependency with Peking. To the west Urumtsi stands within 400 miles of the Russian border, with which it is connected, as already stated, by the Tian Shan north road. Beyond this frontier the lines of modern railway made, and in the making, which connect European Russia with Chinese Turkestan, are too well known to require to be mentioned here.

Having endeavoured to indicate briefly the present general aspect of the communications which unite Chinese Turkestan with the outside world, let us now turn to another connection which has strong claims to attention.

Among those who have devoted time to a study of the area under review, it is well known how intimately connected in the past Chinese Turkestan was with India. But by people less interested this important point is not perhaps fully realised. It is a matter of history, to which reference has already been made in a previous chapter, that it was from our great Asiatic dependency that the teachings of Buddha first entered China. It was also from the same direction that the early Græco-Buddhist art, relics of which Dr Stein has been chiefly instrumental in disinterring, reached Chinese Turkestan: and we now also know without any doubt that it was from Northern India that the western end of this area was at one period colonised, and in addition received a language, a literature, and a script. The first reliable evidence of this latter was discovered by Colonel Bowen in his well-known find of birch-bark leaves in 1900, and since that date Dr Stein has largely increased the debt owed to him by all students of Central Asian history and archæology by other and even more valuable discoveries.

At what exact date intercommunication between China and India first took place is still a debatable question. Chinese records place the event about 100 years B.C., when commercial relations with Shintu, or Thianchu, as India was first called by them, are on record.

Sir Henry Yule, however, gives reasons for supposing that the Hindoos knew the Chīnas, as they were called in the laws of Mănu, as degenerate Kshatriyas, centuries before the date assigned by the Chinese themselves. Pauthier, in his edition of Marco Polo, also says "that people from India passed into Shensi, the westernmost part of China, more than 1000 years before our era, and at that time founded a state named Tsin, the same word as our China."

The story of the actual introduction of Buddhism into the latter country has already been told, and is not without interest, for Chinese Turkestan was the channel through which it flowed.

After having dwelt somewhat fully upon the introduction of Buddhism into China, the question may naturally be asked, What effect has this had upon the moral wellbeing of the millions who have at various periods professed its obligations? Ethically one of the purest and most elevated forms of religion the world has known, it was at one time the state religion of China. That it may in its early form have answered the purpose of a moral force is probably true. That it does so now I am afraid is not the case. In the present day it retains no inward vitality, nor is it a religion any longer in the broadest meaning of that word. Impossible, even impertinent as it may seem, to attempt to judge the hidden forces which guide the conduct of an alien race, there is no room for such an imputation here. If religion means anything it means some moral force by which men shape their daily conduct through life, one which is sufficiently strong to enable the willing spirit to overcome the weak flesh. Can it be maintained that Buddhism in

China still retains this power? I fear not. Interesting as it might be to follow the gradual decay of this almost divine faith, it is beyond the scope of this chapter.

Present-day administration in Chinese Turkestan varies little from that in force in China proper, except that for the headmen of villages, so great a factor in Chinese rural organisation, Begs and native heads of tribes are substituted.

Wise in their generation, the Chinese are content to supervise and control, leaving to their own chiefs the immediate government of the home life of village communities and that of nomad tribes. As mentioned previously, the centre of administration is at Urumtsi, where the Fu-tai, or governor, resides.

Below the governor are three Tao-tai, intendants of circuit, who are stationed at Kashgar, Ak-su, and Kuldja.

Lower again in the official scale come the Ambans, answering to district magistrates. Attached to all these officials is the army of clerks, interpreters, and functionaries, always considered necessary to uphold the dignity of magisterial life in China.

The above officials constitute that portion of the administration which is in the hands of Chinese. Under them again are the actual working heads in touch with the people, and these are all natives of the dominion. The most important in rank are the Begs, heads of districts, for they are the responsible go-betweens where the administration and the natives come in contact.

Under the Begs, where necessary, come the tribal

headmen, such as the Ming bashis, heads of thousands; Yuz bashis, heads of hundreds; and On bashis, heads of tens.

In addition to the civil officials, there are also military commandants, of grades according to the size of the garrison they command.

Unlike those who serve in China proper, who are rarely allowed to remain more than three years in one place, both civil and military officials have usually served most of their time in Chinese Turkestan.

The civil magistrates appear to be drawn from no particular part of China. During the course of our journey throughout the southern portion of the dominion we met men who by birth came from Honan, Hunan, and Hupeh.

Of intercourse, other than what is absolutely necessary, between Chinese and native officials, we found no trace.

The former look with undisguised disdain upon the latter, whom they invariably refer to contemptuously as *ch'ant'on,* turban-headed. The manner assumed by an Amban in speaking to his native entourage would, if used by an Englishman to a native in India, be described at least as "unconciliatory"; by the native press, probably in far stronger terms. The Ambans either did not or pretended not to understand a word of Turki. Considering that many of them had spent the greater portion of their lives in the dominion, this can be attributed only to a wilful desire to keep aloof from all intercourse with the subject-race. Judged by our own method of treating Asiatics, this must tend to weaken the central authority, by preventing mutual understanding. It is, however, open to argument whether such a method is not more suited to subject Eastern races not highly developed. There would seem to be occasions in our own dealings with Asiatics when we are prone to sacrifice the authority while drawing no nearer to the mutual understanding. The curious point in the Chinese administration of Eastern Turkestan is in the financial arrangements which provide in a far-off dependency a regular monetary system, with coinage complete, while withholding any such system from China itself.

The question of currency in the latter country has long been calculated to drive the would-be reformer to despair.

It is unnecessary now to do more than call to mind that in the interior of China to-day there is no current coinage. The medium of all barter is the tael, a weight of silver, not a coin. For the masses, copper "cash" of various degrees of debasement are coined by provincial mints. These circulate within confined limits all over China, but for trade purposes and for travellers, lumps of solid silver are still a necessity. In Chinese Turkestan, on the contrary, the system is, comparatively speaking, modern, though not simple. They have there a common coin answering to the dollar of the China coast. This coin is the miskal, which circulates in one, two, or three miskal pieces. These have the appearance of a clumsily made florin. Ten miskal are equal to about 3s. Other monetary terms are used, though there are no equivalent coins, such as the pung, equal to five copper Chinese cash, and the tengeh, eight of which go to one sar, which latter is also worth about 3s. Copper cash of Chinese pattern (*ta-chien* or *man-chien*, as they are called) and yamba, large silver shoes worth about £7, 10s., also circulate—the former among the poorer natives, the latter only among the wealthy merchants.

It is no easy matter to state definitely the system of taxation in any Eastern country, especially where Chinese administration is in force; but the basis of the one in use in Chinese Turkestan is that of a capitation tax, with certain tithes upon produce.

We were unable to ascertain the amount of the capitation tax with absolute exactitude, but such information as could be obtained shows that it is levied in sums varying from 5d. to 11d. per male head only. With regard to the tithes, the following lump sums were given as specimen payments, and may be of interest, although not tabulated:—

At Polu, a well-to-do village situated on the northern slopes of the Kuen Lun mountains, 2000 tengeh (about £37) is paid per annum as taxes to the Chinese Amban at Kiria. At Cherchen, the fairly rich oases already alluded to, 8000 tengeh (about £150) is the annual land tax chargeable to the revenue. In addition to this sum, an amount equal to 4000 tengeh (£75) is paid by the shepherds and nomads of the surrounding district. As if this were not enough, incredible as it may sound, the townspeople are subjected to still another tax. I was assured by various sellers in the bazar, under solemn pledge of secrecy, that the Amban took for his own "squeeze" two tengeh out of every ten tengeh worth of goods sold on market-days in the bazar. As this sum represents roughly 9d. out of every 4s., it is apparent that even an Amban must live, and that right well.

The industries of Chinese Turkestan are few at present, and of little except local importance. Of those that might become more widely known, the chief is mining, next the wool industry, the skin trade, and last, cotton-growing. Of minerals this area holds a good quantity. The gold industry has already been described. Whether the mining, which now proceeds in the prehistoric manner we saw at Sorghack, could be made to pay by the introduction of Western methods, I am not able to say. The presence in that district of two American gentlemen who hailed from the vicinity of Chicago leads me to suppose that expert opinion upon the subject will soon be available.

In addition to gold, copper, iron, and jade are all worked in more or less remunerative quantities. Should the time ever arise, as I believe it will, when the attention of the Chinese or foreigners is turned to the development of the mineral wealth of this outlying dominion upon European lines, scientific exploration and the exploiting of its results in a modern manner might lead to a large increase in the revenue derived from Chinese Turkestan.

If this opinion be endorsed by time, one of the difficulties to be met in the early stages will be that of labour. Both naturally and by environment, the Turki is either pastoral or agricultural in his habits. In disposition he is lazy and without ambition, content to exist, provided he can do so at no great personal inconvenience. Excluding the inhabitants of Polu, the natives engaged in the gold-mining industry are of a lower type than those remaining as cultivators in the oases. Nor are there sufficient good labourers to meet a large increase. In the event of a European reorganisation of the mining industry, it would, in all probability, be found more advantageous to import Chinese labour.

The military organisation of Chinese Turkestan is rather worse than in most parts of China at the present day. Putting on one side the new foreign-drilled army nursed by the well-known Viceroy, Yuan Shih Kai, in the vicinity of the capital, the remainder of the Imperial forces scattered throughout the various provinces are still quite ineffective—that is, should they be called upon to meet European troops.

In spite of what has lately been heard of the high pitch to which Yuan Shih Kai's men have been trained, I have no hesitation in saying that even they, unless officered by Japanese or mixed with Japanese troops, would make a poor show against good European soldiers.

From Kiria in Chinese Turkestan to Tai Yuan Fu in Shansi province, 250 miles from Peking, altogether a distance of some 2000 miles, including such towns as Su-chou, Kan-chou, Liang-chou, and Lan-chou, no soldiers were seen either in numbers, quality, or armament that a single foreign brigade with field artillery could not account for. In Turkestan, such garrisons as there are occupy either small forts in the vicinity of the towns, or the towns themselves. The latter are usually built on the lines of a Chinese city with, in some cases, the addition of a surrounding moat. The garrisons vary in nominal numbers from the 3000 at Urumtsi to a few score at such places as Toksu, Korla, and the frontier post of Tashkurgan towards the Pamirs. In *actual* numbers they vary still more. At Kiria the Amban himself informed me that the garrison consisted of one *liang* of infantry, 500 men, and some *ma-ping*, cavalry. No discourtesy to him is intended when I say that after being there three days I do not think there were fifty men all told.

At Chakalik the same story was again repeated. Putting the actual number of Chinese troops garrisoning Eastern Turkestan at 8000, it may safely be inferred that barely 5000 would be found present on an emergency. And of these 5000, a medical inspection upon European lines would suffice to cast 50 per cent for old age, opium-smoking, and other causes. Were Chinese official statements as to the number of troops present accepted as facts, no doubt the garrisons would be put at 15,000 or 20,000 well-armed men. The troops who form the garrisons are drawn chiefly from the provinces of Hunan and Hupeh. Spending as they do years in one place, the men eventually deteriorate even more than their provincial brethren in arms in China proper.

Of local Turki troops there are none, nor would they make soldiers under Chinese instruction.

The internal political relations of Chinese Turkestan are probably in as close touch with Peking as are those in such far-away provinces as the Kwantung, Yunan, or Sze-chuan. During the course of our journey a considerable number of officials were met with on the great north-west road which traverses Kansu province. These were either proceeding to or returning from Urumtsi. The telegraph line from Peking to Kashgar is the one outward sign of Imperial interest which Eastern Turkestan enjoys. It is kept in repair, well-staffed, and in good working order. In addition to the telegraph, the Imperial courier post still survives. By it the transfer of information or special orders is extraordinarily rapid. An Imperial despatch, wrapped in the well-known yellow silk and tied round the waist of a succession of mounted couriers, will reach Liang-chou in Kansu province under nineteen days from Peking. The time usually taken for the same journey by well-equipped travellers is forty-three days.

The external political relations of the dependency are confined by geographical necessity to two foreign Powers. From the situation of Chinese Turkestan this will, in all probability, always be the case. Of the two Powers it should be apparent, even to Celestial obtuseness, that from Russia there is everything to fear, from England nothing. Yet the closest scrutiny is necessary before any sign can be observed that this fact is realised. Before proceeding to discuss the present position of these two Powers in the area under notice, it may not be amiss to glance for a moment at their importance as apparent to natives on the spot.

The visible authority of Russia is for ever held prominently before the eyes of the inhabitants, both in the position occupied by the Consul-General at Kashgar, and by that of his colleague at Urumtsi. The very real local power exercised by these two officials is made to appeal to Asiatic notions of authority in its most practical form when required—viz., that of force. On the other hand, the position occupied by the British representative at Kashgar is looked upon by those who are accustomed to compare such details, where they never cease to be discussed, as inferior in every way. There may possibly be sufficient reasons for the continuation of this state of affairs, but they are not apparent to the man on the spot. However good they may seem to be at a distance, few who have travelled in Chinese Turkestan, or who possess even an elementary acquaintance with Asiatic methods of thought, will agree with them.

Though no direct reference has hitherto been made to the neglect on the part of China to safeguard her most distant colony, the fact cannot be overlooked in any allusions to Chinese Turkestan.

There are two reasons which suggest themselves for the apparent apathy of the Imperial government. The first is that it is aware of the hopeless nature of the task should it endeavour to take the necessary precautions. The second, and probably the true one, is that it is too apathetic, and, having been accustomed for so long a period to trust to the forbearance of its neighbours, will not now arouse itself.

It may also be that the retrocession of the Ili province in 1882, after its temporary occupation by Russian troops, may have helped to lull Chinese suspicions. Be the reason what it may, there is no slight chance that the future will bring forth a rude awakening. It is acknowledged that Russia holds Chinese Turkestan in the hollow of her hand, and with no intention whatever to suggest immediate or even likely action on the part of those who guide the Asiatic policy of that nation, it may be of interest to indicate future possibilities.

In the event of any such action being taken as the absorption of Chinese Turkestan, it is probable that Russia might be content merely to overawe at first Kashgaria and Ili. The former territory was still considered as belonging to the Kokhandian Khanate after the Russian conquest at Kokhand in 1864. The Mohammedans there did in fact pay tribute, amounting to some thousands of pounds a-year, and such a gradual advance would be more in keeping with traditional Russian policy. The aim of those answerable for that policy has always been to secure as far as possible the toleration of the Mohammedan element in previous Central Asian conquests, for, as they are well aware, in the feelings entertained for Russia by the faithful lies one of the chief dangers of Russian expansion in Asia. It is difficult to say if we ourselves suffer in less degree from the same feeling at the hands of Mussulmans. It is usual to suggest that we do,

—partly on account of the well-known toleration shown for the religious feelings of all our subject Asiatic races, more perhaps on account of the facilities provided under government auspices for the millions of devotees who make the pilgrimage to Mecca from our Eastern possessions.

In discussing the political relations of Chinese Turkestan it is unavoidable not to include in any such review those of the neighbouring territories which border that country. The future of Tibet is another eventuality which cannot but affect the political relations of Chinese Turkestan with whoever is the dominant power at Lhasa.

Although at the present moment China is once more acknowledged to be in full possession of her authority at the capital, it is impossible to say how long it may be before fresh schemes for upsetting that authority may not be set on foot. Last time the efforts of Dorjieff the Buriat were sufficiently near to being successful to give cause to ponder what the sequel might have been had an open adoption of the wishes of the Dalai Lama been forced upon the Tibetan council. It does not require much prescience to suggest that the triumph of the pro-Russian party in Tibet would probably have been followed at no remote date by the proclamation of a Russian protectorate over Chinese Turkestan. In whatever form Russian interests were displayed, the results would have been most serious to ourselves, even though no open attempt were made to enter Tibet. In drawing attention to some of the more interesting questions connected with the future of the area under discussion, no attempt is made to suggest novelty. None of these questions are new: all have been possibilities ever since Kokhand was absorbed by Russia rather over thirty years ago, but there has been a perhaps unconscious neglect of Chinese Turkestan as a factor in Central Asian politics. Events which have happened during the last few years in the Far East have recast most of the political problems which they affect, and it behoves those interested to reconsider their own judgments and opinions in the light of the entirely new perspective through which these problems must be viewed.

There is one point which cannot be too strongly insisted upon when we remember very recent events both in Manchuria and Tibet, and that is, the danger of reckoning upon either the intention or ability of the present Chinese Government to carry out its undertakings.

Recent utterances, both in the press and verbally, in Imperial Chinese edicts are calculated to inspire confidence that at last the Golden Age has come, and that China has arrived at the point when she may be left alone to safeguard her own and foreign interests both at home and abroad.

Nothing could be more opposed to facts, and unless due precautions are taken to safeguard the interests of individual nations, instead of trusting to Chinese authority to do so, we, for one, may find ourselves severely handicapped when the occasion for action suddenly arises.

Before concluding this chapter I would like to lay before my readers two points of view bearing, though indirectly, on the future of Chinese Turkestan. Concerning neither do I propose to offer any opinion; at the same time, both are worthy of earnest consideration. From the first point of view: there are to-day distinct signs that a more hopeful era is about to dawn in Asia, heralded perhaps by an Anglo-Russian *entente*. Few political movements would be more welcome to those interested in the East, but we may not forget that international agreements, though a sign of mutual goodwill, are not binding for all time. And now for the second point of view. In defending the increased military expenditure in India as late as March 1906, the present Viceroy made the following remarks in answer to protests by a member of his Council against any increased expenditure. This member was a well-known native gentleman. "I am afraid," said the Viceroy, "I cannot follow the honourable member in his conclusion that these dangers, our Asiatic differences with Russia and the dismemberment of China, have disappeared for ever. He has told us that the tide of European aggression in China has been rolled back for good, that the power of Russia has been broken, and that her prestige in Asia has gone.

"I am afraid these are mere assumptions, which I can hardly accept. I am afraid I feel much more impelled to consider what effect the Russian reverses may have on the pride of a high-spirited military race, and I wonder in how long or how short a time she may feel confident of recovering her lost prestige."

CHAPTER XI.

SACHU—MARCO POLO'S ACCURACY—A HOSPITABLE RECEPTION—THE INTRODUCTION OF WESTERN IDEAS—THE TEMPTATION OF LUMP-SUGAR—A DISPLAY OF MARKSMANSHIP—CHINESE CARTS—A NERVE-SHAKING ORDEAL—A DECAYING TOWN—STREET-STALL BARGAINING—THE INTRICACIES OF PAYMENT BY "CASH"—SILVER *SHORS*—MOHAMMEDAN RISINGS—IN THE TRACK OF WAR—COMFORTLESS LIVES—A MUD-BRICK FORT.

SACHU (literally sand district) is the most advanced western outpost that China possesses, and the town is said to date from the first century A.D. In those remote days the city was a fortified post planted to keep in order the marauding Huns, always a terror to China. From about the seventh century it has been known as Sachu—the original and only name by which the town is locally known is T'ung Huang. According to Palladius, in the time of the Emperor Kien Lung the district was colonised on a vast scale, and as late as 1830 it numbered about 100,000 inhabitants. Marco Polo refers to it as the point of arrival after thirty days spent in crossing the desert, and if in the present century any further proof of the extraordinary general accuracy of this renowned traveller were necessary, it is of interest to note that the same journey occupied us twenty-nine days. The town is described by

Marco Polo as situated in the province of Tangut. This was the name of an independent kingdom, to which reference has already been made in an earlier chapter. It comprised, so far as is known, a considerable portion of North-Western China, corners of Mongolia, of Eastern Tibet, and of Chinese Turkestan. It supported for many years a local dynasty known to the Chinese as Hsi Hsia, which flourished during the eleventh and twelfth centuries. T'ung Huang, to give the town its proper name, stands on the right bank of the Tiang Ho, a river flowing north from the lower ranges which reach on the south to within seven miles of the city. It has already been said that the first view was an imposing one, and after visiting such so-called towns as Chakalik, Cherchen, and Kiria, this is not to be wondered at. Further inspection, however, in no way lowers this impression, and in the well-to-do appearance of its inhabitants the town will bear comparison with any this side of Liang-chou.

T'ung Huang boasts both outer and inner walls which enclose an area 1000 by 800 yards square. The inner are 30 feet high with towers every 50 yards, affording good flank defence. The walls are solidly constructed of mud-bricks and are 20 feet thick. There is one double gateway in each of the outer walls and at right angles to it. The gateways are equally strong, and are closed by massive wooden gates clamped with iron. The inner walls enclose a kind of sanctuary, inside which are the *yamen* and all the official buildings. The garrison is nominally one regiment 500 strong, with some cavalry, but neither are in any sense of the word soldiers, nor do the full numbers exist. We had five told off for our personal use, nominally as a guard. They were, with one exception, confirmed opium-smokers, and on their first appearance not prepossessing. When they began to understand that they were there to do some work, and not for appearance sake, they served us as useful hewers of wood and drawers of water.

Our reception by the local magistrate was most cordial, as was the treatment we received throughout the course of our stay. After the first official call the magistrate repeatedly visited our house in his private capacity, bringing with him on several occasions his one child, a prepossessing little girl of seven with unbound feet. Not the least shy, she had, even at that age, the charming manners usually found in the educated classes in China, and, while her father drank numerous cups of tea, and amused himself by asking many and most intelligent questions concerning our journey and Western ways, the little maid played about and ate the last of our chocolate. Not the least of our indebtedness to the magistrate was due to his kindness in causing some of the local merchants to exchange Chinese silver for our remaining rupees. The question of money is invariably a difficulty when travelling away from the beaten track. So far it had been imperative to carry rupees; and the fact of having a *yakdan* full of silver is in itself an unfair temptation to those whose ideas of *meum* and *tuum* are not based on civilised standards. At Kiria we had been able to get rid of some of our rupees, and here again we were able to barter more.

The Chinese New Year festivities were already in full swing at the date of our arrival at T'ung Huang. At this season work of any kind is altogether abhorrent to the Chinese; so our friendly reception by, and constant intercourse with, the chief magistrate were all the more marked.

It may be as well to state, once for all, that I received at T'ung Huang an impression never afterwards effaced during the remainder of our progress through China. This was that, with a few local exceptions, Chinese officials remote from the poisonous influence of the capital are not only expecting the coming of Western ideas and practice, but are eager and anxious that these should come. But of this more anon. The oasis surrounding the city is a fertile country, which, besides providing for the wants of T'ung Huang, sends its agricultural products to support An-si-chou and other less prosperous towns farther east. Of trade there is a considerable amount, if we remember that the situation of the town makes it to all intents and purposes a *cul-de-sac*. To us, one of the most welcome signs of the adoption of European ways lay in the fact that we could buy American cigarettes, which were on sale in the streets. Articles of cheap German manufacture, such as buttons, needles, and suchlike, were also offered for sale; and it was gratifying to find that the well-known British house of Ilbert & Co. of Shanghai was represented by their cotton goods.

A small fortune awaits a working watchmaker at T'ung Huang, and his time would be more than fully occupied. It was a surprise to find so many

Chinese in possession of watches, but not that most of them required mending after seeing the treatment these delicate articles received from their inquisitive owners. There is a thriving colony of Andijanis, who have a large *serai* in a small quarter of their own. The chief articles sold by them are Russian ironware, basins, mugs, and so forth, common bright-coloured cottons, and cheap cloth materials. They also do a fairly large trade in skins. Their house in the *serai*, which is above the local level of comfort, was distinguished by glass windows and an iron stove of Russian pattern which burns coal. The chief magistrate had so far wisely adopted civilised customs, for he also possessed a duplicate stove which greatly added to the comfort of his otherwise chilly Chinese reception-room. Coal in small quantities is brought from the mountains to the south of the city.

Our first visit, after settling down into the quarters provided, was to the chief magistrate, and we found him, surrounded by the usual crowd of hangers-on, about to receive the New Year calls of all the minor officials. Unwilling to intrude, we endeavoured to postpone our call, but this was not at all in accordance with the hospitable feelings of our friend. He made us come in and sit down while tea was got ready. When it appeared, an amusing incident happened, which, though against the writer, honesty compels him to relate. It is well known that one of the cravings most difficult to satisfy, to a person accustomed to wine and suddenly deprived of it, is that for something sweet. Any one who has for a length of time been in the habit of taking sugar with tea is also aware of the craving which ensues if the habit has to be broken. Now, not only is the writer habituated to wine, but he must also plead guilty to being fond of sweet things, and the deprivation of both for some time past had been severely felt. Wine we had not intended to use, but the saccharine tabloids, which we had hoped would last until they could be replaced, had also given out. On the appearance of our host's tea, served of course in Chinese fashion, we were most agreeably surprised to see among the little dishes which usually accompany the ceremony some of lump sugar. That it was Russian, and imported from the West, mattered little. Lump after lump began to disappear both in our tea and as plain bon-bons; and so easily are the habits of civilisation cast aside, that on our host leaving us for a minute upon business, I could not resist the temptation to pocket half a dozen lumps. Being temporarily alone, I fondly imagined that my greed had passed unnoticed, but I reckoned without thinking of the prying eyes never absent from the various peepholes in the paper partitions and windows of a Chinese room. After remaining an hour, during which time our host changed into various garments, each finer than the last, in order to do honour to his local guests, we departed. This dressing and undressing was as good as any play, for it was made in full view of his own establishment, who, to the tune of eight or nine dressers, took a lively interest therein, and of ourselves. As we rose to go, another retainer stepped forward and ceremoniously handed to his master a small packet. Turning to me with a smile, the magistrate asked, without a trace of malice, was I fond of sugar, and would I accept this small present *to take away?* I hesitated guiltily for a moment, but Layard's loud laughter made the confession easy, and there and then I disburdened my conscience, much to the amusement of the old gentleman, who must have known all the time.

Although T'ung Huang is not within the boundaries of China proper, the country surrounding it to the north and east is sufficiently civilised to boast roads. True, they are merely Chinese roads; but they enable the traveller to make use of carts, also to do without a caravan of animals; and the trade of carter is both a recognised and a lucrative one. Thanks to the magistrate, we were soon able to arrange to hire what we required to take us to An-si-chou; but the disposal of the remains of our own caravan was not so easy. For the few days of our stay the yard at the back of our house was full of would-be purchasers, but for the most part curiosity and the holidays accounted for their presence. Our guns and rifles were as ever a source of interest, and nothing would satisfy the magistrate but a public display. In the middle of one of his many calls, after he had been admiring the guns and trying to understand the way they worked and the use of the cartridges, he suddenly invited me to step outside. Now, in another country this might have been taken as a prelude to something more exciting than the killing of a few pigeons; but by this time we were fast friends, and, knowing what the magistrate required, I prepared to give him as good a performance as my inferior skill and the pigeons would allow. Our house stood at one corner of the inner city wall, and on the latter was a picturesque turret whose overhanging curved roof was a favourite roosting-place for the scores of semi-wild birds which hovered over the town. Accompanied by our host and his friends, and followed by a large crowd of the townsfolk, we sallied forth, and I took up a position not too far from the wall. Hardly had the crowd time to understand what they were about to see before Layard had put the pigeons up, and as the leaders swung over the city wall I took the first pair. To our relief, and to the huge delight of the crowd, down they both tumbled,—one inside the wall, the other almost at our host's feet. Having seen the effect of a gun, nothing would satisfy the latter but a second display with the rifle. Though we assured him that neither the place nor the surroundings were at all safe, he airily waived all objections aside; and seeing that he was bent upon having his own way, we thought it better to accommodate him. Sending to the house for the lid of a box, we made an extempore target against the city wall, hoping that the wall would turn out as solid as it appeared to be. As I withdrew a hundred yards to shoot, Layard, by way of amusing the crowd, took a cap from the head of one of them and placed it in the centre of the board. The owner appeared rather flattered than otherwise at this attention, and stood smiling by while our preparations were made. As soon as the range had been cleared, I fired. Now a .500 express bullet is a somewhat killing projectile even at longer ranges: fired at 100 yards distance into a cap and a soft board, the result may easier be imagined than described. Again the crowd applauded loudly,—all save the owner of the cap, who now rushed forward to retrieve what remained, amid the jeers of all his friends. Luckily in China reparation is easily made in the shape of "cash," a full handful representing a few pence. With these the owner of the mutilated headgear soon retired, probably to become ever after the hero of the foreigners' visit.

In spite of the delay incidental to the New Year feastings, after three days all was ready for a fresh start. While at T'ung Huang we got rid of all unnecessary baggage, and it was with a much curtailed kit that we loaded up the two carts we had hired to take us to An-si-chou. The Chinese cart is pre-eminently for use, not for show. The two we had were of the usual rude kind, but solidly put together, and, though guiltless of springs, capable of standing any amount of knocking about; also, which was equally important, of carrying the still somewhat large amount of *yakdans*, gear, instruments, &c., which we could not do without. The carts were not the well-known narrow Pekin ones, but had the broad gauge six-foot axle. The roof of the cart, sides, back, and front, if the traveller so desires, are covered with thick matting, forming ample shelter in all weather, and affording a certain amount of warmth and protection from the severe cold and

Our Carts at the Gate of Hsia-kou, N.W. Kansu.

Buying Bread and Eggs at a Wayside Eating-house, N.W. Kansu.

biting winds of that upland country. Horsed by three ponies or mules, and driven as only Chinese carters can drive these unruly brutes, the rate of progress is about two-and-a-half miles to three miles an hour. The system of travel in vogue on the great north-west road is to start about 5 or 6 P.M., then to drive all night and as far into the following day as is necessary to cover each particular stage. A more uncomfortable and senseless fashion could not have been invented, nor could any but Chinese, whose nerves are conspicuous by their absence, make such journeys. To be jolted and bumped for twelve or even sixteen hours at a stretch, day after day for three or four months on end, is beyond the capacity of most Europeans to stand. Yet such is the fate of all whom duty or the emperor's fiat may send to make the journey from Peking to the Hsing Chiang. Throughout this weary pilgrimage delicate ladies, and even little children, are called upon to suffer—if not the tortures of the damned, at least as good an imitation of them as this world can provide. True, sedan-chairs can be used,—though upon this road they very rarely are, probably owing to the impossibility of procuring carriers. So also can saddle-animals; but the extreme rigour of the winter in the elevated districts through which the road runs in the far north-west prevents any one so exposing themselves where there is a choice.

That we preferred to retain ponies to ride was chiefly in order that we could cover more ground, or, if necessity or inclination bade us, temporarily quit the track. In yet another way we declined to be bound by Chinese custom, and that was in the method of making our stages. Much as our carters pressed us to travel at night, we firmly and once for all declined. Apart from the discomfort of such a proceeding in mid-winter, we had not already travelled so many thousand miles to be led, as it were, blindfold through China. Our system was to rise and start as early as the light would allow, then to travel as long as it continued; but before night came on we insisted upon reaching some shelter. As usual with the Chinese, once convinced that we intended to have our own way, they very soon adapted themselves to it, and we had no trouble. In one sense we did occasionally suffer, and that was by not always being able to use the recognised stages to halt at. At these there is usually a choice of inns, though, where most only varied in the degree of dirt and general decay, we lost little by having to use the solitary one found at the places where we halted. Between T'ung Huang and An-si-chou the country is wild open moorland. On the south-east of the track the lower spurs of the Nan-shan ranges approach within six or seven miles. Every twenty-five or thirty *li* are unoccupied watch-towers of mud-brick. To the north a bare plain stretches in frozen solitude to the horizon. Not a tree nor a human habitation was to be seen throughout some of the days' marches. Supplies, of course, there are none, except at the night's halting-place; and then hot water is about all these provide. In five days we reached An-si-chou. This is another walled town, but far inferior both in appearance and in the well-to-do aspect of its inhabitants to T'ung Huang. It is situated on the main great Chinese north road, which connects Peking with Kashgar; and it owes the small importance it possesses to being the point at which travellers must take in supplies before commencing the ten desert stages to Hami.

Even with these advantages the stamp of decay lies heavy upon the town, nor does the present magistrate strike one as likely to make for improvement. His *yamen* was in poor order, and his city walls likewise,—two things by which the prosperity of most Chinese towns may be judged. Besides being cracked and split in several places, the walls on one side are almost covered by the drift sand which the wind has piled level with the top.

We only remained at An-si-chou one day, in order to bargain for fresh cart-hire. But we were agreeably surprised when our carters expressed their willingness to continue with us as far as Su-chou. The latter town is seventeen days' march from An-si-chou, and is the first city within the boundary of China proper. This boundary is not passed until Chia-yu-kuan is reached. The latter is a so-called fortress, twenty miles west of Su-chou, to which reference is made in the next chapter.

Having concluded our bargain for cart-hire and made the necessary purchases of meat, vegetables, bread, and such things as were obtainable, we took the road for Su-chou. One of the few amusements during this portion of our journey was found in the bargaining at the street stalls while engaged in our marketing. In China it is necessary, if the traveller would not be mercilessly robbed, to think in "cash." It may be asked—How is it possible to think in any other way when making ready-money purchases? But the "cash" of China, it must be remembered, is a definite coin, not a collective name for money. Among the poverty-stricken millions who form two-thirds of the population it is the only coin they ever handle or see. The actual purchasing value of one Chinese "cash" has, I am almost bold enough to affirm, never yet been arrived at by any European. And for the following reason. The calculation of so many "cash" (*man-chien* = big "cash"), as they are locally called in North-West Kansu, to the *liang-yin-tzu* —*anglicè,* tael—decides the value of the "cash." Now the tael, as is universally known, is a measure of weight, not a coin. And the ratio of "cash" to the tael is never the same. Not only does the number of "cash" to the tael vary in separate towns, but even daily in the same town if it is a large one. And to add insult to injury, so far as the calculations of the guileless foreigner are concerned, two kinds of "cash" are legal—viz., large and small "cash." Were it possible to say how many of each made up one tael, again, the foreigner, provided he were a financial expert, might be able to compete. But it is not so. Custom alone is the guide, and to add the final straw to the foreigner's already breaking back, or rather reeling brain, so debased is the copper coinage of China that "cash" which may be manufactured or found in circulation at one town will not be accepted as payment by the inhabitants of the next. The custom is to mix with the *man-chien* or *ta-chien*, both meaning the same, big "cash," so many small ones or inferior "cash," but how many or upon what basis the percentage is calculated no one but the particular stall-keeper with whom one is bargaining is prepared to say. Experience is the only guide and patience the only weapon to enable one to secure the right to include many or few. To a poor Chinaman the practice of this simple virtue is one of the main preoccupations of an otherwise singularly dull life. To the European, to be obliged to await this settlement a dozen times in an hour is maddening, but it is also the finest training that a weary mortal can undergo to enable him to obtain that command over himself which, we are told, is necessary before he should undertake to rule kingdoms.

A word of warning to future travellers in this far country may not be wasted as to the necessity for most careful examination of the silver which they carry on the road for larger payments. These lumps of silver, known as "shoes," vary in value from about £7 English a-piece to those worth a few shillings, and are used for more extended payments than the "cash" transactions. All banks, and many big *hongs*—merchants' businesses—keep and supply their own silver shoes, and, to their credit be it said, these are usually of standard value. But in the street the lumps of silver that may come into a buyer's hands, especially if he be a foreigner, and therefore fair game, are not above reproach. We were once defrauded by being given lumps of lead silvered, which no one would take again. That the smallest silver transaction means hours wasted during the course of a day is nothing to a Chinaman. One will frequently offer a small piece of silver in payment for a few sticks of charcoal at a street shop. It must be weighed, and the change, if in silver, also. One passes on to buy fresh meat from a Mohammedan butcher at the next stall, again presenting the silver just received, and at the same time stating its value. "Two liang-yin-tzu?" says the butcher. "Not so. This piece is only worth 2000 cash. Where are my scales? Let us see." Patiently one waits, attempting to calculate mentally from the look of the butcher how much he dare rob one of. Much weighing and haggling now goes on, though the result is a foregone conclusion. "Yin liang, chiu pei chih shih pa"—"One tael, nine hundred and seventy-eight cash"—sings out the man with the scales. "Mai pu mai?"—"Will you buy or not buy?"—says the butcher. There is neither alternative nor appeal; so, sorrowfully accepting a dead loss of 300 cash upon the last transaction, one shoulders one's piece of sheep to disappear in the crowd. Upon the other hand, the banking system of this far-away province leaves little to be desired, while it fully justifies the reputation for business aptitude and strict honesty enjoyed by those engaged in that undertaking in China.

Upon our arrival at Su-chou it was necessary to obtain money, and although arrangements had been made with the Hong Kong and Shanghai Bank to transfer a certain sum to their agents at Lan-chou, it was uncertain whether any of this money would be available before reaching Lan-chou.

From An-si-chou I telegraphed to the China Inland Mission at Lan-chou, asking that the Chinese agents of the Hong Kong and Shanghai Bank there might be instructed to forward a certain sum, to be at Su-chou by the time we should arrive. Upon reaching the latter town and inquiring at the telegraph-office for any message, a telegram was handed to me in which I was informed that it was only necessary to go to a certain native bank, disclose my identity, and ask for the sum I required This I did, and upon signing a receipt in English the amount was at once handed to me, weighed out in silver shoes of irreproachable value. Here, then, is a business transaction which could not be better executed even in London. Yet this was not so far from the heart of Asia. Around us at the time, the life, the people, their ways and methods, were centuries behind what we in Europe know, yet in this one particular phase of Chinese life, a phase be it said which is the be-all and end-all of Chinese existence—trade—what more up-to-date arrangements could be desired? It is these astounding contrasts, representing the high and low water-marks in the Chinese character, which are the despair of all Europeans who desire to understand them. There would appear to be nothing that a Chinaman cannot learn to do, and, moreover, do better than most Europeans. From running a modern man-of-war, one of the most intricate machines human intelligence ever has invented, to washing clothes: who can excel him at his best? But European methods he will not have, and why not? Some day, perhaps, the secret will out. Meanwhile, intensely interesting as such speculations are, it is said by Europeans in China that that way madness lies.

Between An-si-chou and the frontier of China proper, the character of the country remains much the same as that through which we had passed since T'ung Huang. At a general height of between 4000 and 5000 feet above sea-level the district is for the most part wild moorland covered with tussocky reed-grass, at certain seasons bog for miles. Though, as it is at mid-winter, covered in snow, the appearance of the country is naturally not prepossessing. It would afford in many parts a fine area for cattle-raising. The soil, generally speaking, is by no means poor, and the climate very healthy.

Unfortunately for its future prospects, the Chinese are eminently an agricultural, not a pastoral, race, and although many more cattle than is usual in China were seen, their numbers bore no proportion to the possibilities of the country.

Dotted sparsely over the land, the villages and small walled towns form each its own little oasis, the whole strip of North-West Kansu resembling in this respect the cultivated belt between the Kuen Lun and the Takla Makan desert.

From another point of view there is a striking dissimilarity. It has been said in a previous chapter that the surroundings of the Turki inhabitants of

Southern Chinese Turkestan are, and have for many years past been, most peaceful. In North-West Kansu, on the contrary, the face of the land is stamped with the seal of war and rapine. Not only was this the case outside the border, but throughout the breadth of Kansu, Shensi, and Shansi provinces up to the Yellow River, the same dreadful evidence is to be seen of the ravages made by the various Mohammedan rebellions.

What untold misery is hidden in the history of the two main risings Europe has never heard. Of the last, which chiefly centred round the towns of Ho-chou and Si-ning towards the western border of Kansu, faint echoes did reach the West, chiefly through the accounts given by European missionaries, such as Mr Rheinhardt, who were forced to play no inconspicuous part in some of the bloody sieges which took place. Of what is known as the first Mohammedan rising no connected account is accessible to Europeans; probably, indeed, no accurate description either of losses in battle or of those incidental to the long years of disjointed pillage which succeeded the actual rising could be given even by the Chinese. Nor is it possible here to attempt to do more than outline the successive phases in which the power, first of one party, then of the other, made itself temporarily victorious.

The anti-Chinese feeling prevalent to this day among the more fanatical Mohammedans of the north-west has always existed, and once more it burst forth in 1861 in the province of Shensi. The actual cause is usually considered to have been a quarrel between the Chinese and Dungani (Chinese

Mohammedans) over the division of some spoil, the result of the defeat of a rebel chieftain. Whether the Mohammedan rebellion in Shensi had any connection with the Panthay rebellion in Yunan and the south-east of China five years previously is uncertain. Be that as it may, the effect of the Shensi squabble was to set light to a conflagration which spread from the Yellow River, the border-line between Shensi and Shansi provinces, to the farthest confines of Chinese Turkestan, and which lasted altogether for nearly sixteen years.

Owing to being unsupplied with artillery, the rebel Mohammedans were unable to capture any of the chief cities, and although Si-an Fu, the capital, was besieged for two years, it did not fall. In the country districts the triumph of the Mohammedans was complete, and from 1861 to 1870,—by which time the Chinese troops had only succeeded in clearing the province of Shensi,—men, women, and children were ruthlessly massacred, walled towns and villages were put to the sword, while those who escaped fled for their lives to wander and starve in the mountains surrounding their ruined homes.

The country-side has not even now recovered from these horrible cruelties. Everywhere, to this day, traces may be seen of the heavy hand of the Mohammedan rebels. In the mountains those who did succeed in escaping lived for years an existence which can only be compared to that of beasts. Hunted and harried by marauding bands of rebel Mohammedans, the Chinese character was seen at its worst. Whole villages fled at the approach of small foraging parties of the enemy, and whatever manhood the hunted fugitives may once have possessed seems to have entirely failed them. I have, myself, been told stories by men who remembered as boys being roused from their sleep and hurried away at night into the surrounding mountains. Nor did the Chinese local authorities, who were answerable for the safety of these miserable peasants, rise in any way superior to the general panic. Such garrisons of wretched militia as there were, shut themselves up in the smaller walled towns, there remaining, either to be massacred in their turn, or until the withdrawal of the wandering rebel bands allowed of their emerging.

In the year 1870 Li Hung Chang, a name well known to Englishmen, who, it may be remembered, was first brought to notice by the part he took in helping General Gordon to suppress the Taeping rebellion, received orders to proceed against the Mohammedans of Shensi and Kansu. He had hardly started with his foreign-drilled troops when the massacre at Tientsin took place, and he was recalled, but without withdrawing the troops. Such was the fame that these men had already earned that the rebels at once withdrew into Kansu, and in Shensi peace was at last more or less restored. General Liu, who had been posted to succeed Li Hung Chang, for some reason remained inactive for the next eighteen months, content with guarding the Shensi-Kansu border. Another Chinese general, Tso by name, in the meantime continued the task of clearing the rebels out of Kansu province. He is said to have had under his command nearly two hundred battalions, or about 100,000 troops. By the beginning of April 1871 all Kansu east of the Yellow River was practically free of Mohammedans, the Chinese being also in possession of Lan-chou and Ning Hsia. The chief Mohammedan centre and hotbed of rebellion was then, as it still is, the town of Ho-chou, already referred to as figuring prominently during the second rebellion in 1889. It stands some seventy miles south-west of Lan-chou up the valley of the Yellow River, and the aim of the Chinese was now the capture of this stronghold. By 1873 the advance of the victorious troops had brought about the fall of Su-chou, the last and chief city of China proper, and in 1874 the advance was commenced across the desert strip to Hami.

The latter stage of the first Mohammedan rebellion becomes, from this point, intermingled with other and more stirring events in Chinese Turkestan. These events culminated in the well-known rising and defeat of the sovereign power of Yakub Beg, but, however interesting, are too prolonged to be dealt with in detail here.

Continuing their slow but methodical advance westwards through Turkestan, the Imperial troops succeeded in capturing in succession Kucha, Aksu, and Maral Bashi. In the meantime Kuli Beg, the son of Yakub, and the murderer of the latter, Hakim Khan, had destroyed by their mutual quarrels any remaining chances of successful opposition upon the part of the Dunganis of Kashgaria. After the capture of Maral Bashi, the main lines of advance upon Yarkand and Kashgar were open to the Chinese, and these two remaining Mohammedan strongholds were at their mercy. Both fell towards the end of December 1877, and before the year was out Khotan, the last town of any importance, was in their hands. So ended the great Mohammedan rebellion, which, incredible as it may seem, had lasted for sixteen years, and thus the authority of "the son of heaven" was once more firmly established from Peking to Kashgar.

It was near the small unwalled town of San Tao Kou that we first began to realise the extent of the misery which follows in the train even of civil war. For some days previously ruined villages had become not uncommon, and where the inhabitants still dwelt they had built for themselves fortified farms and towns practically unassailable, the meaning of which there was no mistaking. Crossing a small half-frozen stream, the most pitiful scene of desolation met our eyes. The bank was thickly wooded, and the stretch of country beyond fairly so. Freely scattered over it were numerous ruined buildings, roofless farms, and country houses. Not the little farms, these, of the poorer class, but the comfortable homes of well-to-do men, who once lived in a style now quite unknown in these depopulated regions. Even the orchards were still standing in places, and from the traces of the walls there was no difficulty in arriving at the size and pretensions of these roomy farmsteads.

In the midst of such depressing relics of the ruthless cruelty of the last rebellion, we found two wretched families now existing. They had taken possession of one of the deserted farms, or, poor people, were perhaps the rightful heirs to its roofless walls; and there they were endeavouring, with apparently doubtful success, to win back the comfortable position they had once maintained.

The picture of the town of San Tao Kou is clearly printed on my mental negative, for in addition to recalling the scenes which have just been narrated, it has other and more personal memories. Before reaching San Tao Kou I had been somewhat seriously unwell, and for some days past the piercing winds which swept over this arctic upland had become almost unbearable. To them must be added the cold in the hovels we stopped at, which, after so long exposure, was most trying. At noon, inside what did duty for a room, the temperature was only 23° Fahrenheit; at 6 A.M. it was 7° Fahrenheit. Thanks to the ceaseless care and nursing of my companion, the delay caused by my attack was confined to a few days only, by which time I was again able to take the road.

It might be thought that in reaching China we had once more regained the comforts of civilisation, but this was far from being the case. A more comfortless life, from a European point of view, than that led by the lower orders in China it is difficult to imagine. And, during this portion of the journey, we were of necessity obliged to conform to the habits of those with whom we consorted. Including the evils of overcrowding —to which we were not subjected—almost every necessity of existence, as we look upon them, is absent from the life of millions of the masses. To mention only one or two things: privacy of any kind is unknown. From the moment when a Chinaman enters this world to that upon which he leaves it, he is never, except by accident, alone. A closed door, artificial light, warmth, except upon the *kang*, upon which in winter he lives, are things unknown. Sanitation is undreamt of. To that other blessing which we are taught is only second to godliness, no Chinaman of the poorer classes aspires. To add to such a list would not be difficult, but the patience of my readers might become exhausted were it to be continued. As a specimen of the wilful callousness displayed by these inscrutable people, let one more example suffice. As is well known, it is not the custom of the East to trouble overmuch as to the source or cleanliness of its water-supply, but in this respect, next perhaps to the Korean, the Chinaman may be said to out-distance them all. In most of the inn-yards we had the pleasure of inhabiting, the well usually stood in the lowest corner. The yard itself would invariably suffer in comparison with any muck-yard at home. Pigs, cows, fowls, and ponies are bred and born, live and die there. Every traveller uses the centre of the yard as a place to deposit his kitchen leavings; and beggars of all degrees of dirtiness find in the precincts of the inn-well a place set apart by providence for the annual spring-cleaning.

It may appear strange that such a cesspool does not levy a heavy toll upon the cheery carter folk, not to mention the occasional foreigners unlucky enough to have to use Chinese inns; but no doubt the secret lies in the tea-drinking habit, the blessing of the country. Cold water a Chinaman hardly ever touches: boiling water he can almost invariably find ready for him as soon as he enters an inn-yard. To this fact, and to this only, must be attributed the freedom his constitution enjoys from the presence of germs which would kill at a mile.

Two days before reaching Chia-yu-kuan we halted at the little village of Chih-chin-hsia (pure gold gully). From the name it may be imagined that gold is found there, and our friend and late host, the chief magistrate of T'ung Huang, who here caught us up on the road, informed us that it was, and in no inconsiderable quantity.

The view of Chia-yu-kuan (the jade gate barrier), as the fort is approached across a bare stony plain from the west, is somewhat imposing. The frontier fortress in the Great Wall of China, this gate has for centuries played an important part in the history of that nation. Sir Henry Yule has described how all the ancient embassies and trading caravans, many of which latter passed as embassies to pander to the pride of early Chinese emperors, were compelled to stop at this far-famed spot. It was here that they had to await permission from the mighty Emperors of Cathay to enter China. And before entering the, to them, massive gates of the fort, they were forced to give a full description of each individual member of the calvacade. Only then was the right vouchsafed to enter that wonderful country, miraculous tales of which had penetrated to their own distant lands.

It was at Chia-yu-kuan that the embassy already mentioned in a previous chapter, which was sent by Shah Rukh, was so hospitably entertained. It was there, too, that the delays began which prevented Benedict Goës, one of the earliest and most earnest of mission fathers, sent from the court of the Emperor Akbar at Agra, from ever reaching Peking. In Chinese eyes a certain halo of romance has always clung to this far-famed spot,—chiefly, no doubt, on account of its remote situation, but also because for centuries before the sea-route to China was thought of, Chia-yu-kuan was the true threshold of their country in all communications with the West.

Let us see what justification remains in this twentieth century for a reputation so long maintained.

It has been allowed that a first impression of the fort is imposing, but are not all impressions worthless that will not stand the test of deliberate analysis? If we fail to apply such tests, what right have we to make use of impressions as guides whereby to form a judgment? And though no sane man presumes to judge by impressions alone, there are cases where it is impossible to apply any more explicit test. Particularly of the land of which we are now speaking may it with truth be said that the knowledge of its peoples, government, and ways, gained by most foreigners, is only by impressions derived from a superficial study of it at second-hand. Of the comparatively few willing or able to instruct Europe as to the real *status quo* in China, some, for a reason which the writer is altogether unable to follow, persist in presupposing that China must not be judged by a European standard. Yet if this be the case, by what standard is she to be judged? The mere fact that such gropings after national reorganisation exist, and that they owe their inception to the nineteenth and twentieth centuries, is surely a sign that it is the intention of those who initiate such changes to force comparison with the methods they see in progress around them. If, then, we base our judgment of the progress of other nations towards enlightened rule and general conditions upon a modern standard of comparison, surely we ought to apply that standard also to China. Once let it be considered sufficient that *some* progress has been made, that a distinct advance in national evolution is evident, and all standard of comparison is lost.

If there is one hard truth which history has over and over again confirmed, it is that neither in the life of an individual nor of a state can there be stagnation without decay, and nowhere in the history of the world is this truth more plainly exemplified than in China. In this twentieth century it is an accepted canon in the laws which govern the evolution of nations that none has the right to stand still, even though it would. And though perhaps not written in such blunt language in the *aide-mémoire* of present-day statesmen, this truth has been none the less universally adopted.

Should the comparisons drawn in the following

chapters be considered too severe between things as they are and things as they ought to be, the writer can only plead good intent. Although the position of candid friend is usually a thankless one, it may be assumed in the present case that it is adopted from the best of motives.

All this time the reader has been left most unceremoniously in the cold, enjoying his first view of the old wall of China. Let me now invite him to approach and enter through the gates of Chia-yu-kuan.

The so-called fortress is in reality a mud-brick fort of a kind far inferior to such as are to be seen at Lahore, or in other Indian cantonments, where they have long served as mere quarters. The walls enclose an area some 120 to 150 yards square. On the north and south sides these are double. The outer walls are twenty feet high and four to six feet thick. East and west there are double gates of solid aspect, while the inner wall is thirty-five to forty feet high all round. Three big gate-towers of the usual Chinese type are chiefly instrumental in giving the place the imposing aspect referred to. One of these towers surmounts each gate, and the third stands in the centre of the fort. Inside the walls is to be found a collection of the most squalid hovels, with one official residence of an equally dilapidated kind. Round the highest wall runs a narrow parapet for defensive purposes, but being built within four feet of the summit of the wall it is inaccessible, except in three or four places. From the point of modern defence the whole place is pitiable. Guns there are none. The garrison consists of a half-score withered old men, of the usual type of soldier seen in these parts, and they are the proud possessors of wooden jingals. One other item of defence remains to be catalogued, and with no intention to hurt the feelings of the trusty garrison to whose charge is committed the most advanced outpost their mighty empire possesses, this must not be passed over. At intervals of a few yards along the top of the walls, piles of small round stones are heaped as ammunition for the purpose of repelling assault! Could even Chinese conservatism go further? Standing by one of these heaps to gaze over the north-west frontier, one could not but recall the accounts of the amazing superiority of the Russian artillery over that of the Japanese at the battle of the Yalu. But here was no question of artillery. We were still in the days of David and Goliath.

CHAPTER XII.

SU-CHOU—POST-HOUSES—BEACON-SIGNALS—THE FEAST OF LANTERNS—KAN-CHOU—A COLOSSAL FIGURE OF BUDDHA—TOWN DEFENCES AND FORTS OF REFUGE—THE QUESTION OF CHINESE MISSIONS—MONSEIGNEUR OTTO—POSSIBLE RAILWAY ROUTES—LIANG-CHOU—THE STORY OF THE DEATH OF YÜ-HSIEN.

THE day after crossing the old frontier of China at Chia-yu-kuan our party reached Su-chou. Known to Marco Polo as Sukchu, the latter town is also mentioned by other well-known travellers of the fifteenth and sixteenth centuries. To Marco Polo, practical merchant as he was, the chief point of interest would appear to have been the rhubarb, which was then, and still is, one of the main sources of trade in West Kansu.

Other and later travellers have also left record of their passage through Su-chou under various quaint names. The embassy sent to China by Shah Rukh, from Herat, about 1419, relates some interesting items of the customs of the day. Among these the account given of the *yam-khana* or post-houses is worth recalling. According to Yule, from the time the embassy reached Su-chou until it finally entered Khanbalik (Pekin), the party were supplied with everything by the Chinese authorities. They were lodged at the *yams* or post-houses, of which, he says, there were ninety-nine between Su-chou and Khanbalik, and every night they found not only provisions but servants, beds, night-clothes, &c., awaiting them. "At every *yam*," the account continues, "they brought four hundred well-caparisoned horses and donkeys for the use of the travellers, besides fifty or sixty vehicles."

At every post-house the travellers were presented with sheep, geese, fowls, rice, flour, honey, wine, arrack, garlic, pickled onions, and vegetables. At every city the ambassadors were invited to a banquet. On these occasions there was always a vacant throne with a curtain hung before it, and a fine carpet spread in front. The Chinese officials and the ambassadors sat down upon this carpet, while the rest of the company stood behind them in ranks, like Mohammedans at their public worship. A man standing behind the throne then proclaimed something in Chinese, and the mandarins proceeded to *kôu-tôu* (*Anglicè* kow-tow) before the throne, in which the envoys were obliged to follow them.

Another and no less interesting account of local customs, is given by a Turkish dervish, a great wanderer, about 1560 A.D. To Sir Henry Yule we are again indebted for its preservation. Having travelled across Asia by the usual route of Samarcand, Bokhara, and Taschan (Tashkendt), the dervish found himself eventually at the frontier of China proper. "Then," he relates, "the question is put to the merchants, 'What they bring, whence they come, and how many of them there are?'"

And now comes the interesting point of the tale: "The answer being given, the king's guards pass it by signal—by smoke if in daylight, by fire if by night—to the next watch-tower; they to the next, and so on until in a few hours the message reaches the king at Cathay; a thing which would by any other communication require many days. The king sends back his orders in the same manner and with equal rapidity, saying whether all shall be admitted, or only a part, or the whole put off."

Strange as the above account may sound, it has confirmation from an entirely different source —viz., in a story told by Shah Rukh's embassy already referred to. It is here related that "the town is so placed that the next *kargu* (tower) is in sight from it; and when any important event occurs, like the approach of an enemy's army, the men on watch immediately light a fire, and this being seen from the next *kargu*, they make haste to light another. And so the signal passes from one to another, till in the space of one day and night a piece of news passes over a distance of three months' march." Yule also tells of the continued existence of both post- and fire-beacons between Yarkand and Peking. The distance is more than five months' journey as usually travelled, but he states that an express went in thirty-five days, and under very great emergency in fifteen.

Miraculous as these accounts may sound, even if we allow a considerable discount in the figures quoted, it should not be forgotten that the methods of passing news in use to this day by the natives of Australia, South Africa, and elsewhere, are almost as inexplicable.

One other mention of Su-chou must not be omitted, for it marks one of the finest efforts of missionary work which is known in China.

About 1602, Benedict Goës, a Jesuit missionary, was sent to China by the Emperor Akbar. Chosen specially for the work by Jerome Xavier, who had himself not long previously been despatched from Goa at the emperor's request to enlighten him upon the truths of the Christian religion, Goës represents the most heroic type of mission worker. The story of his effort to reach Peking, where the Jesuit brothers were then labouring, is a page of mission history of which men of any creed might well be proud.

Leaving Lahore in the Punjaub in the beginning of 1603, this devoted man arrived at Su-chou, the frontier of China, towards the end of 1605. During this time he had successfully accomplished the most arduous portion of the journey across Asia, only as it turned out to be there kept waiting for permission to enter China, until that permission came too late to find him alive. His death appears to have been the result of disease, not improbably brought on by the hardships he had endured. It was contracted during the heart-breaking delay of fourteen months at Su-chou. But it is not altogether certain that he did not die of poison at the hands of the Mohammedans there, by whom he was detested.

Whatever the cause was, Su-chou was the scene of the death of this noble man. It is related of another of the most famous Jesuit pioneers,

Matthew Ricci, who was working at Peking at the time of Goës's attempt to reach that capital, that his principles as a missionary "appear to have been to stretch conciliation as far as possible; and to seek the respect of the educated Chinese by the display of superior scientific attainments." Without venturing for a moment to criticise the methods now in vogue among missionaries in China, it may be said in all simplicity that no more obvious or likely way could be found of winning over an educated people, such as are a vast proportion of the Chinese.

Our own arrival at Su-chou was unmarked by any incident. The town is a fine specimen of its kind, and retains evidence of having once enjoyed greater prosperity than it does now. The walls are forty feet high, with flank defence towers every hundred yards. The area they enclose is some one thousand yards from east to west by seven hundred from north to south. One peculiarity there is, in the fact that there are three, instead of the usual four, massive gateways. The area included by the walls is not entirely built over, the western side of the town being sparsely occupied. The thickly inhabited portion, and that where all the main trade congregates, is, as remains the custom in most large cities of China, confined to the four main streets which meet and cross at an ornamental drum-tower in the heart of the town.

To us, straight from the wilds, the busy streets and hustling crowds of Su-chou were at first rather oppressing, especially so as it was the eve of the celebrated Feast of Lanterns, for which all the country side had poured into the town.

The inn-yards were for the most part crowded, and it was not without difficulty that we could make our way along the heavily-thronged thoroughfares from one inn to another. Though invariably treated politely, except for such jocular remarks upon our personal appearance as any yokel crowd might make, we were surrounded by gaping crowds the moment we stood still. A European in Su-chou is very rarely seen, and to many of the villagers no doubt we were altogether a new experience.

After some trouble we found an inn which was nearly empty. It was one of the sort called in these parts a *kuan* or officials' inn, where the ordinary Chinese travellers do not go. Rejoicing in the prettily-sounding name of the "Yu-fu-dian," or Elm Tree Inn, we considered ourselves lucky to have found it. The following day, after calling on the head magistrate, we gave ourselves up to enjoying the crowds and the street scenes. Su-chou was very much *en fête*, and never-ending processions of what appeared life-size figures, but were really children dressed up, were carried about the streets, followed by grinning and good-natured crowds.

No little originality is displayed both in the grouping and setting-up of these human waxworks on the iron frames. Borne by many sturdy coolies, the framework upon which the figures stand must be of considerable weight, and how the children keep so steady under the swaying and jostling it is difficult to understand. Upon first sight we were under the impression that the figures were inanimate, but an amusing incident which happened at a low barrier served to undeceive us. At the end of a narrow by-street it was necessary for one of the processions to pass underneath the wooden archway, and in endeavouring to do so part of the framework caught. In a moment the hitherto motionless figures became very animate, and it was only by the dexterity of the bearers that a complete collapse was saved, much to the amusement of the crowd.

While these processions were perambulating the town, followed by the rough elements composing the crowd, the merchants, shopkeepers, and more wealthy *hongs* were busy setting up temporary street arches, as well as various quaint and, in some cases, artistic devices destined to contain lanterns as soon as darkness fell. Seen by daylight, these erections were not always handsome, but as we viewed them at a late hour, after dark, gazing on the now fairy-like town from high up on the central tower, the effect was most pleasing. The latter is of three storeys, in the well-known style never departed from in China, with sloping deep eaves, which support the heavily-groined roofs. Round the eaves lights sparkled in a continuous line, and from them huge lanterns, of variegated colour and design, swung gently in a faint breeze. Running up at right angles to the tower were the four principal streets, throughout whose entire length stretched a brilliant vista of lantern-decked arches. In the lesser streets and more distant purlieus, scattered and irregular lanterns shed a more feeble light, which gradually softened into utter darkness beyond the inhabited quarters of the town.

Standing on the topmost storey of the tower, it required but little imagination to recall the opening scene in that well-known operetta, "The Geisha," and whoever has sat enthralled at the opening chorus in his comfortable stall in a London theatre, can form a very true idea of the real thing as we saw it that night in the crowded streets of Su-chou.

Much as we enjoyed the Feast of Lanterns, it was from another point of view unwelcome. At Su-chou it was necessary to make a fresh arrangement for cart-hire, and hard as the carter class in China work, like the rest of the lower orders there, to them a holiday once taken is a sacred thing.

It was not until the third day, and then only under pressure from the *yamen*, that we could obtain carts and make a start. Between Su-chou and Liang-chou is a distance of rather over 300 miles, which, owing to the slow rate the Chinese cart travels, and to the miserable state of the so-called track, occupied our party seventeen marches. It is not so much that the gradients are not sufficiently considered, for in this respect the Chinese have not much to learn, but that of the roadway they take very slight, if any, notice. So long as a Chinese cart can be bumped and hauled along, no matter how severe the strain upon the animals may be, no Chinaman troubles his head. In many places systematic repair would work wonders; but it is a well-proved fact that although the Chinaman can make almost everything, he neither can nor will keep up anything.

Another great drawback to speed in North-West Kansu are the sunken roadways, which form for scores of miles the most common type of track. At times over twenty feet deep, these cuttings are so narrow that two carts frequently cannot pass. Here and there a dug-out is made for this purpose in the narrowest cuttings. In the wet season, and when the snow which lay everywhere when we first entered China proper has melted, many miles of the route would be bog and wellnigh impassable. Up to the Wu-shi-ling, the highest pass climbed anywhere between Peking and Su-chou, situated between Liang-chou and Lan-chou, the country is only semi-cultivated and sparsely settled. The narrow strip of North-West Kansu, through which the great road runs to Su-chou, is nowhere more than 100 miles in width until nearing Liang-chou. On the north-east this strip is bordered by the Gobi desert, along the edge of which flows the only river of any consequence in these parts, the Hei-ho. Rising in the Nan-shan, the latter crosses the main route near Kan-chou, then runs parallel to the route for some distance, to disappear finally north and east into the desert. South-west of the great road, for most of the distance to Lan-chou, the gigantic ranges of the eastern Nan-shan shut in the strip of Kansu already mentioned. Behind the Nan-shan lie the easterly terraces of the highest tableland in the world, Tibet.

Being of an average height of 5000 to 6000 feet above sea-level, the climate of North-West Kansu inclines towards severity in the winter, with a correspondingly mild summer.

In January, at the time we passed, the wind is at times piercingly cold. Snow is not excessive, although the lower Nan-shan ranges were thickly covered while we were at Liang-chou at the end of February. Yet a week later, crossing the Wu-shi-ling, there was only a little snow at 10,000 feet above sea-level.

Shortly before reaching Kan-chou, the third of the Fu towns (those of prefectorial grade) in North-West Kansu, our party met the first European we had seen for six months. Sitting one day sunning myself, carter fashion, on the shafts of my cart, I noticed some vehicles approaching in the opposite direction, and walking ahead of them what I took at first glance to be an unusually tall Chinaman. A second look, however, showed something in his walk decidedly European, and such he proved to be. Unfortunately for both parties, we were denied the pleasure of a long talk. Mr Derring was making for Hami and Chinese Turkestan on behalf of the Bible Society, who hope to find opportunities of there extending their sphere of work, and the spot we happened to meet at was about half-way through our respective stages for that day. He was able, however, to give us some news of the world, for we had been entirely cut off from communication of any kind since leaving Leh in Kashmir; and after a quarter of an hour's chat by the roadside we parted.

Two days later Kan-chou was reached.

As all Chinese towns are practically a copy of one another, it is unnecessary to weary the reader with a description of it. To us its interest was chiefly confined to the fact that there is there a small Belgian mission, where we were most kindly received by the brother in charge, who was able to give us an old Belgian newspaper. Here we first read the news of the day, to a limited extent it is true, but what the sight of even an old newspaper means, only those who have been cut off entirely from all communication with the outside world for six months can realise. Coal of excellent quality is found near Kan-chou, as indeed it is throughout North-West Kansu. At Su-chou petroleum-oil is already worked under the superintendence of a gentleman who has for years served the Chinese Government. Mr Splingart is a Belgian by birth, but holds Chinese rank. Well known throughout the far West, Lin-Ta-Jen, to give him his Chinese name, is the right-hand man of the Viceroy, and it will be through his instrumentality that railways, mills, and such modern mechanical appliances as eventually find their way to this far-distant province, will owe their inception.

Two days south of Kan-chou, the monotony of the daily march was agreeably broken by the finding of an exceedingly striking Buddhist temple, near a small walled town, Shan-tan-hsien by name. The temple ("Ta-fo-tsu-miao" in Chinese, "great Buddhist temple") stands at the base of a low range of mountains, where it is picturesquely placed against the hillside. The area enclosed by the walls is built up in five terraces, forming in the usual fashion five individual sets of temple buildings, which yet are connected by steps.

The glory of the temple is a colossal figure of

Buddha, some fifty feet in height, which is not cut out of rock, but is built of stone and plaster. The figure is seated in the usual fashion with eyes fixed, one hand on each knee, rested against the hillside. Access to any part of the figure can be obtained by ascending to one terrace oı another. The representation of the sainted founder of the great renunciation is kept in very good repair. The huge head of the figure is gilded all over. It has a startling blue wig and bright red lips. The eyes, fairly natural, look like glass, but are not within touch even from the top gallery of the terrace.

For the sake of comparison the following dimensions may be of interest, though to introduce such prosaic details into the contemplation of so absorbing a representation almost causes a feeling of shame. The ears are each seven feet long. The head sixteen to eighteen feet high. The neck twenty to twenty-four feet round. In the temple buildings we found some unusually artistic specimens of Chinese wall-paintings; and although at the time we passed a few old priests were considered sufficient to watch the whole enclosure, there is no doubt, from the evidence of money spent, that the temple must be richly dowered, or Buddhism must still have many devoted followers in this particular district.

Like the Japanese, the Chinese are wonderfully endowed with the eye for a beautiful landscape, and equally with their more up-to-date neighbours, are unsurpassed in the faculty they enjoy for choosing just the right spot to indulge the spirit of contemplation in its most ideal form. Few who remember Sir Edwin Arnold's beautiful description of the palace prepared for Yasôdhara after Siddârtha had wedded her but would recall them as they lingered on the terraces of the "Ta-fo-tsu-miao,"—not that the one could for a moment compare with the other, but to the common folk, who spend their holiday in this modern Vishramvan, and choose to enjoy the view it offered, the charm may be as great. Leaving the temple, we were, as so frequently happens in this land of surprises, rapidly brought face to face with a striking contrast. At Shan-tan-hsien, the small town already mentioned, we reached the end of our stage and had to spend the night. Anything more squalid, not to say filthy, than the appearance of the place it would be hard to find. Down the middle of the chief lane, itself a disreputable-looking spot, ran a small stream, and this appeared to answer the double purpose of main drain and municipal water-works. Whether because it was partially frozen we escaped the myriads of germs which must have lurked in its shallows, I do not know; anyhow, the recollections of the temple would be even more charming than they are had Shan-tan-hsien showed any desire to live up to it.

In an earlier chapter mention has been made of the entire neglect of any military precaution for safe-guarding the communication with, or the advance of, an enemy from Chinese Turkestan. Not only are the garrisons deficient in numbers, munitions of war, in fact in every necessary requirement, but no endeavour has been made on the part of the Chinese to take advantage of natural features, which in modern war play so prominent a part in deciding the fate of battles and incidentally of nations.

How far China is vulnerable on her north-west border may to some extent be gathered from the enormous expenditure she has incurred during the course of her history to retain possession of Chinese Turkestan. No other reason, except perhaps that of national pride, can be imagined for the constant drain she is willing to meet. Moreover, history goes to show that a China confined to Kansu, and deprived of Mongolia and Eastern Turkestan, is but half an empire. Yet, while apparently recognising this fact, her rulers past and present have never allowed conviction to carry them farther than to build the Great Wall.

Throughout almost the whole of her vast northern boundary, stretching from the Pamirs to the Pacific, at the mouth of the Tumen river south of Vladivostock, fortunately for herself, China is defended by a great natural buffer in the shape of vast deserts. To reach the heart of the country, armies from the north must enter either through Manchuria at one end, or through North-West Kansu at the other end, of this huge stretch of territory.

Manchuria has already been the scene of at least one serious attempt, and no man can say with any certainty how remote may be the period when a similar attempt may not be made at the other end of the frontier. It has always been a subject for difference, in expert opinion, whether it is strategically sounder to await the advance of a possible foe on the hither side of such natural defences as a desert country offers, or to occupy available positions on the far side, connecting these by means of railways with the defender's advanced posts.

A Remnant, 2000 *years old. The Great Wall of China in N.W. Kansu.*

Old Watch-tower on the Great Wall of China at its far north-west extremity.

Such problems are found on our own frontiers, as for example in that part of Baluchistan through which the railway now runs to Nushki, and may some day to Seistan. Again, between Quetta and Kandahar does a somewhat similar problem arise, and on the north-east frontier would arise were Russia in occupation of Chinese Turkestan.

In the country under discussion, China possesses a long line of fertile oases, practically unfortified, which stretch from Ili and from Kashgar to Lanchou in Kansu. Along this line nature has decreed that armies are bound to move whose aim is to enter China. The question therefore of the advisability, not to say necessity, of taking advantage of all possible natural positions hardly admits of argument. It may then be accepted as granted that China would long ago have ascertained, and have placed in a state of defence, such positions as there are. Unfortunately, the obvious is nowhere less studied than in China, and far from having made any attempt at fortifying her one vulnerable line of attack, I am bold enough to suggest that to-day she has no idea of the existence of such natural positions as there are.

To turn from modern defensive works to forts of refuge, such as are still found dotted everywhere in North-West Kansu, is perhaps too severe a trial of my reader's, and especially of a military reader's, interest. I will, however, ask any who feel thus to remember that it has been the writer's aim to chronicle what he did see, not what he might have seen.

The previous history of a country-side, peaceful

or otherwise, may usually be read in the character of its towns and villages. Our own border marches tell a tale even to this day in the remains of the fortified ruins which still linger in remote parts. Nothing is more striking in most portions of China than the peaceful character of its villages over thousands of square miles. But in North-West Kansu all is changed. It is no exaggeration to say that from An-si-chou to the Wu-shi-ling hardly a village or farm exists but is in some way or other prepared for defence.

The Fu (prefectorial), Chou (departmental), and Hsien (district) towns are enclosed, as is the usual custom, by defensive walls and strong gates, but even these have been more solidly constructed than in towns farther south. Double, sometimes triple, gateways defend the exits; and at Kan-chou a stream and marsh just outside the walls are also turned to advantage.

Setting aside the towns, the feature of the country-side is undoubtedly the forts of refuge and defensible posts—defensible, that is, where modern weapons are not employed—which are scattered not only along the main route but on both sides of it wherever human habitations exist. From small forts a few yards square with ten-feet walls, these posts run to miniature fortresses, which, allowing for the differences of surroundings and available building material, resemble nothing so much as the mediæval castles of our own feudal days. Varying as they do in size and massive appearance, the dimensions of one which is here given suggest some idea of the invincibility of these refuges, if only the hearts of their defenders had been strong in proportion to their ramparts. The fort described stands at a village named Pa-pa (eight streams), a few miles west of Liang-chou. This district exhibits some of the most pitiful

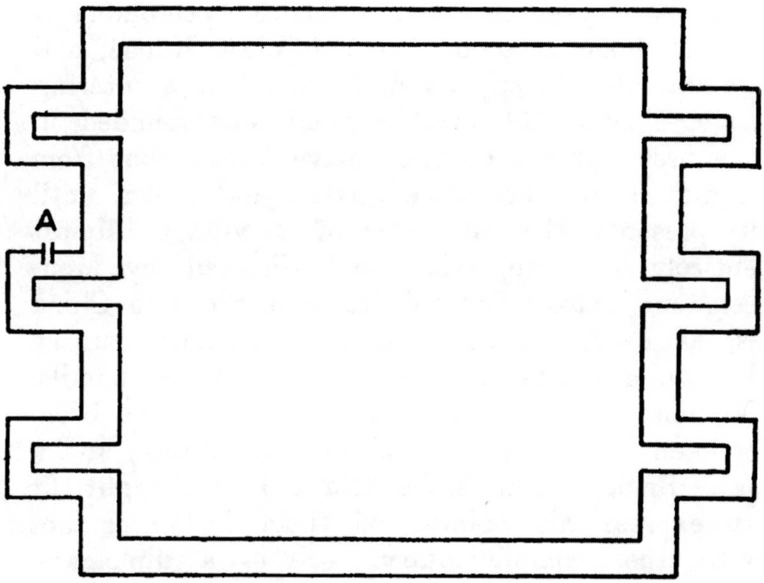

ONE TYPE OF FORT OF REFUGE IN NORTH-WEST KANSU.

Area, 90 square yards. Walls, 35 feet high, at top 3 feet thick, at bottom 15 feet thick. They are made of rammed earth and mud-bricks, and have solid buttresses for flank defence. "A" is the only entrance, a small postern door, 6 × 4 feet. Inside are the hovels of the inhabitants.

examples of the wholesale destruction caused during the early Mohammedan rising, though why such places did not afford the safety sought for by the wretched inhabitants can only be laid to the charge of their own cowardice.

Seventeen days after quitting Su-chou, we

were approaching the town of Liang-chou, and had already sighted the two fine brick pagodas which adorn the site, and are well-known landmarks for some miles round. On the north-west side of the town a European mission-station has been established for thirty years. It is presided over by Monseigneur Otto, Vicaire Apostolique of the Catholic Mission to North-West Kansu, and we intended to pay a visit to him before entering Liang-chou. The establishment was founded in the first instance by two native priests sent from Lan-chou, and has since thriven and grown until it presents the character of a village, almost entirely self-supporting, and directed by Monseigneur Otto. The subject of missions in China is, as every one acquainted with that country knows, a somewhat thorny question to handle. Volumes might be, and in some cases have been, written for and against these institutions; and a late British Minister to China has thought fit to express his opinion of them in terms not altogether complimentary. From a diplomatic point of view, no doubt, considerable trouble is caused by the presence and behaviour of a certain class of missionary in China; but the lesson the writer would derive from this fact is not that the missionary is not wanted, but that most strict and searching care should be exercised in the selection of those who are chosen.

Setting aside for the moment all other side issues, it is impossible for any professing Christian to raise objections to the spread of God's Word among the heathen.

1. FRÉDERIY, Holl.
2. LAUWAERT, Belge.
3. OTTO, Mgr.
4. TER LAAK, Préfet Apostol, Holl.
5. DE PEUTER, Belge.
6. FAN POECK, „
7. CALBRECHT, „
8. HEIREMANS, Belge.
9. WANG, Chinois.
10. SPRONKEN, Belge.
11. DESMARETS, „
12. JAMART, „
13. CCH'ENN, Chinois.
14. JADOUL, Belge.
15. MORTIER, „

The R.C. Mission near Liang-chou, N.W. Kansu.

From the writer's own experience there are men quite unfitted for the profession they have adopted —as missionaries; so in every other walk of life, where many have unfortunately mistaken their vocation. But there are also earnest devoted men, whose one and only thought is to carry out the original command to preach the Gospel; and in doing so, in the opinion of the writer, these men are laying a priceless foundation which will some day bear fruit. Of the secondary benefits the presence of such missionaries affords, not the least is the medical knowledge they diffuse in a land where treatment is still in vogue such as people in Europe would scarcely credit. One other point may be noticed, possibly unfamiliar to those whose sympathies do not altogether run with missionary enterprise in China.

I venture to assert that nowhere in the world is the personal element more valued or more necessary, as applied to any work, than in this land of contradiction. In the doctrines of their great sage, Confucius, the highest moral principles are to be found. These, if acted up to, would furnish as high an ethical code as any the human mind has ever conceived, but unfortunately they rarely are.

The chief use of the sage's aphorisms is confined to engraving them as food for the eyes on temple doorways, or to quoting them as embellishments to the eternal essays and philosophical discussions so dear to Chinese educated minds. None the less in that country is an upright man respected and honoured to the full, whether he be a high official struggling to stem the torrent of corruption which threatens finally to sweep away all attempts at the regeneration of public and magisterial life, or whether he be a village elder known throughout his own little world as a man of just and honest purpose.

It is from this point of view that I would plead for the real missionary, in the conviction that the sight of such men, the work they do, the self-sacrifice they exhibit, the wholly unselfish lives they devote to their work, must and does appeal even to the intensely realistic nature possessed by most Chinese.

During the two days spent with Monseigneur Otto, we began to realise once more the delights of civilisation. Though nothing could be simpler or more modest than the mission surroundings and daily life, it was a great pleasure to enjoy once again the companionship of educated Europeans. The bishop himself is a remarkable man. In the course of many conversations he told of his arrival in China thirty years ago; and the impressions and recollections of so shrewd an observer upon all matters connected with Chinese life were full of interest. Though Monseigneur had never since quitted the country of his adoption, he had kept himself altogether *au fait* with European affairs. So much so that after our first meeting I was under the impression that he had not long returned from furlough. Thirsting for English news we had eagerly devoured the last Shanghai French papers, where we found full lists of what was at that time our new Liberal Cabinet.

Monseigneur was not only ready but eager to

discuss the characters of those Right Honourable Gentlemen, with whose names he was familiar; and unknown previously as many were outside our own country, there were very few of whom he had not heard.

At the time of our stay the mission contained some three thousand to four thousand converts and sixteen priests, but the number of the latter were above what is customary owing to the arrival of a fresh batch from Europe only a few days previously. It was intended to further strengthen another station at Tsin-chou, south of Lan-chou—hence the temporary increase.

The mission premises represent a Chinese village of the local type, with the addition of two churches—one quite new—the schools, and the quarters for the priests. In these schools the children are first taught French and grounded in the elements of their new faith. After some years, and if of promise both in character and intelligence, they are brought on to learn Latin. Eventually, but not until after fifteen years' close study and training, the pick of the scholars may be ordained native priests, though very few are so chosen.

Leaving Monseigneur Otto and the fathers, whose kindness and hospitality nothing could have exceeded, we started again for Liang-chou on the third day. During our time at the mission-station the snow had never ceased to fall. It was a morning of brilliant sunshine, and the surrounding country as well as the lower ranges of the Nan-shan, three miles distant, presented a most beautiful panorama in their spotless covering of white.

Liang-chou, as has already been stated, is likely to take a prominent place when, and if, the development of this far-away province commences.

A railway being the first necessity, a suitable track must be found. It will be seen by a glance at the map that the great highroad runs from Peking *viâ* Tai-yuan-fu and Ping-yang in Shansi to Si-an-fu, the capital of Shensi. From Si-an-fu the road continues north of the Wei river valley *viâ* Ping-liang to Lan-chou and Liang-chou. This is the main road which for centuries past has seen the passage of embassies, armies, merchants, and officials, to and fro between the capital and Chinese Turkestan Along it inns are found throughout the entire distance, and by the traffic which unceasingly drags its laborious way over its hilly length many thousands of the lower orders find a living. This route is impossible for a railway, owing to the fact that any such track would be obliged to face numerous cross ranges, also that the natural drainage of this area runs at right angles to any such proposed course.

There are, however, two other more direct though less used tracks connecting Liang-chou and Lan-chou with Peking. Of these the most northern, after quitting Peking, runs north-west to Kalgan. Hence, turning almost due west, it reaches Kwei-hua-cheng, continuing across the Ordos country north of the Yellow River to Liang-chou. It is by this route that camel-caravans travel, and by it the mission's heavy stores, and the priests who had lately come from Europe, had reached their destination. The journey occupies sixty-one days. The main difficulty of this track is the want of both water and supplies throughout most of its length, though these deficiencies would be no bar to the construction of a railway. There is the other consideration to be thought of—viz., that after leaving the vicinity of Kwei-hua-cheng the country traversed offers no hope of paying local traffic.

For the conveyance of goods there is an alternative and subsidiary route to the above. This is found in the Yellow River, which is made use of by the Tientsin wool and skin merchants returning after buying at Si-ning and other localities. Boats are chartered at Chung-wei, half-way between Lan-chou and Ninghia, which can descend the stream to Pao-tu, not far from the great southward bend where it divides Shensi from Shansi. The third line of connection between Peking and Liang-chou runs from Tai-yuan-fu in Shansi *viâ* Wu-pao in the Yellow River, Sui-te, Ning-tiao-liang, Chung-wei to Liang-chou. This route is much used by the opium-traders, who come every season from Chili and Shan-tung provinces.

They are well mounted and frequently do double marches, treating their animals most carefully. They take thirty-five days. From Chung-wei to Ning-tiao-liang the route is at present only the usual bridle-path; but I was informed that it could be made into a cart-track but for one bad torrent which runs into the Yellow River not far from Chung-wei.

The question of railways is at present arousing so much attention in China, that it may not be without interest to devote a few lines to the subject. The eventual opening up of the resources of China depends, as is well known, upon the acceptation by that country of modern means of transport. It may not be as well known that, from the engineering point of view, China is by no means an easy country to link up with railways.

For the most part mountainous, the level plains are confined to a more or less limited area north of the Yangtze river, and south of the Yellow River from Si-an-fu to Kai-feng-fu.

Most of Western and Southern China presents most difficult problems to the would-be constructor; nor is the task made easier by the fact that the physical composition of the area now immediately under discussion is composed of loess. Of a pliable soft constitution, this loess offers unusual difficulties, owing to the extraordinary configuration of the face of the land where it predominates. The subject is fully discussed in a later chapter, being merely mentioned here as it forms one of the chief points which will guide the choice of railway track between Si-an-fu and North-West Kansu. Whether the future North-Western Railway of China is likely soon to be an accomplished fact, the writer, not being a prophet, cannot say; but there is no harm in attempting to indicate the most likely track. Over the central and eastern portion of this track our own journey took us whilst exploring the wilds of central Kansu.

It is perhaps necessary to inform the reader unacquainted with the present position of railway construction in China, that the Peking Hankow

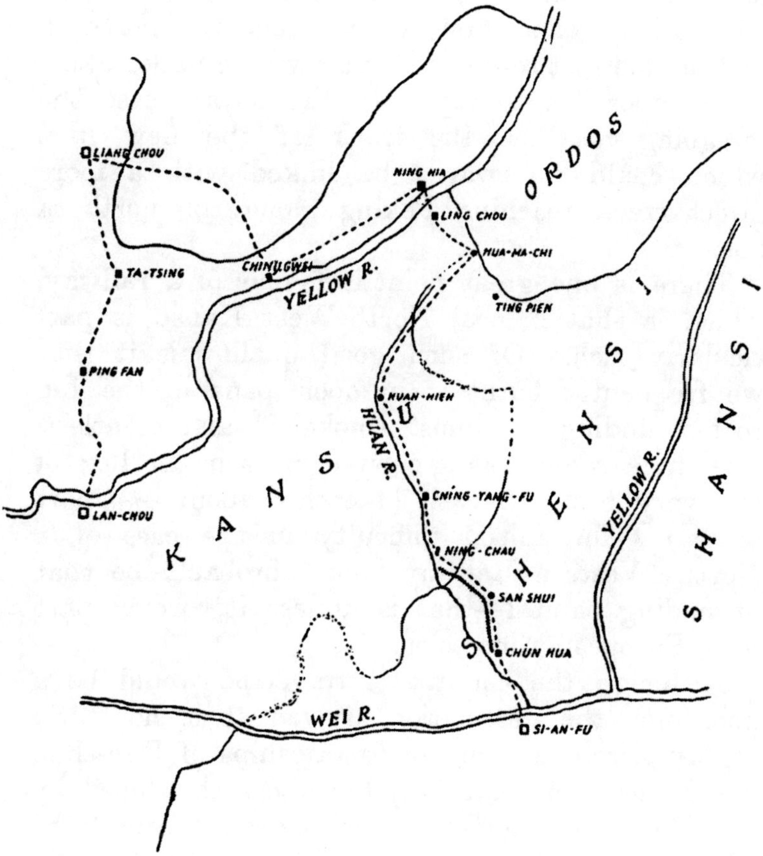

Possible trace of the railway line from SI-AN-FU to LANCHOU.

.... Railway

trunk line will eventually link up with Si-an-fu. The latter is such a very important centre that it must be connected with the capital; and whether it in turn will be put in direct communication with Liang-chou first, or whether the northern and most direct route to Peking will be undertaken, it is impossible to say. In the former case the foregoing may be the track of the new line, which could afterwards be linked with a more direct track reaching Peking along the northern border.

There is one great point in favour of a railway, which is that in coal North-West Kansu is particularly rich. Of such good quality is it that we frequently burnt it in open pans in the inn rooms, finding it almost smokeless and scentless. The price round Liang-chou is 6 cash per lb.; of the very best, 12 cash (1 cash = about $\frac{1}{800}$ part of 2s.) The initial difficulty in the case of a North-Western Railway would probably be that of finding capital—that is, unless it formed part of a European concession.

Although the country it traversed would be a poor one, the destination arrived at is not. So highly prized are the magistrateships of Kan-chou and Liang-chou that they have been christened by the Chinese respectively "the gold-mine" and "the silver-mine." It is owing to the chance of rapidly accumulating wealth, as well as to the fact that such posts, from their remote situation, are safe from the too exacting control of Peking, that aspirants to magisterial honour are tempted to travel so far afield.

Liang-chou itself is a town in every sense of the word. It has a population of 15,000 to 20,000 souls, and shows all the usual signs of prosperity. We found here the first English mission—one of the China Inland branch. It is at present the frontier post, but it is hoped that farther progress towards Chinese Turkestan may not long be delayed.

At Liang-chou we became possessed of an item of information interesting perhaps to those who took part in the Boxer rising of 1900. During that brief but somewhat stirring period, few names were as widely known to foreigners, or more execrated by them, than that of Yü-Hsien, Governor of Shansi, and murderer of the unfortunate missionaries, who to the number of forty-five perished in a day at Tai-yuan-fu.

Among the conditions of peace which followed the rising, it may be mentioned that several high Chinese officials were condemned to death by Imperial decree. But as the execution of such decrees was not intrusted to any European tribunal, much doubt has existed whether they could be considered anything more than the usual "saving of face." Of the ultimate death of Yü-Hsien, we were informed at Liang-chou there can be no doubt. The following is the somewhat strange story told by a native Christian, a Chinaman, who accidentally happened to witness the final scene. Immediately after the publication of the edict referred to, Yü-Hsien was banished to the farthest confines—in other words, to Chinese Turkestan. He had reached Liang-chou in Kansu, and there found in the governor a fellow-provincial and old schoolfellow, neither having met for years. Asked by the latter to remain a few days, Yü-Hsien was only too pleased to consent. Unfortunately for him, this step cost him his life. The second day of his visit an order was received from Peking that upon the arrival of Yü-Hsien at Liang-chou, he was to be put to death · and a more unpleasant command for his old friend and schoolmate to have to enforce it is hardly possible to imagine. The governor having given the necessary orders, our informer related, retired to his *yamen* and himself took poison. Early the following morning — probably warned, and by then resigned — Yü-Hsien came out into a courtyard in the front of the house where he lodged, and there the executioner told off was waiting for him. Whether the nerve of the latter failed him at the thought of the status of his victim, our informant could not say; anyhow, after striking one badly aimed blow at Yu-Hsien's neck, the man threw down the sword and ran, leaving the wounded ex-governor lying in the yard. A moment after a minor military official came out from the house, and this man, encouraged by his still living master to make an end of the horrible scene, himself cut off the ex-governor's head. So died Yü-Hsien,—a man of brutal character, who was perhaps more responsible than any other Chinese official for the rise and spread of the Boxer rebellion.

CHAPTER XIII.

NATIVES OF WESTERN KANSU—OPIUM-SMOKING—THE PEKIN EDICT—TRAVELLING CARTS—LAN-CHOU—A BRIDGE OF BOATS—A SURPRISING DINNER-PARTY—THE MEETING OF EAST AND WEST—COMIC-OPERA ARMY MANŒUVRES—FAIR WOMEN AND FAMED TOBACCO—PRIMITIVE MACHINERY—THE FUTURE OF KANSU AND SZE-CHUAN.

THE inhabitants of Western Kansu vary so little from the ordinary Chinese of the north, that any detailed description of them is unnecessary. The population may be divided into two classes. The first are those who live by agriculture, and who are in settled possession of such land as is under cultivation; the second, those who live by, and on, the main road.

It might be thought that the latter class would form a small minority of the general population, but although statistics on the point would be impossible to come by, personal observation leads me to think that the proportion of each would not be far short of equal. The dwellers on the land are either settlers since the rebellion days, or descendants of the unhappy people who bore the brunt of those never-to-be-forgotten times.

From An-si-chou to Lan-chou, even the larger towns owe a large proportion—if not the chief—of such prosperity as they enjoy to the passing traffic, in the shape of having to provide stores and supplies to the never-ceasing string of travellers, officials, and merchants who frequent the road.

The towns in their turn take what means of subsistence the surrounding districts can produce, but, judging by the amount of transport carrying only the necessities of life, as well as from inquiries made, it appears as though sufficient supplies were not produced on the spot to meet the demands of the through traffic as well as to supply the local inhabitants.

The people of Kansu met with in the journey impressed us favourably, especially the carter class. As a rule, these were friendly and open-minded compared to the ordinary Chinaman of the interior, progressive and not anti-foreign.

On consideration it is natural that they should be so. The through traffic on the great road is composed of people from almost every part of Northern China, besides others, who to the Chinese are almost foreigners. It also provides the opportunity of studying all classes, from governors and high officials of provinces to ordinary merchants; also, though far more infrequently, it affords the chance of coming in contact with the actual foreigner, and he of various nations.

One blot, and that no small one, lies on the people of Western Kansu. It is that men and women are to a fearful extent habitual and confirmed smokers of opium. From personal observation I should have placed the percentage high, but had I not had the best authority for saying so, not as high as it would appear to be.

Monseigneur Otto, who, as already related, has spent thirty years of his life in China, and a large portion of that time in Kansu, reckons six men out of every eight of the population as confirmed in the habit. Opium-smoking is sometimes compared to the unnecessary drinking common to most European nations. But this in no sense represents a true perspective. It is well known that opium is largely in use among other Asiatic races, some of our own native Indian soldiers being of this number; but that it can for one moment be considered in China as merely a harmful excess confined to a small minority of those who use the drug is not the truth. Without statistics it is useless to attempt to draw exact comparisons, but it is only necessary to travel for a few mouths in Western Kansu to see how all-embracing in its fearful effects the habit is.

Facilis descensus Averni is a maxim with which we are all familiar, and in the sense in which it is generally used it applies to nothing so aptly as the career of the immoderate opium-smoker. During the last year efforts have been made to control if not to extinguish the evil; and if high-sounding edicts from the Imperial brush could accomplish the impossible we might hope for better things.

Worthy of all praise as such attempts are, there would be more hope of ultimate success had moderation been shown in the commencement of the crusade. Unfortunately the edict has gone forth that in ten years opium-smoking will no longer exist in China, and in this form the experiment may be said to be doomed. Let us suppose for the sake of analogy that a bill could pass through both Houses of Parliament suppressing not only the abuse of beer-drinking, but the use of beer within the same limit of time. Would any sane person expect to see aught but failure accompany such a preposterous attempt? Yet the task to which the rulers of China have yoked themselves is a thousand times more impossible.

Setting apart for the moment the political side of the question involved in the Imperial edict referred to,—that is to say, whether there is any intention on the part of the Chinese Government to do more than free themselves by the issue of such an edict from the charge that they must first remove the beam from their own eye previous to demanding the cessation of the import of Indian opium into China—in this case the mote which is in their brother's eye,—let us glance briefly at the history of the opium question in the Flowery Land.

One hundred and forty years in the history of an Asiatic race is an inappreciable space; though it is just that time since opium first became a bone of contention between England and China.

In the autumn of 1856 a ship flying the British flag, *The Arrow*, was lying at anchor in the Canton river, suspected of smuggling opium destined for the market at Canton. As the result of some years of international squabbles upon the opium question, the Chinese captured *The Arrow*, hauled down the British flag, and imprisoned some of her native crew.

This incident was practically the cause of the second war between the two nations, so that opium has its roots deeply fixed in the international soil upon which we stand to discuss the question with China.

From 1856 to the present day the import of Indian opium has continued, and although the amount that thus reaches China is a mere cipher in comparison with the quantity of the home-grown drug, yet the first steps taken by the Chinese Government in the anti-opium crusade were to request that the import of Indian opium might cease.

There is no possibility within the limits at command of discussing in detail the various clauses of the Pekin Edict, published in 'The Times' of November 23, 1906. They are far too comprehensive, and would need to be dissected in detail in order to show the improbability of their being carried out as they stand.

It is allowed by the Chinese authorities, who, it may be said incidentally, do not as a rule err in severity in the enumeration of national faults, that forty per cent of the Chinese use opium. Had the percentage been raised considerably, and the forty per cent tarred as *abusing* the use of opium, perhaps we should have been nearer the real figures. Whatever these may be, it should be remembered that the abuse of this drug is not confined to the lower orders. On the contrary, it numbers among its slaves—those most hopelessly addicted to its use—the highest and most powerful in the country.

Not only as consumers do we find such men but also as producers. Much of the land upon which opium is grown is in the hands of magistrates and even higher officials. As the most productive crop, in spite of its paying in places double taxation, the area under the poppy is annually increasing in China. In some parts good wheat-land is turned into poppy-land, with the result that whole districts, formerly capable of raising sufficient food-stuff for local requirements, must now import.

Nor are the vested interests in favour of the drug less strong in other ways.

It is well known that no Chinese magistrate could exist upon the miserable stipend he receives. It has hitherto been his business, and that of no one else, how he supplemented his income; and one of the chief sources was, and still is, in the extra royalties or "pickings" which can be dragged in an ever rising scale from village opium-dens.

The few examples quoted only serve to indicate some of the vested interests which will be found in the inert mass of those lying in the way of any attempt to curtail the supply or use of opium.

Whether the Chinese Government, hitherto a synonym for conservatism of the most harmful kind, is likely to succeed in the crusade it has initiated against opium-smoking time alone can show.

If it is willing to supply adequate guarantees that the attempt is a sincere one, made solely for the good of the people, then indeed has China awoke to the evil and it is England's destiny once more to stand for progress and the right and to help to the utmost of her ability.

The strip of country traversed throughout this portion of the journey should be divided for the purpose of gauging its agricultural value into two distinct districts.

The former consists of the country north-west of the Wu-shi-ling, already referred to as the highest point between Peking and Urumtsi, and the latter of all the country south-east of the pass.

The difference lies, perhaps, not so much in the fertility of the soil as in the more general settlement of the southern portion which naturally ensures a heavier production. In any case the two portions differ materially, and that much in favour of the southern. From An-si-chou to the Wu-shi-ling there are fertile belts, also many hundreds of acres of land far superior to much that is heavily cultivated in other portions of China. Were the same ceaseless care bestowed on much of what is now waste and bog-land as is given, say, to the eastern portion of Shan-tung, a notoriously poor province, the result would, I venture to think, be astonishing.

Of water there is no lack at certain seasons, but irrigation would need the same care and forethought as is bestowed upon it in other parts of China. Of what can be done by this means, the famous irrigation works of the Chengtu plain in Szechewan province are the standing example.

The cost of labour in the area under description

would be found to vary more than usual, as it was required in town or country. Taking as an example Lan-chou, the provincial capital, the presence there of a large number of officials who employ a correspondingly increased number of servants and hangers-on, is one cause which tends to raise the price of wages.

The existence of the extensive tobacco industry is another. Away from the town labour is naturally cheaper, but anywhere "on the road" prices are apt to be higher than in an ordinary agricultural district in China. It is a well-known fact that travellers on the whole are good payers, and the tips expected by the carters, the innkeepers, and others connected with the road, maintain a higher scale of payments than in ordinary Chinese life.

Most of the travelling is done by means of broad two-wheel carts, known in other parts of the East as *araba.* They have an axle-width of sixty inches with wheels either fifty-three or seventy-eight inches high. Some of the travelling carts in use by high officials or even well-to-do merchants, though cumbersome, are fitted up with no little comfort. Invariably roofed with matting, most have besides both front and back shut in with the same materials or with heavy curtains. I have seen some carts boarded fore and aft, with a small wood door and glass window. The inside is also made as comfortable as circumstances will allow. On the floor are felts, cotton-stuffed mattresses, and cushions, to the depth of ten or twelve inches; while the sides within the matting are hung with heavy blankets or curtains. Small charcoal braziers are carried, as well as brass hand-warmers; and these, with a lantern, candles, and the inevitable pipe, do all that is possible to render bearable the monotony of a journey which few beside Chinese could stand.

The Peking cart is sometimes used, but when seen has more often than not been placed on the wider axle.

For agricultural work the carts are drawn by cattle or mules. On the road, either by ponies or mules.

As a carter, the Chinaman born to the road is *facile princeps*; and it was one of our daily pleasures with a certain set of drivers to watch them swing in through the narrow inn-yards, thread their way with a cracking of whips like pistol shots through a maze of loose animals and empty carts, to pull up exactly at the most convenient angle, with back to the hovel door, to enable the baggage to be unloaded. Strings of camels are to be seen here and there, and these are sometimes in charge of the wild-looking tribesmen from the Sirtin border towards the Tsai Dam.

On the last two days before reaching Lan-chou the route ran through a bewildering mass of low hills and valleys of loess formation, whose average height is about 6500 feet above sea-level. This district is sparsely populated owing to lack of water, but it contains another and curious type of fort of refuge. These are only found at rare intervals when collections of farms are spread in some valley in which water allows of cultivation and human existence. In general appearance the refuges are more like a miniature of the well-known fortress at Gwalior in Central India than anything I have seen.

The usual site is on the summit of the steepest and most isolated hill-top in the vicinity of the farmstead.

Hère, perched some 400 to 600 feet above the valley, such refuges are almost impregnable. The usual approach to them is by a mere goat-track up the most steep and least accessible spur which runs from the hill-top. Owing to the gradient, never less steep than 1 in 4 or 1 in 3, the approach is simply a series of sharp zigzags, to mount which it is necessary for the ordinary man to use both hands and knees. When the top has thus been reached, it is seen that the summit of the hill has been artificially flattened; also, that the sides of the fortress, which from a distance appear to be walls, are in reality the sheer scarped hill. In some of the forts there are two walls, the lower made by leaving a small berm at the foot of the first wall. The hillside is then again scarped all round to a depth of twenty feet or more, which represents a second wall. To obtain entrance, a tunnelled way is usually driven from outside the lower wall right into the interior of the fort, but there are some into which I have climbed where the only method of obtaining entrance was, in old days, by being drawn up in a basket on a rope, or in the present day to ascend by means of holes cut for the hands and feet in the sheer wall.

After traversing the intricate stretch of loess

country, in which the curious forts described above are to be found, the track emerges suddenly into the valley of the great Yellow River, a day's march from Lan-chou.

The provincial capital stands on the right bank, over which the north wall hangs in an impressive and picturesque manner.

By far the wealthiest and most striking town visited by our party anywhere until Peking itself was reached, Lan-chou deserves some description, even at the risk of wearying the reader with a surfeit of Chinese towns.

The capital is situated at the narrowest point in the centre of a basin-like valley surrounded by high hills. At the point where Lan-chou spreads its length along the river-bank this valley contracts to about a mile in width. Here the Yellow River has forced its way through a cross range, and together with the town, which extends at this spot some 1000 yards from north to south, it almost blocks the narrow opening. East and west of Lan-chou the valley has a total length of some nine miles, while it broadens on either side of the town to a width of two-and-a-half to three miles. At the eastern end the Yellow River once more forces a path through the soft loess hills, to continue throughout its vast length a standing memorial to Chinese inertia and hateful conservatism. Commonly known as "China's Sorrow," what a waste of power and means of livelihood to thousands does the neglect of any attempt at control throughout its course entail!

From the north-west Lan-chou is approached by

a bridge of boats or a ferry, according to the season of the year. Opposite the town the river has a width of nearly 300 yards, and at the time of our crossing had not long thawed. The winter passage is made on the ice; and not a few lives are annually lost at the time it breaks up, owing to the carelessness of those who persist in attempting to make use of the ice-road long after it is unsafe.

The annual construction and opening of the boat-bridge is attended with no little *éclat.* The chief magistrate and others take part in the ceremony, which may in a small way be compared to the ancient Venetian custom, also a yearly one, of the marrying of the Adriatic by the reigning Doge.

On arrival we were met by Mr Andrew, the head of the China Inland Mission, and one of its other members. To Mr Andrew's kindness we owe a debt of gratitude not easily repaid; and the week spent in taking a thorough rest in the hospitable home over which Mrs Andrew presides will always remain as one of the brightest memories of our long journey.

Previous to starting from Leh I had made arrangements that our party should be met upon reaching Lan-chou by two orderlies from the Chinese Regiment at Wei-hai-wei, also by an old and valued *ma-fu* (groom) of my own. At Lan-chou we found the party safely installed awaiting our arrival, and heard with regret that Captain Ruxton, of the Chinese Regiment, who had brought them with him, had been obliged, owing to the delay in our arrival, to return alone to Peking.

During the week spent at the capital our time was fully occupied in seeing as much of the life of the town and its busy population as possible.

The usual exchange of visits with the high officials took place, and we were most hospitably entertained by the Nieh-Tâi (provincial judge) at a Chinese dinner, in the unavoidable absence of the Viceroy.

The Nieh-Tâi takes rank in Chinese magisterial precedence next but one to the Provincial Governor. He is therefore an enormous power for good or evil, enlightenment or anti-reform, throughout the wide territory over which his powers extend. Fortunately for the area over which our new friend exercises jurisdiction, even more for the sake of the members of the missions at Lan-chou and throughout the province, the Nieh-Tâi of Kansu bears a high character.

Upon our arrival at his official *yamen* to accept his hospitality, in such state as we could muster, he received us himself in the most courteous manner. In appearance he is an old and venerable-looking gentleman of high class, sixty-seven years of age, and, as we soon discovered, pro-foreign in his ideas and hopes. So openly does he expose his opinions that he has had constructed in the *yamen* three semi-European reception-rooms, where our dinner took place. The right-hand man of the Nieh-Tâi is a certain Mr Chiang, who combines in his own able person the offices of head of the provincial telegraph department, that of secretary to the *wai-yuan* (bureau for foreign affairs), besides which he is secretary to the Nieh-Tâi. Mr Chiang is an enlightened and progressive Chinaman of a good type. He was born at Hong-Kong, and is by birth a British subject, though he naturally does not care to say too much about the fact in public. During the 1900 rising he was most friendly to the China Inland Mission, incurring no little odium among his compatriots owing to the constant visits he paid to the mission. Mr Chiang speaks English fairly well, lapsing into Chinese if the right words will not come.

Another of the four Chinese officials at the dinner was a gentleman who spoke excellent French. He had been on the staff of the Chinese Ambassador in Paris for five years, and evidently retained most tender memories of his time in the gayest city in the world. As we know, it is the unexpected that usually happens, and never was this more forcibly brought home to the writer than when he found himself a guest at a Chinese dinner in the far west of Kansu, discussing with his neighbour at table the art treasures of Versailles and the Louvre gallery, not to mention some of the more mundane joys to be found in the French capital. The other and chief host at the dinner was the second grandson of the Nieh-Tái who, when the old gentleman retired after about an hour, took his grandfather's place. The latter is a well-born lad, and looks it. He has been taught a little English by a member of the China Inland Mission, but cannot yet talk it. Besides Captain Layard and myself, the other guests present were the members of the mission. It was not without some difficulty that we were able to persuade Mr Andrew to accept such an invitation, and then only because he allowed himself to be guided by our view of the matter.

Referring for the moment to the question of influence which missionaries in China can exercise. In the opinion of the writer, the higher the class they can influence the more likelihood of a permanent impression being made, and surely the more fixed that impression will be for good.

If such intellectual men as the Nieh-Tåi and his staff are ready to receive and recognise in a friendly spirit those who in such far-distant places stand for all that is ideally best in the European ethical code, would it not be a direct surrender of an advantage which ought to be seized to neglect every opportunity of meeting such men ?

It was by means of such arguments that we were able to persuade Mr Andrew to waive his personal feelings that his place was not at such a gathering, and to allow that our view was correct. Nothing could have been more marked than the respect paid to the members of the mission who accompanied us, —Mr Andrew, Dr Julius Hewett, Mr Preedy, and Mr Kennett.

The suite of rooms already referred to where dinner was served were nicely furnished, decorated in good taste, and painted white. The windows opening on to an inner courtyard were of glass, and here a large crowd of the usual *yamen* loafers remained during a considerable part of the meal, with their faces glued to the panes.

The room walls were hung with Japanese-made maps, well executed, of various foreign countries. Also, with large cards of numerous wild and domestic animals, such as are seen in Board schools, equally well got up, and having under each their scientific names in Latin. The meal itself would have done credit to the Ritz, being *à la Chinois* for the most part, but beautifully cooked; and to make matters quite easy for us, forks and spoons were provided as well as ivory chop-sticks.

Here for some two hours East and West met simply on the plane of educated men, and a more interesting and at the same time instructive little experience I have rarely taken part in. Hardly worthy of mention in itself, the episode is merely quoted as an example of what a little Western experience will do, even in the farthest wilds, when imbibed by educated and progressive Chinese gentlemen. In such types as are represented by Mr Chiang and the official connected with the Chinese Ambassador in Paris lies the hope of the present advance of China upon modern lines. If encouraged by those in authority, and if upheld at all times and on every possible occasion by the sympathy and backing of the Ministers of the great European Powers at Peking, there is no saying but that in the end some impression may be made upon the hide-bound conservatism usually to be found among the Chinese official class.

Among the innovations introduced under the present Administration is a so-called modern police force. This consists of a body of six hundred men, of whom four hundred are old soldiers, and two hundred fresh enlistments. The force is dressed in the new style of clothing,—in their case of a black colour. In this uniform the ancient and grotesque "target" coat gives place to a not unpleasing short coat and breeches of a semi-Chinese cut, but the latter garment is tucked into the usual worthless cloth boots. The pay of these men is said to be from three taels sixty cents to four taels thirty cents per man. This is a considerable advance upon the old style of wages, and the probability is that the men do receive the larger portion of it.

The troops, of which there are some 1500 to 2000 men, are "foreign," drilled by Chinese instructors, and badly armed. They are in possession of a few old mortars, which are pulled by ponies; and to show how easily incorrect reports arise, I may say that these were reported to us by a European, before we had seen them, as machine-guns on mules.

During our stay we had plenty of opportunity of seeing the troops at work, and at Lan-chou they are kept at it. The main barracks, or camps as they are usually called in China, are situated outside the town, beyond the east gate. Here we visited the square mud forts, surrounded each by a dry moat, and also watched the troops at drill. The men were on the whole a fairly good stamp; a few bore the unmistakable mark of confirmed opium-smokers. The drill was confined almost entirely to firing endless volleys by companies with blank cartridge, also to independent firing in a few simple parade formations. All the men were armed with the old muzzle-loading cap musket. No officers were present on parade, only drill-instructors and non-commissioned officers. The latter, to the number of one or two per company, carried no arms, but instead a bright red triangular flag, two feet six inches by two feet wide. The men wore a short black coat like the police, with the addition of a scarlet apron right across the front of the coat. In the apron are two small pockets for ammunition, useful no doubt, but a finer mark than the apron to draw a bead upon up to a thousand yards' distance could not have been invented. For the information of the uninitiated, it may be added that the movements were performed "on markers," also that a very useful beating of the men by the instructors went on all the time. As the weapon used was a good solid stick, like a pace-stick, even the wadded black coat can have been but slight protection. Among the camps we inspected was one used by the cavalry (*ma-ping*, horse soldiers). It was said to contain one *chi* (two hundred men), but actually held between twenty and thirty.

In one of the infantry camps visited we made the acquaintance of a junior officer. Him we asked if there were any modern rifles. He replied that there were, and at once sent for one, explaining at the same time that each *chi* had its two hundred rifles, but that they were always kept locked up, and the men trained with the old kind. Typically Chinese as this procedure is, it has even a worse side than might at first be apparent. In China most things which are kept locked up have a knack of disappearing before long for cash received. As regards the training with the old rifle, comment is needless.

Among the arms kept in reserve is the ancient "two-man" tripod gun. This is not even a hammer gun, but is fired by applying a piece of burning rope to the touch-hole.

Lan-chou from across the Yellow River.

The Tobacco Industry of China—a Modern (!) Press at Lan-chou.

There is a modern arsenal at Lan-chou which employs about a hundred men. They are looked after by a foreman trained at the well-known Shanghai arsenal. Eight taels a-month is the handsome wage paid each man, while the foreman receives thirty taels.

The manager was a pleasant gentleman from Shansi province, who, after showing the way round, entertained us to tea. Very little work is now done beyond the turning of old Chinese jingals into a somewhat modern edition of the same thing. In another part of the arsenal buildings we received a great surprise on being shown the complete and most costly machine plant for an entire European wool factory.

It transpired that the plant had been erected fifteen years ago by a former progressive Viceroy, at an evident expenditure of thousands of pounds. There are engine-houses and engines, looms, carding machines, cleansing and pressing machines—in fact, all the necessaries of an up-to-date factory worked entirely by steam-power; even the leather-driving belts of the machinery, some two feet wide, still remained; and though the whole is now in indifferent repair, no doubt much of the machinery could still be made use of. The Viceroy ordered the plant from Europe, and his successor stopped it working after a short period. The latter has now passed away, and the present Viceroy has commissioned Mr Splingardt, the Belgian gentleman already mentioned as in the service of the Chinese, to bring out from Europe two mechanics capable of looking after the whole factory.

The town of Lan-chou is known throughout China for two things: the first, the beauty of its women; the second, the fragrance of its tobacco. If the overwhelming superiority claimed for both these distinctions were to be judged by a European standard, less, perhaps, would have been heard of the one in Chinese poetry, and of the other wherever votaries of the water-pipe do congregate.

Known throughout the whole of China for its excellent tobacco, the town subsists to a large extent upon its manufacture. As it happened, we had an unusually good opportunity of becoming acquainted with the product of the industry, as before arriving at Chakalik in Chinese Turkestan we had consumed all the English tobacco brought from Leh.

At Chakalik we received, as a present from the Amban, a small quantity of the finest Lan-chou tobacco of the red kind. I have seen it stated that this cannot be smoked except in the Chinese water-pipe, and am aware that it is intended for consumption in that manner. At the same time, necessity knows no binding laws, and for a considerable period our briars were fed with nothing else, though we found what we called "the desert mixture" an improvement upon the plain Lan-chou tobacco. The mixture contained three parts of common Turki tobacco, something like that used by the Boers, with enough of the very pungent red Chinese to give it a taste.

Like most things in China, the Lan-chou tobacco industry is still worked on prehistoric lines, and it is difficult to say what the increased value of the trade might be were more modern methods introduced. Taking as one example the caking of both qualities. In course of manufacture the tobacco requires pressing in order to attain the flat oblong shape in which the cakes are packed for despatch all over China. This phase of the preparation is carried out in an open yard of the usual kind, where filth of every description may or may not accumulate. So also is another and earlier phase—viz., that of picking over the raw leaf. Women are chiefly employed at this work, the open yard again supplying the workshop, and the exceedingly dirty floor the sorting place.

The only machinery in use for pressing—though the word in no sense can really be applied—consists of an enormous rough beam, some thirty feet in length and eighteen inches to two feet in diameter. The beam is up-ended upon a supporting structure. At the base huge stones are fastened under the beam in order to weight it down, while at what may be called the hammer-end more stones are placed on the baulk, ropes also being attached. The structure resembles, on a gigantic scale, the usual erection common throughout the East for drawing water from a well. The bale of tobacco, already partially pressed, is now placed in a rough wood casing underneath where the top-end of the huge beam will fall, and the latter is jerked up and down, after the manner seen in pile-driving, by three or four men laying on to the ropes attached to the beam.

Were the tobacco industry at Lan-chou a mere local trade there might, even in Chinese eyes, be some reason for still retaining these archaic methods, but when it is said that the export trade permeates to the farthest corners of their vast empire, even to Singapore and such distant places where wealthy Chinese can afford to pay for what they consider a luxury, the wilful retention of such a hopelessly antiquated system can only be described as a fresh injustice, if not to "ould Ireland," at any rate to Europe in general. There are two kinds of tobacco made, known as the red and the green, nor is the colour by any means faint, strange as it may sound to our ideas. The red tobacco is known as *shui-yen* (water-pipe), the green as frosted, from the process which entails not picking the leaf until the early frosts have touched the plants.

As a specimen of the wages earned it may be interesting to note that the amount paid to the women who follow the industry is 300 cash a-day; but at Tsin-chau, a neighbouring town where the industry is also a feature, the women in winter receive 400 cash a-month and their daily food.

In this apparently abnormal difference may be read the secret of the hard struggle for actual existence which confronts so many of the lower orders in China. Daily bread, or, it should be said, daily rice, is the be-all and end-all of existence to millions, and once assured, any extra remuneration is more or less of a luxury.

Before quitting Lan-chou mention should be made of another town with which it is intimately connected. The latter stands close to the Tibet border, and both politically and from the point of view of trade, Si-ning has a considerable importance.

As the place of residence of one of the high Buddhist dignitaries, Si-ning is also a religious centre, ranking not so very far behind Lhasa. Connection is maintained with the Tibetan capital by means of traders and pilgrims who pass between the two points. It has also importance as the centre of such authority as the Chinese representatives there can maintain over the wild people of the Koko Nor.

The future prosperity of Kansu province, and that of its perhaps better known neighbour, Szechuan, are features in the exploitation of China which will loom largely in a few years' time.

As the interior of the vast empire becomes gradually opened up to European trade, the former province cannot be ignored by our own merchants. Already fed to some extent by trading houses established at Tientsin, the advent of a railway will give those who have been bold enough to push their business so far a much increased stake in Northern Chinese markets. At the present moment it may be said that Russia commands the trade of Chinese Turkestan, also that she is prepared to make a bid for that of North-West Kansu. It may be said that both in bulk and importance the amount of merchandise which Chinese Turkestan at present takes is insignificant, yet while aware of the fact I still see in the future a prospect worth striving after.

Geographically the natural limit of trade expansion in North-West China is bounded for Russia and for our own merchants by the strip of desert dividing Hami from An-si-chau. As far as An-si-chau should be made safe ground for our importers. Chinese Turkestan may at present be considered as out of reach.

In a previous chapter mention has been made of the mineral wealth, coal, oil, and possibly some gold which North-West Kansu contains. In the event of these being found to the extent the writer believes them to be present, sufficient wealth should be put in circulation locally to allow of a large increase in the money available for importing foreign goods. Even now the existence of the wool factory seen at Lan-chou shows what enlightened Chinese minds thought of the prospects of trade so far back as fifteen years ago. And given a free hand and a guarantee from interference, the Chinese merchant makes few mistakes.

Of Sze-chuan the writer is unable to speak from personal experience, but the question of inter-provincial trade between Lan-chou and Chun-king was among those discussed with men familiar on the spot with its difficulties.

The route given as now most generally made use of for inter-communication is as follows :—

Lanchau to Kung-chång on the upper waters of the Wei river, thence to Tsin-chau, situated on the northern side of the Tsin-ling mountains. These are then crossed to Hui, a Hsien town on the uppermost waters of the Kialing river, down which the descent is made to Pai-shui-kiang, Pao-ning, and so to Chung-king itself, on the Yang-tse river. The lower reaches of the

Kialing river are well known. I was informed that boats of six to seven feet draught could reach Pai-shui-kiang, also on good authority that small steamers could make the ascent, but this was contradicted by others who should know, on the score that rapids prevented any steam traffic in the highest waters.

CHAPTER XIV.

A WEEK AT LAN-CHOU—THE PROBLEM OF THE LOESS FORMATION—RICHTHOFEN'S THEORY—CONTRASTS OF SCENERY—DIFFICULT LOCOMOTION — CAMEL CARAVANS — A HISTORICAL RETROSPECT — A DANGEROUS FERRY—CAVE VILLAGES—A REMOTE CATHOLIC MISSION —A QUAINT OBLATION—CHING-YANG-FU—A REMARKABLE TUNNEL —A CHINESE IVANHOE.

A WEEK'S rest at Lan-chou with the, to us, unaccustomed luxuries of a decent roof over our heads, cleanliness, and warmth, had put fresh life into the whole party.

It was now the 17th of March, and since the 4th of August of the previous year, the day upon which our caravan moved out of Srinagar, we had marched almost daily, camped nightly, always pushing ahead. Enjoyable as such a life is, in spite of the natural obstacles which cannot be evaded, constant exposure, and the thousand and one small troubles incident to such a chance existence, cannot but tell on the physical endurance of the most robust. At Lan-chou more than half the journey had been safely accomplished, and the results had so far been satisfactory. Before us now lay only the crossing of China, and as at last spring seemed to be approaching, we looked forward to the continuance of our outdoor life for another two months with feelings of hopeful expectation. The usual route followed from Lanchou to Peking has already been described. In order to cover new ground altogether, our intention was to strike north and east for Peking, across Kansu, Shensi, and Shansi provinces, where roads are unknown and where towns hardly exist.

In the researches into the commercial and physical conditions of Northern China, made by Baron Richthofen, the eminent geologist, so long ago as 1870, was included a most detailed account of the loess formation, nowhere more capable of being studied than in the area under discussion.

To any student of physical geography few more interesting problems are afforded than that of the loess formation, which overlies almost the whole of North China, nor is any apology necessary for quoting *in extenso* what Baron Richthofen has written of it. From experience of a very wide extent of country, and including as they do the matured opinion of one of the best known scientists where the nature of this stratum is concerned, his views may be taken as one of the most important contributions ever made towards the understanding of this curious physical occurrence.

"Every one who has walked in the vicinity of Ching-kiang, on the Yang-tse river," wrote Baron Richthofen, "will recollect the yellow hills which surround that city, in which the Ching-kiang branch of the grand canal is deeply cut. They consist of loess, which is there about 200 feet thick. The same formation composes a large portion of what is generally called the great plain, and it forms probably a broad belt, intervening between it and the surrounding hills. It appears not to exist in Southern China or Sze-chuan, and is but little developed on the Yang-tse above Nanking, and on the Han, but spreads over all the northern provinces, covering everything where it has not been carried away by water. In Shansi I found it spread equally over table-lands 6000 feet high, and valleys several thousand feet less in altitude. Along my route through Honan it composes the table-land between Ju-chau and Honan-fu, and envelops on all sides the lower portion of the ranges of the Sung-shan. The bottom land of the Lo-ho is bounded on both sides by vertical cliffs of loess, and the same formation reaches, on the southern side of the valley, to the height of more than 1200 feet. The southern bank of the Yellow River consists entirely of loess.

"The peculiar feature of this formation is to spread alike over places which differ much in altitude, and, therefore, to fill the gaps between hills, to smooth away the uneven surfaces of the mountainous countries, and to create the conditions for agriculture and prosperity where they would not exist without it. From descriptions given by Chinese, who apply the specific name of *hwang-tu* to the loess, it appears that the same formation exists on a still grander scale in Shensi, making up the slopes of the broad valley of the Wei river and the entire country of the Ordos; and it spreads, probably as a cover of great thickness, far into Kansu and Central Asia. It is the loess which gives to the Hwang-ho its

Pillar, 91 feet high.

A specimen of the loess formation in the Huan-ho Valley, E. Kansu.

yellow colour. Large quantities of it are washed down from the hills by every rain, and are carried by the rivers into the plains, and ultimately into the sea. The sediments which constitute the great plain, and render the Gulf of Pechili and the Yellow Sea so shallow, are chiefly derived from the destruction of the cover of loess.

"The loess is among the various substances which would commonly be called 'loam,' because it is earthy and has a brownish-yellow colour. It can be rubbed between the fingers to an impalpable powder, which disappears in the pores of the skin, some grains of very fine sand only remaining. By mechanical destruction, such as is caused by cart-wheels on a road, it is converted into true loam. When in its original state it has a certain solidity, and is very porous, and perforated throughout its mass by thin tubes, which ramify, like the roots of grass, and have evidently their origin in the former existence of roots. They are incrusted with a film of carbonate of lime. Water, which forms pools on loam, enters therefore into loess as into a sponge, and percolates it without in the least converting it into a pulp or mud. The loess is everywhere full of organic remains, but I have never seen any other than land-shells, bones of land animals, and the numberless impressions of roots and plants. It is not stratified, but has a strong tendency to cleave along vertical planes. Therefore, wherever a river cuts into it the loess abuts against it, or against its alluvial bottom-land, in vertical cliffs, which are in places 500 feet high; above them the slopes recede gradually in a series of terraces with perpendicular front faces. Where the river washes the foot of such a wall the progress of destruction is rapid; the cliff is undermined, and the loess breaks off in vertical sheets, which tumble into the stream, to be carried down by the water. Such is the case along the southern bank of the Yellow River near Kung-hien and Sz'shui-hien, and probably in many other portions of its course. The beds of the affluents which join the river in these places are no less deeply cut into the loess, and ramify into its more elevated portions like the roots of a tree, every small branch a steep and narrow gulch. It would lead us too far astray from the objects of this letter to describe more in detail the exceedingly curious features which the scenery of a region composed of loess presents. Among the most noteworthy is this, that it gives habitation to many millions of human beings. You walk on the richly cultivated bottom-land of a river, and yet do not see a single human dwelling. But as soon as you approach the precipitous wall of loess on either side, you find it thronged with people like a beehive. They live in excavations made in the loess.

"As regards the mode of origin of this formation, the loess of China, like that of Europe (where it exists on a comparatively small scale), has been supposed to be a freshwater deposit. This supposition is erroneous as regards the loess of Northern China, because it extends equally over hills and valleys, and does not contain freshwater shells. Others have therefore considered it as a marine deposit. This view is more erroneous even than the former, because it would presuppose the whole of Northern China to have been submerged at least 6000 feet beneath the level of the sea in a recent epoch, while there is abundant evidence to prove that such has not been the case. Nor can the theory current in Germany, that the loess of that country was produced by glacial action, be at all applied to the loess of Northern China, from various obvious reasons too lengthy to explain here. Unbiassed observation leads irresistibly to the conclusion that the loess of China has been formed on dry land. The whole of that vast country, which was covered by a continuous sheet of loess, before this had undergone destruction was one continuous prairie, probably of greater elevation above the sea than the same region is now. The loess is the residue of all inorganic matter of numberless generations of plants that drew new supplies incessantly from those substances which ascending moisture and springs carried in solution to the surface. This slow accumulation of decayed matter was assisted by the sand and dust deposited through infinite ages by winds. The land-shells are distributed through the whole thickness of the loess, and their state of preservation is so perfect that they must have lived on the spot where we now find them. They certainly admit of no other explanation than that here hinted at, of the formation of the soil in which they are imbedded. The bones of land animals, and chiefly the roots of plants, which are all preserved in their natural and original position, give corroborative evidence. This is not the place to carry these geological deductions further than I have done. I hope that what I have said in regard to the loess will contribute to direct the attention of travellers in Northern China to this interesting formation, from the study of which we may expect valuable data for the knowledge of the condition of things in China in prehistoric and early historic times.

"The practical importance of the loess is based on some of its prominent properties. In the first place, it is a productive soil. If Northern China had a more favourable climate it would rank among the most productive countries in the world, on account of the general distribution of the loess. It is very probable that it did rank high in this respect in early historic times, when the mountains were wooded and kept the climate moist. The entire surface of the loess is at present under cultivation. But owing to its property of being easily percolated by water, it needs more frequent and prolonged rains than most other kinds of soil, and if rain fails in time of sowing, then the tilled ground will be carried away by the winds, the seeds exposed to the sun, and not germinate at all. I travelled for days through regions where such had been the case this year, and the otherwise fertile country had an extremely arid aspect. Another important property is the tendency to vertical cleaving. It creates the conditions for cheap dwellings, of which a large proportion of the population avail themselves. To it, too, is due the rapid progress of denudation. The rivers which carry away the loess separate it into its

The Ordinary Hill Track through the loess formation near Ching-yang-fu in E. Kansu.

constituent parts—viz., the sand, the loam, and the carbonate of lime. The latter is probably carried in solution into the sea, while the very fine sand and the loam are separately redeposited, creating here an arid soil, and there a fertility which exceeds that of the loess itself. The sandy regions prevail where the rivers emerge from the mountains, while the rich alluvial loam is carried to the lower country. It would be of interest to have a geological map of the great plain, with the formations of loess, sand, and alluvial loam marked separately."

The portion of these provinces through which our route lay consists of a series of plateaux of an average height of 4000 feet, scored and cut in all directions by valleys, stream-beds, and dry gorges, almost entirely composed of loess.

The only regularity, from a geographical point of view, is found in two open valleys which run nearly due north and south—the first containing the telegraph-line from Ping-liang to Ning-hsia, which we traversed near the village of Wang-chia-tan-chuang; the second is the Ping-yang valley, from whence we crossed into the valley of the Huan-ho.

As usual in a loess country, the absence of trees and undergrowth is most marked; at the same time, stretches of quite another character were found. Near Ping-yang, in Eastern Kansu, the hills are utterly devoid of trees or even bushes, but the valleys and low hillsides are under cultivation; and there are grassy coombs where several thousands of sheep and long black-haired goats were seen grazing.

After leaving Ching-yang-fu, which stands just inside the eastern border of Kansu, an entire and striking physical change in the nature of the country-side occurs. The low banks of the stream we were following were covered with beautiful turf, the valley-sides became wooded and filled with brushwood, and the country seemed to lose to a great extent its loess character. As we proceeded, the wooded area increased; and though the effect was sombre, owing to the absence of foliage not yet out, the contrast to the bare loess hills was very marked. By the afternoon of the same day we found ourselves riding through a district which resembled the country near Aldershot on the side of the Ash ranges.

Although the face of the ground did not vary, the track, such as it was, still leading over ridge after ridge and descending into valley after valley, yet as far as the eye reached could be seen trees, brushwood, and thickets of thorn. Strange as it may sound so to describe any loess country, especially in Northern China, the view which lay before us as we crossed from ridge to ridge reminded one of nothing so much as the Surrey hills round Godalming or Hindhead in their dreary winter garb. A week before it had been impossible to imagine such a country in East Kansu. Even when the Catholic brothers, at the tiny mission of San-shi-li, near Ching-yang-fu, spoke of "Plateaux avec des forêts et des lacs bien près et beaucoup de sangliers de cerfs et de léopards,"

Stone Staircase of 500 steps, leading up to a Mountain Temple near San-shi-li, in the Huan-ho Valley, E. Kansu.

it hardly appeared credible; yet, that day as we rode there, before us was ground such as might well hold all the game mentioned.

Pheasants so common we had never seen in China, as they basked on the banks of the streams or rocketted across from one valley-side to the other. Oak, hawthorn, and other trees of that tribe, wild apricot, cedar, evergreens, lilac, and many more shrubs, made lovely spots of colour, and such contrasts as one had never hoped to see in this wild district.

Another and, as it seems from Richthofen's description of the loess districts he had visited, an unusual occurrence, was the quantity and wide distribution of the rocky outcrop met with. True, it was almost entirely confined to the stream valleys and the ravines in their vicinity; but all round and on both sides on the adjacent plateaux was the pure loess.

Many of the most charming bits, from the point of view of a lover of nature, were seen where the rock cropped through. In one valley a huge mass of broken *débris* had fallen from the overhanging cliff, almost blocking the narrow track which wound alongside the stream. All about the face of the cliff the wild apricot-trees were just bursting into bloom; and mingled with them, clinging, as they invariably do in that country, in most inaccessible holes in the cliff-sides, was the dark rich green of the cedar—both shown up even more vividly by the dull red of the broken rock-face behind them.

Penetrating into Shensi, between Ching-yang-fu

and Fu-chou, the character of the country again changes—lapsing into the more bare and treeless loess as before. The ravines which score the plateaux are more steep and the gradients of the track, if possible, more unkind than ever.

From Fu-chou up to Yen-an-fu the valley sides and bottoms are again covered with brushwood.

From Yen-an-fu to the Yellow River the loess once more lies bare, exposed to the eye. From the summit of a local pass some forty miles west of the Yellow River a typical view, and a fine one, of that country is obtained over ridge after ridge of dust-covered hills, if such a *coup-d'œil* can be considered a view at all. East of the Yellow River the conformation is the same—treeless at first and equally broken, with occasional red soil showing up.

Some fifty miles east of the river the extraordinary transformation once more occurs.

Before reaching a large village—Shih-ko-tzu by name—the valleys suddenly became thick with brushwood which, as we progressed, rose on both sides, spreading over the rounded hill-crests where is also much coarse grass. East of the same village commences the iron and coal district, which continues more or less as far as Cheng-ting-fu on the Lu-han railway.

Such is briefly the physical character of the country during the latter portion of our journey, and from this description it may be gathered how exceedingly difficult locomotion is. The two main rivers which between them drain the whole area under description are the Yellow River and Wei

Loess formation in the Huan-ho Valley, E. Kansu.

River — the latter more particularly by means of the tributary streams which feed it. The watersheds through which the various secondary streams flow are as broken and scarred as possible. The plateaux are cut in all directions by valleys, ravines, and gorges; and for this reason it is hard to imagine a more hopeless country to traverse—that is, from west to east, or *vice versa*. Although in a loess country such as is described no large lakes are likely to occur, yet small ones are found in some of the plateaux, and the illustration on another page will give some idea of the local configuration.

As a race there is no difference between the Chinese of East Kansu, Northern Shensi, and Central Shensi and those of the provinces north of the Yang-tse-kiang. Local peculiarities in dress, habits, and dialect are found, as in most provinces, but they call for no special remarks.

The climate over the whole of the area latterly traversed is pre-eminently suitable for a white man. The winters, though severe on the plateaux, are less so than in the far west of Kansu, and the snowfall is never very heavy. In East Kansu we imagined spring had suddenly come about the 20th of March, when a spell of hot days made a *terai* hat almost necessary in the midday sun: this very soon changed, however, and on the 23rd March the north-east wind was as cutting as ever.

The following day at 6.30 A.M., inside an open yard, the thermometer showed a temperature of 31°; the ponds were frozen over, and a biting wind continued all day. On the 25th of March we woke to find the whole country under snow once more, though only half an inch deep. On the 27th March the thermometer registered 84° in the sun at 4 P.M. at a height of 4550 feet above sea-level; and skin-coats and furs were again laid aside as rapidly as they had lately been put on.

The first half of April brings the spring rains, which, though light, are sufficient in the loess soil to ensure abundant crops. If the rains are short or do not come, a bad season is usually the result.

On the 20th April, in the deep ravines and stream-beds, the winter snow was still lying frozen under the shaded banks. Dust-storms and high winds were frequent, and made travelling most unpleasant.

The summer season may be said to last from the end of May or middle of June until the middle or end of September.

The heat in the plateaux at such an average height as 4500 feet above sea-level is never oppressive; at the same time, so shut-in and sunken are the ravines and valleys through which such tracks as there are lie, that for locomotion in summer, day-work would probably be found trying.

The inhabitants throughout the area traversed are not above the ordinary standard of physique,—in fact, I place them lower than the sturdy coolie and agricultural class in Shan-tung. At the same time, they are a fairly hardy-looking race, though the districts are too sparsely inhabited ever to see even small crowds collected in one place.

Cave Farmsteads in the loess near Ching-yang-fu.

Cave Temples in the rock on the Shensi Kansu Border.

From Lan-chou to Tai-yuan-fu agriculture exists just sufficiently to supply the local wants, and in bad seasons not always that. All deficiencies are made up from the Wei valley, but the plateau country being thinly inhabited does not need many crops like the more prosperous southern provinces. In the districts traversed by us wheat is the main staple, being extensively grown wherever the surface, valley bottom, or terraced sides of the loess allow.

Of commerce, except the through traffic between the great north-west road (from Sian to Lan-chou) and the Mongolian border towns, there is none. All the commerce which passes from the coast, Peking or Tientsin to Lan-chou, and Chinese Turkestan, crosses the area under description, but either north or south of the plateau country.

Of industries there are very few. The area is entirely agricultural or mineral, the latter to an extent not even yet acknowledged. Coal, iron, oil, and probably other minerals, are found in various sections on the route; but as yet, except in Shansi, these have hardly been exploited at all.

Labour in East Kansu and the Shensi plateaux is scarce. In Shansi, in the coal and iron districts, it is abundant.

Of animals for pack-work there are few. On the plateaux and valley farms, cattle are usually used for ploughing, donkeys and mules for pack transport. A large number of camels are seen working on the north to south pack-trails, chiefly between San-yuan, near Si-an-fu, and Tsing-pien on the Mongolian border, or on other trails in the same direction farther west.

Vehicles are of course unknown throughout the area traversed by us. From Lan-chou until the edge of the coal district was reached at Tai-chu-yu in Shansi, a bustling little town of some local importance, wheeled traffic is practically out of the question.

Though numerous camel caravans were met with, there did not appear to be any advantage in their use which pony or mule transport does not provide. In fact, we came to the conclusion that the latter were preferable even when there was a choice. The only natural advantage that the use of camels might possess—viz., the carrying of a large load—is negatived on these tracks by the extraordinary narrowness of the loess cuttings through which at times they run. All the camel-loads seen were cut down to narrow flat packages, and were laid as even as was possible on the animals' backs. Even then there were places where it hardly seemed as though a camel-train could pass, or could round a corner, the alternative being to be hurled over the edge of the *khud* if the pack struck with the inside load against the hill.

The early history of the eastern portion of the country through which the latter part of our journey lay is that of China itself, so far as the earliest history of that wonderful nation is known. In the 'Shu-king' (the Chinese historical classic), the people of Meaou are mentioned as being in rebellion in the reign of the Emperor Yu-Shun,

Single-arch Stone Bridge, Huan-ho Valley, E. Kansu.

about 2255 B.C. These Meaou were the original barbaric tribes inhabiting what is now Shansi.

Shansi and Shensi a little later, 2203 B.C. to 1766 B.C., formed part of the Imperial province then known as the Ki province, under the names of Liang and Keh.

The Tae-yuan plain mentioned at the same period as having been "set in order" after a great flood, probably *the* flood referred to in the Christian Bible, is that portion of the present Fen-ho valley between Fen-chou and Ping-yang in Shansi.

The Liang province of the same era was made up of part of the modern provinces of Sze-chuan and Southern Shensi. In those days it teemed with wild animals, furs and skins forming the principal articles of tribute. Rhinoceros hides were conspicuous, as valuable for armour and defensive equipment.

The same settlement of the country, about the dates already mentioned, included territory as far west as modern Tibet, then known as Seih-chi, also as far as Kiu-sow to the west of modern Kansu.

Ping-yang in Shansi was the then capital of the Imperial domain.

In 1106 B.C. the completion of Tsung-chow, the modern Si-an-fu in Shensi, is recorded: it stood in what was then known as the country of Lo.

The basin of the Wei river is also known historically as one of the earliest settled and most important parts of China.

In 1100 B.C. the princedom of Yen, of which the capital was in the site of the present city of Peking, is mentioned as having been conferred on the Duke of Shao, who acted as co-regent to his nephew the Emperor Ch'eng of the Chou dynasty, with his brother the celebrated Duke Chou, a great historical character familiar to all Chinese students.

Again, during the reign of the Emperor P'lng Wang, *circa* 770-719 B.C., of the great Chou dynasty, the capital of the then existing kingdom was moved from Si-an-fu to Ho-nan-fu in Honan province.

Shensi province, so far as is known, may be said to represent the Ch'in state, which in the fifth and fourth centuries B.C. extended its boundaries and consolidated other feudal states into one empire, its ruler founding a new dynasty —viz., that of Ch'in—about 200 B.C. It is a moot-point if this state did not give to the present empire the name of China.

Sze-chuan province was known at least as early as the above, from the commencement through it of an overland traffic with India, by way of Assam and Burmah. It was at that time known as the Shu state.

In 67 A.D. Buddhism was introduced into China, and in later years, during the fourth, fifth, and sixth centuries A.D., the overland route through Chinese Turkestan to India saw many pilgrims and devotees passing to and fro by the way we followed through Central Asia.

About 420 A.D. was the epoch of the northern

and southern dynasties in China when the Toba Tartars ruled the north and Buddhism was a state religion.

From the sixth to the thirteenth centuries, when the Mongols conquered China, various divisions of the land took place, and dynasty succeeded dynasty without leaving any great mark. From 960 A.D. until 1127 A.D. the northern and southern Sung dynasties divided the land and obtained some notice in history.

From the fall of the Mongol dynasty, when they were driven out of China in 1368 A.D. and were succeeded by the Mings, until the present Manchu dynasty occupied the throne in 1644 A.D., is for China modern history.

It was during the Mongol dynasty, perhaps, that the overland route became best known, owing to the travels of the Venetian brothers, written by Marco Polo. But to return to our own times. Throughout the whole of this portion of the journey the cruel effects of the wholesale devastation of that wide stretch of Northern China during the Mohammedan risings are still apparent. Old decayed towns remain, partially inhabited, but retaining not one tithe of their former greatness; though more common still are ruined villages, earth-grown ramparts, and small towns whose interior is now actually ploughed-up ground. As already remarked, what the wastage of life may have been was probably never known, even to the Chinese authorities themselves; but it is as certain as can be that during the score of years that the first Mohammedan rebellion lasted, hundreds of thousands of men, women, and children lost their lives.

The system of administration in the three provinces traversed is uniform with that in force throughout the rest of China, and is too well known to need description. It may, however, be of interest to state that wherever and whenever we visited, or were visited by, the various magistrates of towns passed through, we found them, with few exceptions, capable, enlightened, up-to-date men.

In such out-of-the-way portions of the empire armed forces are not required. Between Lan-chou and Tai-yuan-fu, police work would be the sole reason for quartering soldiers, even in the civilised country; and in China the well-known capacity of the people to govern themselves leaves no excuse.

After leaving Lan-chou our caravan consisted only of pack transport, which in some ways made it easier for ourselves. After bidding good-bye to our kind hosts of the mission, we had once more to face the ferry crossing of the Yellow River—a most tedious and dangerous task. In China the old law of every man for himself is strictly upheld. As applied to this particular case it meant that the ferry-men ran the boat anywhere alongside the huge frozen hummocks of ice which still adhered to the right bank, and left it to us to get on board as best we could. Now to pass sixteen mules and ponies, fully laden, into a ferry-boat without gangways, is at best no easy task. When the shore is represented by enormous blocks of ice hurled together at any and every angle, and as slippery as glass, the ordinary European might hesitate whether the task were possible at all. Not so a Chinaman, to give him his due. According to his lights, the mule or pony that cannot fend for itself is of little use. Once unloaded, for he is preeminently sensible in his methods, ice or no ice, the animal is expected to jump into the boat, and to their credit be it said they eventually always did.

Twice again during the course of our journey to Peking did we ferry over the Yellow River, and all four times in the same primitive fashion, without losing an animal.

From the time we had entered China proper our nightly halting-places had consisted of inns of various degrees of badness. From henceforth, more often than not, the loess caves gave us shelter. A feature of the country are these cave villages, lending themselves most admirably to the nature of the land. But for their use it is difficult to see how the inhabitants could house themselves. Wood is almost as precious as a mineral in many parts, and stone absolutely unknown. Of cave-dwellings in use in East Kansu, the illustration given elsewhere may be taken as a type, though of a superior kind. Some nights found us and the animals huddled together in a mere dug-out, this in parts where dwellings and human habitations of any kind were very scarce.

One of the difficulties met with in crossing Eastern Kansu and parts of Shensi was that of obtaining sufficient supplies for both animals, muleteers, and our men. The tracks we habitually made use of were mere trails leading from village to village where, throughout many days' march, not a single traveller would be met. Though few, our wants taxed the slender resources of the various tiny cave hamlets, and it was often necessary to push on an extra stage to reach a resting-place where we could obtain sufficient grain, water, and fodder.

Throughout the whole nine months of the journey we owed our subsistence chiefly to our rifles and guns. In Tibet and Chinese Turkestan bird life was conspicuous by its absence, but during the latter portion of the time in China we had excellent sport in providing the daily meat ration. If sport is measured by the number of cartridges loosed off, I am afraid our daily efforts can lay but feeble claim to the name. Fortunately this is not the universally accepted test. By the time we had passed Lan-chou our supply of gun cartridges had fallen very low. It was only possible to allow ourselves six a-day; and as the chief and most sporting quarry were wild blue-rock pigeon, which haunted the deep ravines and gullies in scores, it may be imagined that the loosing off of these six cartridges was no light affair.

Eventually the day arrived, and that long before we were within reach of butchers' shops, when our twelve-bore cartridges were altogether exhausted. It was then the turn for the sporting .303 again; and not a few fat pheasants and some hill partridges met their fate at the muzzle of this handy little weapon. To have shot a Tibetan antelope at a height of 17,000 feet and a gaudy Chinese pheasant at a distance of 40 yards with the same weapon, is a sufficiently unique experience in the realms of sport to be perhaps worth relating.

Though the shooting we enjoyed was confined to small winged game, the country traversed supplies other hunting of a more exciting kind.

On the border-line of Kansu and Shensi provinces a tiny Catholic mission lies buried from the world not far from the ancient town of Ching-yang-fu. Here, as already related, from the two brothers in charge we heard stories of boar, deer, panther, and smaller game of all kinds to be found during the winter on the neighbouring wooded hills. The existence of this mission is probably only known to those immediately responsible for its foundation, and was quite a surprise to us. It was, indeed, only by accident that we did not pass without seeing it.

Riding one day ahead of the caravan through the ruins of what once had been a picturesque village, Ma-lin by name, I had paused to admire one of the exquisite stone memorial arches so common in China. In addition to a beautifully carved low balustrade guarding the arches, the front of the pillars of which they were composed was faced with polished black stone, upon which were graven deep Chinese characters. The whole fabric combined, as such arches invariably do, a wonderful impression of solid strength with graceful lightness,—an impression heightened by the row of small bronze bells which hung from the top of the grey fretted stonework, and which the gentlest breeze sufficed to set tinkling. Previous to entering the village we had passed the remains of a picturesque old temple, and no doubt the latter, as well as the archway, were both part of the same story, could we have learnt it. Inquiry, unfortunately, and as is usually the case, proved fruitless. In China those able to do so are seldom anxious to tell the story.

As I was about to move on, my eye caught sight of a Chinese farm-hand, and on looking at him again I was astonished to see in his mouth a distinctly European pipe. At the same moment I noticed over the doorway of one of the courtyards a small cross. The mystery of the pipe was soon explained. In answer to my question the owner of it led the way into a yard, on the other side of which stood a tiny chapel, from whence, as we entered, one of the two brothers in charge was just emerging. Mutual introduction followed, and we were soon enjoying the limited but unstinted hospitality the little mission afforded. Buried in the wilds of Kansu, this has been established for fifteen years. So far as the two brothers were aware, it had only twice before been visited by strangers. In one case the traveller was the well-known mission leader, Dr Martin; in the other it was the Russian explorer Obrutchev.

Thanks to the artistic powers of a former brother, the mission possesses a perfect gem in its miniature chapel. Inside, the latter is profusely ornamented with scroll paintings of no mean merit, and these, with the carved woodwork in which Chinese carpenters excel, and some imported lanterns, give to its interior an aspect of tender care wholly

A Combination House-and-cave-village in the Huan-ho Valley, E. Kansu.

in keeping with the character of the devoted men who are content to spend their lives so entirely cut off from civilisation.

After bidding farewell to our hosts we crossed into Shensi province, and made our way over one watershed after another by hill tracks until we struck the valley of the Lo-ho at Fu-chou. Up this we turned to Yen-an-fu. A curious feature of this district is the cave tombs to be seen here and there cut in the solid rock. That they are or were temples I believe to be the case, though I am aware that during the terrible days of the great Mohammedan rebellion many caves were used as hiding-places by the wretched inhabitants.

From the solidity of the work, and in one case from a curious kind of sarcophagus seen in a temple, it is to be presumed that they are Buddhist remains. That Buddhism still flourishes is shown by the temples in daily use. Most picturesque some of these are, and I was fortunate enough to be the witness of a quaint scene at one of these lonely spots. A little temple stood perched on a rocky bluff some forty feet above a small stream, having at its back a steep thickly-wooded hillside. As I rode past on the narrow winding track, a respectably-dressed farmer had just arrived, either to return thanks for some favour or to ask a boon from the little gilt figure of Buddha which sat enshrined in the usual attitude. Having dismounted, the farmer produced from his saddle-bags six large dough-cakes, an offering which visibly caused the mouth of the ancient priest to water; and as the latter, an old, old man, kept solemn time, beating a small brass incense-pot with a tiny mallet, the farmer made his prayers and his adoration on his knees. Holding in one hand a lighted fire-stick, he lit two small pieces of tissue-paper which lay in his right palm, then gently allowed the burnt ashes to float away. Rising from his knees, he turned to me as I sat outside on my mule, and politely asked if the noise of crackers would frighten the animal, at the same time holding up a packet which he took from a table by the door. As the mule was standing on the very edge of the bluff above the stream, I replied that probably it would, so he quietly bade me depart, and I went. For the rest of the day I could not shake from my mind the idea that in the simple ceremony just witnessed perhaps the key was to be found for the regeneration of this vast empire, for, before everything, what China requires is a firm and honest belief in some moral faith.

One of the most tantalising features of travel in China, far from the beaten track, is the impossibility of learning anything but the merest outline of the past history of its towns and the country traversed.

To the European for whom guide-books are ever prepared, many of which are themselves valuable historical and archæological works, this may seem a blessing in disguise; and no doubt to many the mere fact of being told exactly what views to admire and which ruins to venerate, does to some extent spoil a personal pleasure: at the same time, the reverse side of the question has undoubted drawbacks.

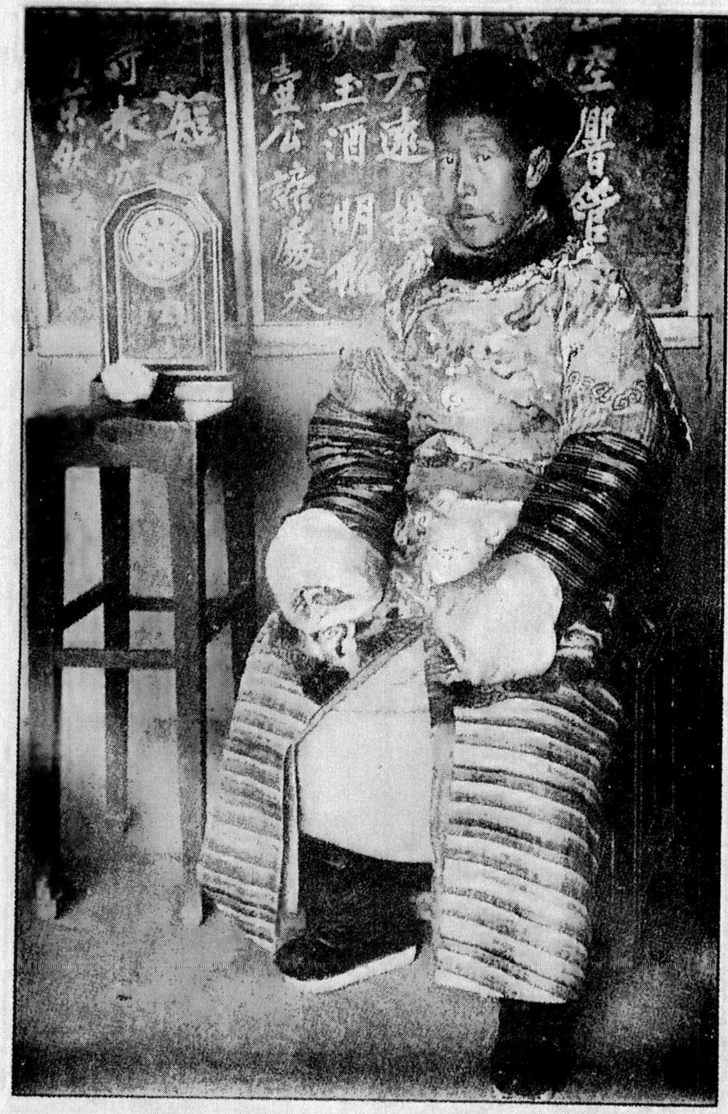

The Wu-Kuan of Ching-yang-fu, E. Kansu.

Pleasant as it is to stand on the ramparts of some city centuries old, hidden away where the foot of a European has hardly ever trod, and there, upon the slender foundation of such scraps of its past as the stranger has been able to unearth from translations of Chinese histories, to build his own airy castles, yet one longs at times for some more definite knowledge of how its inhabitants lived, loved, and died in the years long gone by.

Of such ancient towns, by far the most interesting, both from its position and the undoubted traces it still bears of a venerable past, is Ching-yang-fu, on the Eastern Kansu border.

As a natural defensible site, that of Ching-yang-fu bears comparison with many an old castle still to be seen in various parts of Europe.

Perched upon an almost sheer eminence, three sides of the town are washed by the waters of two small rivers. These, after running past the base of the cliffs which slope from the ramparts, unite at the southern end of the eminence to form one stream, which cuts its way on through a series of wild valleys. On the north side we had approached Ching-yang-fu down a maze of narrow gorges and minor ravines, the track eventually climbing on to a small grave-strewn plateau opposite the outer city walls. Across the plateau it runs for some three hundred yards down a narrow sunken cutting, directly at right angles to the walls, and commanded by them. To reach the latter, a ravine a hundred and fifty yards wide has to be crossed on an artificial causeway fifteen feet wide and some thirty feet above the bottom of the ravine. The first walls are only the outer enceinte of the city, though forty feet high, and so solid that no artillery which even in these modern days could be taken to the spot would harm them. East and west the city walls are scarped from the loess cliffs, which drop almost sheer on both sides two hundred to two hundred and fifty feet to the streams already mentioned. Along the top of the rampart thus formed a crenellated parapet six feet high has been built, which gives a picturesque effect to the massive eminence forming the city. The outer portion on the north side is now either ruins or under cultivation, and across this depressing scene of desolation a winding track follows what was once the main street for nearly three-quarters of a mile. It then confronts the inner enceinte for the last hundred and fifty yards, running straight at the walls as before, but only to find itself upon the wrong side of another wide ravine, crossed again, as in the case of the first, by a solid stone causeway with handsome balustrades, a hundred yards long and thirty feet from the ravine bottom.

Having crossed the causeway, the track enters the inner walls through gates a shade less massive than those in the outer enceinte, but of the same magnificent conception so often seen in large Chinese cities.

Both in the advantage of its position as well as in its natural surroundings, Ching-yang-fu suggests Edinburgh Castle, though the eminence upon which the former stands would easily contain the latter. The city stands at an elevation of nearly 4000 feet above sea-level, and is surrounded on the north, east, and west by high hills which over-top the ramparts by seven or eight hundred feet. These hills are at such a distance as made no matter in the days when bows and arrows took the place of artillery.

Within the inner walls of Ching-yang-fu the occupied area is greater than in the outer city, but that is about all that can be said. Ruin and decay are everywhere stamped on the face of it. A once extensive and handsome *yamen*, the one spot in a Chinese town where an effort is usually made to keep up appearances, is here the ghost of its former self. From the outer gate to the entrance of the reception-room is nearly a hundred yards, but the formerly picturesque archways and intermediate doors are all in ruins. The paved way up which the awed stranger is supposed to approach now merely represents a succession of traps for the unwary pedestrian or equestrian who wishes to conform to Chinese etiquette and to enter under the direct archways.

A mere handful of poorly-clad runners do duty where scores must once have eaten the bread of idleness, and instead of some thousands of stalwart bowmen and swordsmen who would in years gone by have been necessary to guard nearly 5000 yards of rampart, not half a score of withered old men remain.

In addition to the main northern entrance there are various minor adits; but the architectural gem of the city, if it can be so described, is to be found in a very curious tunnel running from inside the inner walls down to the water's edge on the east cliff-face.

The tunnel commences half a mile from the north-east corner of the inner walls, and is burrowed under them to a small open space lower than the city level, but enclosed by separate walls equally high and with a parapet such as surmounts the others. On this space has been laid out what once was a beautiful little garden which surrounds a few exquisite temples, the whole hanging like some swallow's nest half-way between the upper ramparts and the river below.

From the garden the tunnel is continued through the outer walls and hillside, descending to end abruptly at the water's edge, the stream actually washing the bottom of the stone steps with which the tunnel is provided.

No mere burrow is this hidden entrance, but a piece of engineering which stamps its designer and those who laboured at it as constructors of no mean calibre.

Lined throughout its length with stone, and having steps of the same material eight feet wide, the actual tunnel is some ten feet high. Twice between the inner walls and where the tunnel debouches on to the flowing water is it blocked with iron postern doors, and these, together with the steepness of the floor gradient, 1 in 4 to 1 in 3, make its hundred yards of length a somewhat steep climb.

Sitting to ponder over the discovery beside the

Mother, Wife, and Daughter of the Wu-Kuan of Ching-yang-fu, E. Kansu.

swirling water at the lower end of the tunnel, thoughts of the stories these worn stones might tell could they but speak crowded through one's mind.

It was easy to imagine this or that last sortie by some garrison driven to despair after months of starvation; or to picture the stealthy advance up the weird entrance of a band of desperate warriors, admitted by treachery, and ready to sell their souls, let alone their bodies, to obtain a footing within these forbidding walls.

How many a dynasty had staked its very existence upon the continued occupation of this grim old city! How many a scene had these war-worn gateways witnessed of gallant bands issuing forth, bent on beating up a distant neighbour in some bloody fray; returning, perhaps, a dribbling remnant of maimed and defeated fugitives, anxious only for the security of these impregnable walls!

Here, indeed, was the scene of many a romance could the wand of some magician repeople these empty ruins; but what have romance and the British officer to do with one another? Theirs but to reach Peking, not to idle and dream on the walls of such old-world cities. Yet must one other memory of Ching-yang-fu be recorded.

Standing at sunset on the old rampart above the main city gate, I was witness to a quaint scene which vividly recalled the days of Ivanhoe and the castle of Torquilstone.

Approaching the walls came a quaint procession about to cross the stone causeway. Most picturesque it seemed at that distance, and it was easy to imagine oneself looking down from the battlements of some feudal castle in the fourteenth century upon the entrance of one of the knights of the period, with esquires, pages, men-at-arms, and banners. First came two ancient trumpeters, cracking their cheeks over long brass instruments; then twelve standard-bearers, with pennons fluttering from what might well have been lances. Following the standard-bearers came half a score brightly-dressed youths with brass gongs, drums, and more flags, who represented the heralds of old. Then came the inevitable red umbrella and a somewhat sumptuous sedan-chair with eight bearers and running knaves,—in our day-dream the litter of some well-known queen of beauty for whom many a lance had been broken. Around the litter were another score of retainers armed with small pennons; and bringing up the rear came more youths brightly dressed in scarlet, a number of whom carried large wooden swords and ancient halberts, then two mounted officials. Slowly the long and gaudy procession wound across the grey stone causeway approaching the massive gate. As the last of the retainers disappeared within its crumbling shadow the sun sank behind the bare yellow hills, and, like a dream, Ivanhoe and his retainers vanished into the air.

CHAPTER XV.

PETROLEUM AND COAL — CAVE-DWELLINGS — A VISIT TO A MINE — TAI-YUAN-FU—THE UNIVERSITY OF SHANSI—A NATIVE NEWSPAPER —THE KU-KUAN PASS—A GREAT COAL AND IRON FIELD—A RAILWAY AT LAST—SIGNOR PHILIPETTI'S HOTEL—CHINA'S HASTE TO BECOME WESTERN.

THE country through which our route led us after quitting Ching-yang-fu has already been described in the last chapter. Nor is there any need to weary the reader with a more detailed account.

That portion of the province of Shensi through which we passed resembles its western neighbour in general characteristics, being as wild and sparsely settled as is Eastern Kansu. Not until the Yellow River is approached are there any signs of the presence of the wonderful coal-basin for which Shansi province is so famous. Between the town cf Yenan-fu and the river, both petroleum and coal-fields exist; and though as yet these are probably only known to enterprising Japanese, some of whom, we were informed, had not long ago visited Yen-chang, at some future time these valuable deposits may be worth consideration.

A feature of Shensi province is the stone-fronted cave-dwellings. Though at times the houses are not regular caves, they are almost invariably built with their backs to a steep hillside, often in terraces two or three storeys high.

In the case of the latter dwellings, the roof is flat and has a small stone-coping neatly surrounding three sides. The front is supported on three or four, sometimes even five or six, semicircular stone archways, resembling almost exactly in appearance the entrances seen in England to many railway tunnels. These arches carry the weight of the roof, and tend to support the hillside. They are of very solid construction, and have the front of the arch filled in with dried mud or clay, into which is inserted the doorway and lattice-work windows, covered with the usual Chinese paper. The villages thus built have a solid appearance. Even the numerous small temples are frequently placed on an arched platform of the same type. Most of the houses have also a flagged courtyard, surrounded by a wall. The insides of the houses are airy and comfortable, features not common to most Chinese domiciles of the lower order. The walls are plastered smooth, as is the roof, and I have known them ornamented with a narrow dado, also with rude paintings.

Three days west of Fen-chou, a well-to-do Fu (prefectorial) town situated in the rich valley of the Fen-ho, we entered the real coal districts. Although the route followed was still a mere hill-track, streams of mules and donkeys were passed, laden with coal for Fen-chou.

Halted for the night at a well-to-do village, we learnt from our host of the inn of the existence of a small mine only a few *li* off the track. To our surprise he readily agreed to our visiting it the next morning, guided by his son. Sending on the caravan, Layard and I followed the youth over a very bad hill-path, not always safe for riding, to the little valley in which the shafts were situated.

Only one was in use at the time of our visit, and, as usual, the methods employed were most primitive.

The shaft had been driven straight into the hill-side for a few yards, and was 4 feet 6 inches high by 2 feet 6 inches wide.

Soon after penetrating the hill it began to descend at a slope of 1 in 9 for some three hundred feet. The inner end is about fifty feet below the mouth. Throughout its length the shaft is never sufficiently high to allow one to stand up. For most of the distance it was necessary to move either on hands and knees, or crouched up in a most uncomfortable stooping position. At its lower end the shaft widens to ten or twelve feet. In it there is a certain amount of water which is baled into small wooden tubs, and these, like the coal, are hauled up the incline on tiny wooden trolleys with four wheels, each eight inches high. The trolleys have a short length of rope attached, and this the men hook on to another piece tied round their shoulders, so dragging the trolleys out, bending and crawling in what appears a most tiring manner. Each man carries a small oil-lamp unprotected in his greasy cap. The shaft throughout its length is only strutted in one place by rough beams, the coal-seam apparently requiring no artificial support.

At the mouth of the shaft the coal sells at about

1d. a basket, — the latter two feet six inches in diameter and two feet deep. The coal is brittle, and easily breaks into dust. It is not nearly of such good quality as that obtained round Liang-chou.

At the end of an hour's crawling we emerged like blacks; but thanks to a friendly old villager, who invited us to his cottage for tea and a wash, we were soon able to get rid of the worst effects.

Our arrival in the little village was the signal for a general rush to our host's courtyard. No one there had ever seen a European before, and even the women-folk pressed round in open and undisguised astonishment.

Upon reaching Fen-chou we were hospitably entertained by Dr and Mrs Atwood of the American Medical Mission, and felt ourselves at last within touch of civilisation, while eagerly devouring the latest English paper.

The mission suffered severely in 1900, all those at that time in Fen-chou being barbarously murdered. The chief instigator of the atrocities was a man who had received medical treatment from Dr Atwood in the mission hospital: so much for gratitude!

Once having retasted the delights of civilisation, however much the traveller may be wedded to a wandering life, he is usually anxious to reach the end of that particular journey, and this was now our own case.

Nor was there any particular reason for delay. Shansi is, comparatively speaking, more or less known to Europeans, and we had struck the main road from Peking to Si-an-fu, where both inns and supplies were constant and good. Following the valley of the Fen-ho, we reached Tai-yuan-fu, the capital of Shansi, in three days.

Tai-yuan-fu is chiefly known to Europeans in China as having been the scene of the most brutal murders of missionaries during the Boxer rising of 1900.

Reference has been made in a previous chapter to the death of the man chiefly responsible for these atrocities. It may only be a coincidence, but it is perhaps worth recording that nowhere during the course of our travels through China did we meet with less civility than in Tai-yuan-fu. The people appeared to be of an inferior class, and could not be compared with the polite and bustling population of Lan-chou. If looks can be said to be any criterion of civilisation, then do the inhabitants of Tai-yuan-fu not shine, for opium-sodden faces are the rule, not the exception, and the conduct of the people in the streets struck us unfavourably.

Though exceeding Lan-chou, the capital of Kansu, in actual area, Tai-yuan-fu is not by any means as fine a town in natural situation. It boasts a European university where English professors are carrying on an excellent work among Chinese students. But the presence of the university is due to the energy and forethought of Dr Timothy Richard, a man whose name is a household word in missionary circles in China, not to any particular wish on the part of the local Chinese for Western enlightenment.

The origin and aim of the Imperial University of Shansi is described in their own Calendar as follows, and might well serve as the model for scores of such institutions were the Chinese Government really in earnest in the adoption of Western culture:—

"HISTORICAL SUMMARY: ORIGIN AND AIM.

"After the Boxer atrocities of 1900 it was agreed between the plenipotentiaries LI HUNG-CHANG, PRINCE CH'ING, and DR TIMOTHY RICHARD, that instead of an indemnity for the lives of Protestants massacred in SHANSI, an anuual sum of 50,000 taels be levied upon the province for a period of ten years, and the proceeds be used in establishing a thoroughly efficient modern Educational Institution. At the same time edicts were issued commanding the establishment of a university in each provincial capital throughout the Empire, and the provincial government in Shansi was taking energetic measures to establish one in Shansi. To secure higher efficiency, in the new circumstances, Dr RICHARD signed a contract in 1902 for the amalgamation of the Western College, he was pledged to commence, with the Government College about to be opened. That document was sent to PEKING and ratified by the Imperial seal. The 23 Articles of that instrument constitute the Charter and created an IMPERIAL UNIVERSITY with two departments:—

"(1) A CHINESE DEPARTMENT in which all the students of the University reside,—their dormitory arrangements, board and residence, being under the control of the Chinese themselves: 200 of the students attend, and are wholly taught by officers appointed by the Provincial Government.

"(2) A WESTERN DEPARTMENT in which the curriculum, teaching, and educational control are in the hands of Dr RICHARD and a foreign staff in consultation with its Chinese members: 240 students of the University give their undivided attention to purely Western subjects. The aim of this department is to commence with students who already possess Government degrees, trained minds, and tested ability. They are selected from the 10,000 provincial graduates of the first or second degree, and trained for the service of the State through the medium of the CHINESE LANGUAGE. An opportunity is thus open to those who have a certificated Chinese education to pass the preparatory course, and enter on some higher branch of study without waiting till they become the masters of a modern language. All take language as a subject, but all other subjects are taught in Chinese so as to secure a maximum of efficiency in a minimum time."

It would be difficult to define in clearer language or more pointedly in so few words the object at which institutions of such a kind should aim.

To help the Chinese to help themselves along the upward path towards modern civilisation should be the attitude of all who wish them well. Few Europeans are more capable of acting the part of guide, philosopher, and friend, than Dr Timothy Richard.

In addition to the University, the China Inland Mission possesses a station at Tai-yuan-fu, which is under the charge of Mr Morgan, a mission pioneer well known in Northern China. The city also boasts an Agricultural College in Chinese hands, where it is said considerable sums are wasted, and a Police College, worked jointly by Chinese and Japanese, where, I was informed, friction is not unknown over the question of the salaries considered to be their due by the latter.

There is also a native newspaper, the editor of which is an enlightened man who speaks out fearlessly both against the official classes and, where he considers it necessary, the European residents. The paper circulates largely through Shansi, as each Hsien town receives so many copies, as do many of the officials. For those not punctual in the settlement of their newspaper accounts, rumour has it that the editor keeps and occasionally publishes a black list,—a delightfully simple method of obtaining prompt payment which would no doubt help to raise the circulation of some of our own great dailies. After two days' halt at Tai-yuan-fu we once more took the road. There now remained between ourselves and the town of Cheng-ting-fu, on the Lu-han railway, a distance of a little over one hundred miles as the crow flies, but, although the route about to be followed represents one of the main ancient highways of China, words altogether fail to express the vileness of the track, —that is, from a European point of view.

Known to the Chinese from time immemorial as the Ku-kuan pass, the track we now followed is a standing example of what a main route should not be. During the 120 miles which constitute its length this highway crosses four main ranges, on each of which the road is barred, according to Chinese custom, by a picturesque gateway. Between the ranges the track follows the beds or sides of torrents which are rocky to an almost inconceivable extent, and down which it winds, continually rising and falling at steep gradients every mile or less. Anything more maddening to the European mind can hardly be conceived. Were the route in question met with in the wilds of Tibet or Central Asia, no traveller would have any right to complain, but forming as it has for hundreds of years one of the main connecting links between Peking and the interior, its utter neglect is unaccountable—that is, until the weary traveller recalls the fact that he is in China. Throughout its entire length the Ku-kuan teems with traffic, —a constant stream of mules and donkeys was passed who carry merchandise of all kinds for disposal in the interior, as well as vast quantities of coal. As is well known, this part of Shansi is one huge coal and iron field. It was described by Baron Richthofen many years ago as one of the most remarkable in the world. "On the other hand," he says, "the whole of this great coal and iron region labours under two great disadvantages. Firstly, it is situated a distance away from the coast, and from rivers that are fit for other navigation than by small Chinese boats; and secondly, the whole of the coal formation rests, as it were, on a platform raised a few thousand feet above the adjoining plain. Its steep descent to the latter will not form an obstacle, but at least offers great difficulties to the construction of a railroad which will be the only means of ever bringing to account the mineral wealth of Shansi."

That the prediction given above was no mere guess we had actual proof, but that it should have taken thirty years before the hateful conservatism of the authorities was sufficiently broken down to allow of a railway being commenced, would probably have astonished even the author of it.

Rather more than half-way between Tai-yuan-fu and Cheng-ting-fu stands the old town of Ching-hsing. Close to it is the boundary between the provinces of Shansi and Chili.

At the time of our visit the town also marked the rail-head of a small branch line destined to connect the capital of Shansi with the Lu-han line, and eventually with Peking.

Although the construction of this branch is in the hands of foreign engineers, no Englishmen are employed. When it is remembered that the first and most successful of the lines now open in China, that which runs from Tientsin, was built almost entirely by the energy and skill of an Englishman, Mr Kinder, the fact gives cause to think why we as railway pioneers in China should have lost the position we had once won.

Another of the remarkable transformations, nowhere perhaps met with so abruptly as in China, happened the day we reached the rail-head.

For nine months our party had been tramping slowly across Asia, and during the last five days the route had led through country almost as wild, and certainly as inconvenient to get over, as was the greater part of the way. Curious as it may sound, even at Tai-yuan-fu very little information could be obtained about what point or village the branch line had reached,—the Chinese, habitually inaccurate, not caring, and the few Europeans unable to gather any detailed information. The consequence of this, was that upon the morning in question our caravan entered the little village of Nai-kuai from the northern end without the slightest warning of what was before us. Emerging through the usual narrow single street of the village, which might itself have dated from the days of Ham, as might the village surroundings, we were fairly amazed to see right across the southern end a high modern railway embankment, under which the ancient highway meandered by means of the latest thing in archways.

Dumbfounded as we were, the instincts of civilisation apparently lie very near the surface, for the second thought which entered my mind was one of wonder how soon the next train ran outwards for the main-line junction! No sooner was the thought entertained than it was acted upon. Riding up the line a few hundred yards, we found the little terminus, and soon ascertained that if we wished to take advantage of the iron horse there was no time to waste. At ten o'clock each day a train went to Cheng-ting-fu, and by it we determined to travel, leaving the mules and ponies, as trucks were not available, to do a forced march the last forty miles. In less than two hours we were flying down the little branch line of one metre gauge at what appeared to us a terrific pace. In reality the speed hardly reached ten miles an hour, but after the nine months' daily tramp at two and a half miles an hour, one's ideas of pace are hardly to be trusted. Owing to the necessity for following either the valley of the main stream or numerous side ones, the line winds incessantly, and it took us three and a half hours to cover the thirty-two miles which separate Ching-hsing from Cheng-ting-fu.

Arriving at the latter junction at the time when the day's work was drawing to a close, even the afternoon quiet seemed to us, long unused to bustle, somewhat upsetting.

Having rescued our worn-looking saddle-bags and the immediate requisites which we had brought with us in the train, the next object was to find a roof to shelter our party. Searching among the many Chinese inns which have sprung up round the railway-station, we were disappointed to find them all equally crowded, owing to the arrival that day of a Chinese official with a somewhat unusually extensive retinue. From a Russian overseer, whom we had met with on the train, we had learnt of a European "hotel," and thither we finally bent our weary steps to beg for a night's lodging.

The "hotel" consisted of a long, low, white-washed building of mud, roofed with tin; and though a somewhat ambitious name for the little hostel over which Signor Philipetti still I hope presides, it afforded us a most comfortable sanctuary.

One-half of the building consists of the *salle-à-manger*, some fifty feet long. The rest shelters innumerable little Philipettis and the signor himself, and forms the cook-house and store-rooms.

In spite of finding his lot cast so far from his native land, an Italian of the Italians is Signor Philipetti; nor could anything have exceeded his hospitality and his kindness to us. The only available accommodation he could offer consisted of two tiny godowns. That these were only some 10 feet by 8 square, windowless, and bare of any furniture but packing-cases and a plank-bed, made no difference.

Were we not quit at last of Chinese inns and safely ensconced in a "hotel"? Not even the "Ritz" could have made us feel more shy than did the unwonted luxury of the dining-room.

With Signor Philipetti we spent a most amusing evening, taking our first meal in a civilised fashion in the company of two other Italian gentlemen, engineers, and a hopelessly drunken specimen of a different nationality, which shall be nameless. The latter traveller was attempting to dispose of the last few hundreds from a large consignment of arms. It has been said *in vino veritas*, and if this be true, from the remarks let fall by the vendor during occasional returns to semi-consciousness, he seems to have met with no little success in Manchuria with the earlier portion of his consignment. While Layard and I enjoyed for the first time for many months the refinements of table-linen, European bread-and-butter, wine, and such trifles, a large party, composed of the chief officials in the train of the Chinese magistrate, were beginning their Western education, though at a somewhat advanced age, by being shown how to eat a Western meal in foreign style under the superintendence of Signor Philipetti's Chinese interpreter and factotum. Upon the whole, the first meal may be said to have been a success. In deference no doubt to national prejudice, the trial was not made too severe. Although, for example, the many and varied dishes of which the meal was composed were handed round in the orthodox manner, yet once each guest had received the necessary instruction how to help himself in a manner considered by the master of the ceremonies *comme il faut*, then the dishes were left upon the table, and no further check appeared to be laid upon hereditary traits. The only restraining influence was the wish to be considered thoroughly versed in foreign manners and customs. Now and again, however, inbred habits became too strong for foreign veneer, and some unusually tempting morsel would be hastily snatched from the dish and transferred to the offender's plate with knife or fork, — sometimes even, be it whispered, without either of these encumbrances.

To us, fresh from the wilds, and ourselves inclined to fret under conventional restraint, the inclination to follow suit was somewhat strong, but the presence of Signor Philipetti and his companions furnished the necessary counterpoise to any such relapse. Amusing as it was to watch, like many such object - lessons, the dinner - party described above had its moral, and that a somewhat sad one.

Than what we saw that night nothing could be more typical of the vast changes at present being grafted into the life of the Chinese, and, too, of the hasty scramble that is going on to acquire at almost any cost some smattering of Western ways and manners. Unlike Japan, China has not considered it necessary to learn to walk before attempting to run alone, but, imbued with that overpowering measure of individual and national pride which may yet be her ruin, she presumes that she will be qualified to take her place in the world as a civilised nation in as many months as it has cost the Japanese years.

Quem deus vult perdere prius dementat has as much truth as such sayings can usually lay claim to, but, in the present case, let us earnestly hope that the eyes of the merchant class and the respectable lower orders may be opened in time to discern the rock upon which the official classes of China seem fated to drive their unhappy country.

CHAPTER XVI.

THE GROWTH OF A MILITARY SPIRIT IN CHINA—SIGNS OF UPHEAVAL—THREE POSSIBLE CAUSES OF THE SUBTERRANEOUS MOVEMENT—THE EMPEROR—THE DOWAGER-EMPRESS—THE EFFECT OF THE JAPANESE VICTORIES—THE PAST HISTORY OF CHINESE ARMS—KUBLAI KHAN'S UNSUCCESSFUL ATTACKS ON JAPAN—REASONS FOR DOUBTING THE RENASCENCE OF A MILITARY SPIRIT.

THE morning of the day after our arrival at Cheng-ting-fu saw our whole party rejoined and *en route* to Peking by rail. So far as the final stages are concerned, it is unnecessary to do more than mention that we reached the capital on May 6, where we were soon among old friends receiving a most hospitable welcome.

Before concluding the account of our journey, however, it may perhaps be of interest to attempt to answer, as briefly as possible, one question frequently asked by friends at home, who, though they may not have visited China, are yet interested in the future of that land of anomalies.

Without necessarily having in mind any idea of a Yellow peril, it is natural that Europeans should feel some want of enlightenment as to the possibility of the growth of a military spirit in China. In the concluding pages of this book an attempt is made to weigh honestly both sides of this question.

Only by carefully following the teachings of history can any useful lesson be obtained; and if the reader is enabled to formulate his own ideas upon the subject with any greater clearness, after having read the final chapter of this book, the writer will be amply repaid.

When the history of the twentieth century comes to be written, not the least striking international occurrence will be the story of the Russo-Japanese war.

It is a mere truism to say that the history of Asia began to change from the time when the treaty of peace was signed at Portsmouth, U.S.A.; but to what extent this change may affect Asiatics in general is not the purpose of this work. So far as it may be possible, the object in view is to note the effect upon the Chinese,—though in tracing the part which China is likely to play in the reshaping of the East the influence of surrounding nations cannot be ignored.

To any one interested in the present condition of that unique people—whether politically, commercially, socially, or from the military point of view,—it is a matter for much consideration what form the regeneration of her vast millions is likely to take. At the outset it may be asked, What reason is there to suppose that any such movement is in progress? And though Europe is apt to accept as a fact that there is, the question is no easy one to answer.

During the last five years few who have followed events will wish to deny that there have been signs of an upheaval in China; that here and there the old crust has been broken, and that underneath, at the present time, considerable disturbance is going on. But this is not sufficient for those who have any acquaintance with Chinese customs and habits of thought. To such the further question at once presents itself, From what source do these internal rumblings spring? Are they the mere formless emotions of miserable and, for the most part, hopeless millions, ground down by the tyranny of a ruling class who should know better? Are they, again, the first signs of action at the hands of a beneficent and sympathetic ruler, eager to let in light upon the evils under which the millions alluded to suffer? Or do these mysterious workings represent an intention upon the part of a united and moderate middle-class to attain the standard of freedom they are beginning to observe in surrounding nations?

Such are some of the questions which must be answered, and from some such hypotheses must we endeavour to find a starting-point before a true assumption of what is taking place can be formulated.

Now, in dealing with problems connected with China, it is customary for most writers to indulge more or less in generalities—the reason being that it is never safe to particularise upon matters affecting the conduct of this inscrutable race. While admitting the justice of this plea, and while fully aware of the futility of attempting to lay down hard and fast lines of conduct, it is useless to pretend to discuss the trend of public spirit in any people—even in the Chinese

— if we may not assume a probable course of action. It is only by thus postulating some such course that we can place ourselves in a position to judge of the chances of a new spirit arising in China. It is my intention to assume the possibility of a wave of militarism, and to attempt to lay before my readers reasons for and against such a change coming to pass. History has its lessons which he who runs may read, and which may not be neglected. It has, too, the sometimes awkward but always interesting way of repeating itself.

In suggesting three possible causes of the subterraneous movement now going on in China, the writer has endeavoured to indicate those which, on the face of them, have a reasonable chance of being true ones. Let us endeavour to ascertain which of the three is likely to be the most direct cause.

It is a not uncommon error among Europeans to think of the masses in China as ground down by their rulers, and as forced to pass their time in a miserable struggle for existence. And such a description bears just this stamp of truth—that if we persist in regarding things Chinese from the Western point of view, the over-taxation and oppression by the officials might be so described. So also might the existence of people who, to the extent of many millions, live daily on the verge of starvation. But if the millions of whom we thus think have never known anything better? If for centuries custom has sanctioned the one abuse and withdrawn all terrors from the other, are we justified in using such language—even though to Western ideas it states what are facts? From time immemorial official life in the East has been guided by certain assumed canons. That these unwritten laws are as well understood by those ruled as by the rulers is also a fact. So long as the latter are content to comply with acknowledged custom, all is well. Illegal oppression, one-sided justice, the buying of cases, are the rule, not the exception—hence are accepted as necessities of existence in China. But let a ruler, more voracious or less wise than his fellows, attempt to go one step farther than custom allows, and retribution swiftly follows. From the district magistrate of a small *hsien*, who raises a local riot in which he may lose his life, to the "Son of Heaven" who has to face a Tae-ping rebellion which may cost him a throne, no authority is safe from the people, and those wielding it are aware of the fact. In the hands of the masses the remedy lies, so they are content—up to a point.

When we come to examine the second of the suggested causes of the present unrest in China, we are faced at once by a difficulty which could only exist in that country of anomalies. All the world is aware that Kuang-hsu is merely a puppet in the hands of the dowager-empress. Whether the millions who gather on occasions to offer worship to his tablet in their temples are equally well informed, cannot be so definitely stated. It is sufficient for present purposes if we accept the situation, and ask ourselves whether the feelings of that illustrious lady towards the emperor's subjects indicate either sympathy or beneficence. I think if there is one point upon which students of latter-day affairs in China agree, it would probably be in answer to this question. She has been tried in the balance and found wanting.

There remains, then, the last of the suggested causes, and though perhaps incorrect in form—as any definite statement of cause in China is almost bound to be,—it may be allowed to indicate with sufficient accuracy the general trend of feeling which at present stirs the masses of that country. If it be thought that this latter statement contains the germs of truth, we are then brought face to face with the inquiry what form the aspirations are likely to take. In themselves worthy of the sympathy of all who are happy in the possession of an ideal, it is unfortunate that such aspirations cannot be regarded solely from this high standard. If straws serve to show the direction of the wind, it is no less true that recent events in China point in a direction from whence a storm may again arise. With every wish to avoid the imputation of being an alarmist, it is useless to ignore facts when, moreover, as at the present time, these are most pertinent to the question under discussion. If there is one feeling more than another which can be said to permeate the responsible classes—that is, those who lead and who are able to shape what answers to public opinion in Europe,—it is that the foreigner is responsible for the present unhappy state of their country. It is not necessary to say that this falsehood, so widely disseminated, is believed by those who are responsible for it. It is also beside the question. That the ruling classes can make use of such a statement when necessary, that it awakens at least some echo in the hearts of many millions of ignorant people, is sufficient for their purpose. And the danger lies in the fact that under sinister influence it may be made use of to turn aside natural and commendable aspirations from a legitimate to an illegitimate end.

Let us suppose that the danger which an attempt has here been made to foresee should gather force. It may be asked, How will it affect the actions of the moderate party whose fortunes we are endeavouring to follow? It has been remarked at the commencement of this chapter that the history of Asia began to change on the day when the Japanese granted peace to a defeated white race. It is not to be expected, perhaps, that the full significance of such a unique occurrence should dwell over long in the thoughts of Europeans. To the West, which hardly allows its children time to think, that historical moment was merely an episode. But such was not the point of view of the East. To the slow-thinking Oriental that episode was first a wonderful revelation, only half credited, now the most cherished article of his future belief. What effect, then, will the digestion of such a belief be likely to have upon an intensely proud Asiatic race? Allowing that under evil direction the cry of "China for the Chinese" is not considered sufficiently stirring, but that it is thought necessary to couple with it the insane "Out with the foreigners," has not the time arrived to leave generalities, and to discuss actual possibilities?

If it be granted that there is ever so slight a chance of the present unrest taking some such form as is here indicated, the first steps towards carrying out such a policy must be the creation of some armed force as a weapon to be used.

Since the close of the Russo-Japanese war various and conflicting reports have appeared in Europe as to the striking advance made by the Chinese in the reorganisation of their army upon modern lines. Without wishing to reflect in any way on the authors of these reports, it may be said that they are not in every case in a position to judge.

To attend manœuvres, and to follow for a few days the fortunes of a large but picked body of men, does not necessarily furnish even a military critic with the data required to pronounce an opinion upon the condition of the armed forces of a nation. When, moreover, the forces under review are Chinese troops, and when the initial incapacity of all Europeans to gauge the true significance of what they merely see in China is allowed for, it follows that we must go very much deeper than the results of a few annual manœuvres if we wish to ascertain the reality of a new military spirit in that country. Let us begin by consulting their own earliest and most treasured teachers, one of them the man whose doctrines, above all others, permeate Chinese thought.

A disciple of Confucius inquired on one occasion what was essential in the government of a country.

Confucius answered, "There must be sufficient food for the people, an efficient army, and confidence of the people in their rulers."

"But," asked the disciple then, "if we were compelled to dispense with one of those three things, which one of them should go first?"

"Dispense with the army," replied Confucius.

"But still," the disciple went on to ask, "if one were compelled to dispense with one of these two things remaining, which one of them should go first?"

"Dispense with the food," replied Confucius, "for from of old men have died; but without the confidence of the people in their rulers there can be no government."

The above opinion was given by this great sage and teacher some five hundred years before the commencement of our era, and may be considered the guiding principle to the subsequent action of the nation he taught throughout the centuries that have passed away. Neither time nor space is here available to discuss the ethics involved in this pronouncement. It is enough to remind ourselves that no other human being ever lived whose words had such lasting influence in the thoughts, if not on the conduct, of mankind.

Let us now turn to the early history of Chinese military affairs, and, if we can, learn something of the spirit of the past, warlike or otherwise.

Before the commencement of the Christian era, Chinese power extended over what is now known as Eastern Turkestan. That eminent Orientalist, the late Sir Henry Yule, has also summed up the general acquaintance of Roman historians, such as Pliny and Ptolemy, with the China of their knowledge in the following words: "The region of the Seres is a vast populous country, touching on the east the ocean and the limits of the habitable world, and extending west nearly to Imaus and the confines of Bactria. The people are civilised men of mild, just, and frugal temper, eschewing collision with their neighbours, and even shy of close intercourse, but not averse to disposing of their own products."

Though these words express the opinions of men who wrote not far short of two thousand years ago, it would be difficult to outline with greater nicety the Chinese character to-day. Even at this early stage in their history these people seemed to have developed that extraordinary propensity for paradox which ever since has marked them. To be known as anxious to eschew collision with their neighbours, yet to extend their military power over the larger portion of what is now Asia, are two things which seem hardly compatible. In the fifth century A.D., it is known that the Chinese imposed their power upon the King of Ceylon. In the seventh, they invaded India, and, after harrying Behar, carried away the king of that country a prisoner to China. Not only Behar but other portions of India paid tribute to the great Emperor Tai-tsung of the Tang dynasty. The kings of what at that period were known as the five Indies owed him fealty; while his dominions extended in one direction to the Caspian, and in another his power was acknowledged south of the Hindu Kush.

In the eighth century Chinese forces are said to have occupied Ladak, though, about the same period, it was only by a most favourable reception of Arab envoys that China in all probability saved herself from a Mohammedan invasion. Already Bokhara, Samarcand, and Kashgar had fallen before the fierce onslaught of these religious fanatics; and either the face of Nature, in the shape of the Gobi desert, or the reception of the emissaries above alluded to, saved China from the fate of the rest of Asia.

It was in the tenth century that the name of Kitai or Cathay, as it is now generally known, came to the Chinese through the conquest of their country by the Khitans, an alien people who overran Northern China. As has subsequently occurred to other and later conquerors, the Khitans were eventually peacefully assimilated by the people they had defeated in war.

It would be unnecessary to mention the Mongol conquest of China by Chingiz Khan, but for the food for reflection afforded by the fact that it was an emperor of China who pushed his conquest as far west as Hungary. That emperor was Okkodai, the son of Chingiz.

One century later, perhaps the greatest ruler China ever had appeared in Kublai Khan. As a land-empire, the territories which acknowledged his sway will bear comparison even with that of Rome. His immediate kingdom, we are told, embraced China, Korea, Mongolia, Manchuria, and Tibet, with claims over Tong-king and Burmah. His viceroys ruled in Chinese Turkestan, Transoxania, and Afghanistan. The empire of the northern Tartars, covering a large part of Russia, the country north of the Caucasus, and Siberia, was held in fief from him. And, as if this were not enough, the southern portion of his vast dominions included Persia, which then embraced Georgia, Armenia, and part of Asia Minor.

After the enumeration of such wide conquests it may be of interest to make mention of at least one failure met with by the arms of Kublai Khan. On the eastern flank of his unwieldy land-empire lay some small islands, and upon their conquest Kublai set his heart. Zipangu or Jih-pên-kuei, "the home of the rising sun," the modern Japan, was then, as now, peopled by a race whose love of their island home would brook no invasion. Interesting as a detailed account would be, it must here suffice to say that the first expedition sent by Kublai Khan shared the fate of that commanded by Admiral Rojdestvenski, which latter, history as usual repeating itself, was destroyed almost on the same spot as the former; while the second, a larger and more comprehensive undertaking, was in every respect the precursor of our own Spanish Armada. Leaving out the failure to invade Japan, it is indeed hard to reconcile with such conquests the idea of a peace-loving nation averse to arms. Yet writers in the fifteenth century who knew the country, continue to describe a high standard of civilisation and politeness as the leading characteristics of the Chinese.

Another and amusing tribute to the orderliness and uprightness of the ancient administration is given by Yule, who repeats a saying of the Jesuit historian Jarric. Dilating on the subject, the latter remarked, "That if Plato was to rise from Hades, he would declare that his imaginary republic was realised in China."

In 1405 the Cinghalese insulted a Chinese mission, so the reigning Emperor Ching-tsu despatched a naval and military expedition through what are known to-day as the "Straits," including in their itinerary Siam. It is perhaps unnecessary to describe further the military exploits of pre-European days.

From the time when, early in the sixteenth century, the Portuguese adventurers were the first to land there, Chinese military organisation must be viewed from a different standpoint. Hitherto it has been unnecessary to do more than enumerate the varying fortunes which attended the employment of their armies, as such expeditions, however vast the scale may have been, represent more the employment and success of mere numbers than any attempt at organisation or even cohesion. The first occasion upon which Chinese troops were called upon to meet foreign invaders was towards the middle of the seventeenth century. By that date Russian expansion in Northern Asia had reached the Pacific. And when at last Russian and Chinese troops had come into conflict, a short but indecisive series of fights ended in the treaty of Merchinsk. Before the advance of Russia had reached the Far East, Chinese arms had once again been vanquished by an alien people. By the year 1644 the Manchus had established themselves, and the first emperor of the Ta-tsing dynasty ruled at Peking. Under Kien-lung, the third of the Ta-tsing dynasty, who, it has been said, raised the empire to its highest pitch of greatness, Chinese arms were once more in the ascendant. Not only was the emperor successful in Central Asia, where a strong policy was somewhat mercilessly enforced, but he also once again sent troops to invade a part of India. Towards the end of the eighteenth century the Ghoorkhas of Nepaul had overrun Southern Tibet. Meeting with little resistance from a feeble Chinese force sent to occupy the country, the Ghoorkhas were at first successful. When, however, the Chinese authorities realised the seriousness of the situation, strong measures were at once taken. Reinforcing the defeated troops, the Chinese in their turn drove back the Ghoorkhas, upon whom they inflicted more than one blow. When the latter retired upon their own mountain border, not content with their success the Chinese followed, and the unique experience of an engagement fought near the Ghoorkhan capital of Khatmandu ended in the defeat of its defenders.

It is such determined military efforts as the one described above which renders so difficult the task of estimating the reality of the Chinese military spirit. Though it is unnecessary to dwell upon the value of such an expedition as a military exploit, it may not be out of place to suggest in praise of its very inception a glance at the map of Asia.

To set against the successes obtained in Tibet,

we must now turn to a neighbouring country farther south. About the same time as the Ghoorkha conquests, Chinese armies were despatched to Burmah. Though successful in penetrating into the heart of that country, the Chinese troops were heavily defeated by the Burmese. From the commencement of the nineteenth century, intercourse with foreign nations began seriously to be felt. At the time when the century was half gone the Tae-ping rebellion had shaken the foundations of the empire. That it did not finally effect the fall of the Manchu dynasty is no honour to the military spirit of the race. That the Chinese furnish as fine material for soldiers as any Asiatic race is the opinion of most Europeans qualified to judge. From this opinion General Gordon, who saved the Manchu dynasty, never varied.

With the Tae-ping rebellion came the wars between England, France, and China; later on the war with France alone in Tong-king. In Central Asia Chinese military prestige flamed up temporarily owing to the suppression of the Yakub Beg rising, but received another shock owing to the all but successful efforts of Chinese Mohammedans to release themselves from a suzerainty they despised. In the present day we are able to follow the fortunes of their arms from a personal point of view.

The China-Japan war, with its overwhelming disgrace to the former, taught her no military lesson. The so-called rising in 1900 taught European diplomacy something, but China less. It is not our aim here to do more than indicate the possible chance of the revival of a military spirit in China. Whether I am justified in using the word revival I will leave to my readers to determine. The conquests of the past point to some such spirit having once been extant, but that it remains, or can be reintroduced, is not the opinion of the writer.

Before closing this review of the existence or non-existence of any military spirit in the nation, it may be of interest if some personal experience is added. During the last eight years, in conjunction with other British officers and non-commissioned officers, I have helped to create, and for the last six years have commanded, the Chinese regiment which has lately ceased to form part of his Majesty's forces. Constant daily intercourse with the class from which Chinese future armies will be drawn, and hourly instruction of these men in every possible form of the art of modern war, may perhaps be allowed to count as sufficient reason for venturing to offer an opinion upon the point we are endeavouring to elucidate. Not only is such opinion the result of observation drawn from training in time of peace, but it was strengthened by the actual experience of leading these men in war during the rising of 1900.

The opinion formed by General Gordon of the value of the Chinese troops he and other white men led, was confirmed again and again during our eight years' experience. Without analysing the various accounts which General Gordon has left on record, it may be taken for granted that the following is a true summary of his opinion. Led and trained by Europeans, the Chinese would be second to no native troops in the world,—perhaps it may be added, in these more highly nervous modern days, to no troops in the world. But trained and led successfully by Chinese officers they will not be, at any rate within a period of time which practical politics need take heed of.

To enumerate the good points of the material which the nation could produce, it is merely necessary to reiterate a list of military virtues required to form an ideal soldier. Have we not the authority of the greatest master of war the world has ever known for the following description?—

"The first quality of a soldier is fortitude in enduring fatigues and hardships; bravery but the second. Poverty, hardship, and misery are the school of the good soldier." Few Asiatics and no Europeans more closely fulfil these requirements than do the Chinese.

And now for the reverse of the shield.

A late head of the General Staff in France has thus described the part that the staff of an army must play in the present day. Substituting China for France, his words are given *in extenso*.

"Though the art of war may still hold in reserve for some future Turenne, Condé, or Napoleon, those sudden inspirations of warlike genius — those lightning flashes that suddenly light up the tangled hosts and strike the foe at the very point needed to decide the fight—yet there is in the case of actual warfare a task to be done of a totally different kind. I am referring to the preparation for war, the preparatory work of bringing into the field those huge forces that a nation will one day be called upon to set in motion. I am referring to that patient, earnest, ceaseless work that devolves upon the staff of an army. . . .

"Picture to yourselves, then, the stupendous armament of a whole nation; the sudden suspension of all public and private life, the transformation of 'China' into one great drill-ground; the vast masses of men who must be clothed, equipped, and armed in a few days, ay, in a few hours. Picture them speeding along by every railway to the confined spot where in one fearful encounter will be decided the freedom, nay, the very existence of a country.

"All these human waves will appear to roll onward pell-mell, but at the given place and exact minute all will be found in order, each unit in its place, face to face with the foe, and ready for the struggle. And what a struggle!

"You do not imagine that when once those immense masses have been got together they can be moved, or supplied, or fed, or that they can take the field unless all the problems have been thought out and studied, and, so to speak, solved beforehand."

In these words is most vividly depicted the embodiment of a national military spirit, prepared to sacrifice everything in defence of its country's honour. That such a spirit at present exists or can be called into being in China by Chinese, I am unable to believe.

APPENDIX.

RECORD OF TEMPERATURE AND WEATHER.

LEH TO POLU.

Date.	No. of Camp.	Name of Place.	Temperature. 6 A.M.	3 P.M.	7 P.M.	Max.	Min.	Force of Wind and Weather.
			Deg.	Deg.	Deg.	Deg.	Deg.	
Aug. 29	1	Ranbirpur .	...	...	70	76	...	1 S.W. 4 cumulo-stratus. Cloudy early, with hot sun up to 2 P.M., usual S.W. wind later. 10,725 ft., 19·67 press.
" 30	2	Chimray . .	42	57	70	76	28	1 S.W. 5 nimbus. Cloudless up to 1 P.M., later clouded over as if for rain. 11,825 ft., 18·93 press.
" 31	3	Zingrul . .	24	57	40	71	23	3 S.W. 5 cirro-cumulus. Before 7 A.M. clear and fine, up to noon cloudy aud bright alternately. 15,233 ft., 16·70 press.
Sept. 1	4	Tsultak . .	32	60	44	74	27	2 S.W. 2 cirro-cumulus. Clear all day. 15,400 ft., 16·60 press.
" 2	5	Tankse . . .	...	72	58	77	...	2 N.E. early; 2 W. afternoon. Cloudless all day; great change in heat of sun to-day. 12,700 ft., 18·80 press.
" 3	5	"	...	71	56	71	...	Cloudless. 3 W.
" 4	5	"	40	64	57	71	37	2 W. 3 cumulo-stratus.
" 5	6	Muglib . . .	41	67	57	70	39	2 W. 4 cirro-cumulus. 13,250 ft., 18·06 press.
" 6	7	Lookoong . .	35	64	...	60	31	2 W. 3 cumulo-stratus. 13,833 ft., 17·65 press.
" 7	8	Masemick-la, South side	34	49	...	60	27	Cloudy until 2 P.M. 6 cumulus. Afternoon clear. 1 W. 16,417 ft., 15·96 press.
" 8	9	Masemick-la (Rimdi), North side	34	49	...	...	32	Cloudy all day, faint snow for a few minutes. 4 N.E. Biting wind up to 12.30 P.M. Later 2 W.S.W. 7 stratus. 16,800 ft., 15·70 press.
" 9	10	Pamzal . . .	37	...	44	55	31	Fine early, later cloudy, storms on all the high peaks round; rain at 5 P.M., the first since August 3. Wind variable, mainly N.; afternoon W. 14,400 ft., 17·28 press.
" 10	11	Kyam . . .	38	39	36	56	36	After all-night rain cloudy till noon, later hail and rain storm. 5 S.W. 15,316 ft., 16·63 press.
" 11	11	"	44	42	40	57	35	Early fine, later cloudy, hail and rain squalls. 5 S.W. No observations possible.

Date.	No. of Camp.	Name of Place.	Temperature.					Force of Wind and Weather.
			6 A.M.	3 P.M.	7 P.M.	Max.	Min.	
			Deg.	Deg.	Deg.	Deg.	Deg.	
Sept. 12	11	Kyam . . .	40	45	45	54	38	Cloudy all day. Squalls, hail and rain. 5 S.W. alternately. No observations possible.
" 13	12	Kipsang . .	37	54	33	47	30	Snow on ground at dawn, squally up to noon, later clear. 7 cumulo-stratus. 4 W. 16,433 ft., 16·30 press.
" 14	13	Zalung . . .	22	41	29	46	18	Slight snow at dawn. Sunny and still up to 8.30 A.M., then squally till noon. 4 W. 3 cumulo-stratus. 17,050 ft., 15·55 press.
" 15	14	Chuzan-Po .	17	45	31	47	13	Blew a gale last night; slight snow early. 3 S.W. 6 cumulus. 17,200 ft., 15·17 press.
" 16	1	Lurding, 3½ miles east of Lanak-La	22	42	25	56	14	Early bright and sunny; cloudless all day. 5 W. 17,566 ft., 15·26 press.
" 17	2	Shum (nullah)	17	42	25	56	Broke Min. thermo.	Cloudless all day. 3 W. afternoon. 17,416 ft., 15·40 press.
" 18	3	Bukchang (nullah)	26	55	30	58	...	Cloudless all day. 3 W. 17,117 ft., 15·53 press.
" 19	3	"	27	54	30	53	...	Cloudless all day. 2 W.
" 20	4	Thanglay Wenpo	19	49	29	50	...	Threatening snow. 3 W. 7 snow clouds. 17,080 ft., 15·60 press.
" 21	5	Kamure . .	23	44	29	40	...	Slight snow last night, continued slightly up to noon. Early no wind, afternoon 3 W. 16,850 ft., 15·13 press.
" 22	6	Mang-Tzzaka-Tzo	18	38	27	40	...	Early fine, slight snow-squalls from N.E. to 1 P.M., later from W.; 4 snow-clouds. 16,866 ft., 15·73 press.
" 23	7	Chutzar . .	17	40	29	41	...	Sunny and still early. Heavy snow-squalls 9.30 A.M. Wind 2 N.E.; afternoon 4 N.W.; squalls; 8 snow-clouds. 16,816 ft., 15·75 press.
" 24	7	"	19	36	24	47	...	Clear early, 5 W. later. 6 cumulo-stratus.
" 25	7	"	13	45	31	48	...	Sunny and unusually warm up to 2 P.M. All day nearly windless, most unusual. Afternoon 7 nimbus or snow-clouds. 2 W.
" 26	8	Tang-Ma-Tzo	12	41	24	45	...	No wind early, 11.30 A.M. onwards 5 N.W., later W. 3 cirro-stratus. 16,866 ft., 15·75 press.
" 27	9	Kangri . . .	13	34	31	45	...	Early 2 N.E., afternoon 4 W., cloudless all day. 17,300 ft., 15·51 press.
" 28	10	Camp 10 . .	27	39	24	42	...	Cloudy all day, threatening snow. 3 W. 16,933 ft., 15·68 press.

Date.	No. of Camp.	Name of Place.	Temperature. 6 A.M.	3 P.M.	7 P.M.	Max.	Min.	Force of Wind and Weather.
			Deg.	Deg.	Deg.	Deg.	Deg.	
Sept. 29	11	Camp 11 . .	19	31	24	41	...	Snow fell to 2 inches, and lay everywhere for first time. Heavy snow-clouds all day and squalls, surrounding ranges obscured. Early 2 N.E., later 2 W. 16,466 ft., 16·00 press.
" 30	12	Camp 12 . .	23	39	28	45	...	Early 2 E., later 2 W. till 10 P.M. Heavy squalls with snow from N. 3 cirrus, later 8 cirrus. 16,380 ft., 16·00 press.
Oct. 1	12	"	29	26	21	33	...	Snow fell to 2 inches during night and up to 9.30 A.M., sunny later. 2 N.E.
" 2	13	Loong-oon .	15	24	17	33	...	Early 1 N., hazy, later 3 W. 2 stratus. 17,133 ft., 15·56 press.
" 3	14	Chuchun . .	...	27	...	...	...	Early cloudless, 2 E., later 2 S.W. 7 cirrus up to 3 P.M., cloudless then till dusk. 17,516 ft., 15·30 press.
" 4	15	Devil's Plain	11	...	...	38	...	Early sunny and windless. 6 cirro-cumulus, later 3 S.W. with biting storm from the snow-range at 5 P.M. Intense cold on the plain averaging 18·100 ft. 16,650 ft., 15·70 press.
" 5	16	Baba Hatan .	...	30	8	48	...	Sunny and warm early, cloudless, 1 N.W., later 3 cirro-cumulus, 3 W. 15,966 ft., 16·40 press.
" 6	16	"	23	39	20	49	...	Cloudless early, 3 S.W., sunny and warm up to 1 P.M., later 3 stratus. Storm all day upon the Devil's Plain.
" 7	16	"	26	37	21	38	...	Early 2 S.W., 2 cirrus, afternoon 5 cumulus, 3 S.W.
" 8	16	"	27	25	15	39	...	Early 2 N.E. with squalls of sleet and snow, afternoon 3 S.W. varying to N., more snow.
" 9	16	"	19	25	15	35	...	Early 3 N.E., 5 cirrus, afternoon 3 N.W., 5 cumulus. Snow passing away.
" 10	16	"	14	26	14	43	...	Early cloudless, very cold night, forenoon 2 N.E., 2 cirrus.
" 11	16	"	21	32	21	43	...	Early 1 cirrus, 2 N.W. At 11 A.M. it clouded over as for snow with squalls of dust instead, later 7 cirro-cumulus.
" 12	17	Aksu-la, South side	19	Noon. 38	24	42	...	Cloudless early, 1 S.W., sunny, warm morning after unusually warm night *comparatively*, afternoon 3 S.W., 7 stratus. 16,700 ft., 15·60 press.

Date.	No. of Camp.	Name of Place.	Temperature. 6 A.M.	3 P.M.	7 P.M.	Max.	Min	Force of Wind and Weather.
			Deg.	Deg.	Deg.	Deg.	Deg.	
Oct. 13	18	Aksu-la, North side	10	28	19	36	...	Slight snow during the night from N.E. continuing at daybreak. Early 8 cirrus, clear by 11 A.M., 2 S.W., 5 cumulus. 16,250 ft., 15·95 press. Colder this side of the Curzon range.
" 14	19	Googoot-Plain	5	25	19	36	...	Early cloudless, 1 S.W., later 2 S.W., 8 cumulo-stratus. 15,450 ft., 16·37 press.
" 15	20	Atchik-Kul .	8	26	14	...	...	Cloudless early, 1 W. Sunny and warm as usual after sunrise. By 1 P.M. 6 cumulo-stratus, 4 N.W. Heavy snowstorm in Kuen Lun. 15,200 ft., 16·50 press.
" 16	21	Roongo-la .	12	...	17	...	...	Early cloudless, 1 S.W. Later, on N. side of Kuen Lun range, intense cold with 2 ft. of snow. 15,300 ft., 16·45 press.
" 17	22	Zoobechie . .	7	...	...	32	...	Early cloudless, no wind, afternoon 3 N. 5 cumulus. 12,400 ft., 18·50 press.
" 18	23	Gold-Hole (Camp)	...	29	25	...	...	8 cirro-cumulus, 2 N.W. 12,300 ft., 18·60 press.
" 19	24	Kalungri . .	18	...	29	...	...	Early cloudless, 2 N.W. local. 10,400 ft., 20·00 press.
" 20	25	Polu . . .	19	...	...	48	...	Early cloudless, no wind, dust-haze all day from soft grey loess (?) of lower mountain slopes, later 3 N. 8300 ft., 21·70 press.

POLU TO CHIA YU KUAN.

Date.	No. of Camp.	Name of Place.	6 A.M.	3 P.M.	7 P.M.	Max.	Min	Force of Wind and Weather.
Oct. 21	25	Polu . . .	36	44	39	47	...	Temperature taken in the open courtyard. Early cloudless, 3 N.E., dust-haze all day.
" 22	25	"	37	46	38	51	...	Cloudless, dust-haze, 2 N.E.
" 23	25	"	36	50	...	...	...	Cloudless early, 1 S.W., later dust-haze, 3 N.E.
" 24	1	Kurup R. (Camp)	·39	...	44	72	...	Cloudless early, 1 N.E., later dust-haze, thick, 4 N.W. Early twilight, 5.45 P.M. dark. 6500 ft., 23·30 press.
" 25	2	Boghar Langar	38	63	46	5 P.M. 61	...	Early cloudless, 1 N.W., hot sun, later 3 N.W. 5700 ft., 23·95 press.
" 26	3	Kookhiar . .	37	5 P.M. 55	45	61	...	Heavy dust-haze obscuring sunrise. Cloudless, no wind, later 3 N.E. 4600 ft., 25·00 press.

Date.	No. of Camp.	Name of Place.	Temperature. 6 A.M.	3 P.M.	7 P.M.	Max.	Min.	Force of Wind and Weather.
			Deg.	Deg.	Deg.	Deg.	Deg.	
Oct. 27	4	Keria . . .	32	59	47	60	...	Early 1 cirrus, later cloudless, afternoon 3 cirro-stratus, heavy dust-haze, no wind. 4600 ft., 25·00 press.
" 28	4	"	39	55	52	53	...	Early cloudless, no wind, heavy dust-haze all day combined with 9 nimbus.
" 29	5	Silmila . . .	39	48	38	51	...	Early no wind, rising towards desert N.E., at 11.15 A.M. W.N.W., veering to N., finally by 5 P.M. to 3 E. This is the average procedure of wind. Unusually heavy dust-haze all day, limits view to 1 mile. 4500 ft., 25·20 press.
" 30	6	Yaz-Yulgun .	28	38	39	61	...	Though night is clearer than day, the dust-haze is still apparent. Cloudless but for this. There is only an arc of some 90° of the sky not affected by the haze, and that arc is at times partially affected. 7 A.M. 2 S., later 2 W., by 3 P.M. veering to N., after to E. 4600 ft., 25·00 press.
" 31	7	Chikunda R. (Bed)	24	61	45	67	...	Cloudless early, less dust-haze, no wind. 9.30 A.M. 1 N.E. rising, 4.30 P.M. 2 N. A clearer day altogether. 5300 ft., 24·40 press.
Nov. 1	8	Nia	39	66	52	85	...	Before dawn is the clearest time in the 24 hours; there is no dust-haze, later cloudless, by 10 A.M. haze as usual. Early 2 S.E., by 9.30 A.M. veering to W., 3 P.M. 4 N.W., dust and sand flying. 4550 ft., 25·10 press.
" 2	8	"	39	60	50	...	...	Cloudless early, no wind, afternoon 1 cirrus.
" 3	9	Toorat Lungray	35	...	41	...	...	Early cloudless, by 7.30 A.M. heavy dust-haze, later dust-storms from W. 3 W. dying down to 1 W. 5300 ft., 24·40 press.
" 4	10	Sorghack . .	32	42	36	50	...	Dust-haze all day, otherwise cloudless. 2 S.W. 7300 ft., 22·50 press.
" 5	10	"	29	42	34	44	...	Early dust-haze, later 1 cirrus, dull, no wind.
" 6	11	Tŏrŏlŏck . .	27	35	32	53	...	Early 6 cumulus, 1 E., later 6 cumulo-stratus. Afternoon cloudless, dust-haze stronger than usual. 1 N. 8350 ft., 21·60 press.
" 7	12	Yĕ-Yack . .	29	...	23	57	...	Cloudless early, clearer than usual, view unlimited up to 11 A.M. 2 S.E., later 2 N.E., then E., dust-haze all back by 2 P.M. 8000 ft., 22·00 press.

Date.	No. of Camp.	Name of Place.	Temperature.					Force of Wind and Weather.
			6 A.M.	3 P.M.	7 P.M.	Max.	Min.	
			Deg.	Deg.	Deg.	Deg.	Deg.	
Nov. 8	13	Yulgun-Bulack Lengar	26	52	32	61	...	1 cirrus, 3 S.E. Up to noon clear without haze, noon haze all back. 2 N.E. Sun powerful. 7600 ft., 22·25 press.
" 9	14	Tollan-Kojha	27	51	31	48	...	Cloudless, no wind early, by 9.30 A.M. 1 N.E., later veering by W. to 1 N.E. Haze thicker. 8550 ft., 21·55 press.
" 10	15	Kara-Sai . .	35	37	31	50	...	First blow last night since Polu, 3 N. Cloudy early with heavy haze. 2 W. all day, 7 cumulo-stratus. 9600 ft., 20·65 press.
" 11	16	Buko-Bulak .	29	44	31	...	...	Heavy dust-haze to N. over desert. 7 cirro-cumulus, later cloudless. Early 1 W., later 2 N.E.
" 12	17	Boogna Sai .	25	...	26	36	...	1 N.E. Early 2 cirrus, less haze, later 4 N.E., sand blowing high. 4 cirro-stratus, later 3 cumulo-stratus. 8400 ft., 21·65 press.
" 13	18	Milchai . .	24	32	32	37	...	Early 8 cirrus, 1 S.E., later 9 nimbus or snow-clouds, 2 W. Thick dust-haze all round. 7350 ft., 22·50 press. View limit 1 mile.
				In	open	court	yard.	
" 14	19	Kopa . . .	23	34	33	40	...	Dust-haze obscured clouds all day. Early 1 E., at 9.30 A.M. 2 W., later 3 W. 8000 ft., 22·00 press.
" 15	19	"	34	35	34	...	...	Dust-haze early, 2 S.W., later 5 cirro-cumulus. At 4 P.M. thick dust-haze all round.
" 16	20	Tak Bai . .	32	...	30	...	...	Cloudless early, no wind, less haze all day, good view for 5 to 7 miles round, later 1 W. 7 cumulo-cirrus. A clear sunny day, different from the usual, towards sunset snow-clouds gathering. 10,050 ft., 20·30 press.
" 17	21	Achen . . .	29	...	33	59	...	Early 1 S., 1 cirro-stratus, later 2 N.E., dying away in afternoon. Clouded over as if for snow. 9300 ft., 20·90 press.
" 18	22	Soopa Deng .	32	52	34	...	...	Clear from haze early, 7 nimbus for snow, 1 S., later 3 W., dropping towards sunset. Afternoon cloudless. 7300 ft., 22·50 press.
" 19	23	Uzzun Takki	28	...	37	60	...	2 S. early, 3 A.M. very cold off the snow Kuen Lun range 12 miles distant. 7 of Nos. II. and III. blended, later 3 N. 4700 ft., 24·90 press.
		In	open	court	yard.			
" 20	24	Cherchen . .	27	49	33	61	...	4 S. early, all day cloudless without haze, later 2 N. 4100 ft., 25·60 press.
" 21	24	"	24	44	29	53	...	Early cloudless, 2 S., later 2 N.

Date.	No. of Camp.	Name of Place.	Temperature. 6 A.M.	3 P.M.	7 P.M.	Max.	Min.	Force of Wind and Weather.
			Deg.	Deg.	Deg.	Deg.	Deg.	
Nov. 22	24	CHERCHEN . .	21	48	35	47	...	Early 3 S., 4 cirrus, later 2 N.E., 4 cirro-cumulus, afternoon cloudless.
" 23	25	AKH-DING . .	19	44	28	51	...	1 S. early, 5 cirro-stratus, later 2 N.E., 6 stratus. 3800 ft., 25·70 press.
" 24	26	KENG-LAIKA .	18	45	17	48	...	Early 1 S., haze all day, later wind fitful, dying away 2 N.E. 3450 ft., 26·15 press.
" 25	27	Camp 27 . .	12	45	17	45	...	All day 1 to 2 N.E., 3 cirro-cumulus, no haze. 3300 ft., 26·25 press.
" 26	28	Camp 28 . .	7	43	18	57	...	Cloudless all day, 1 S. early to 2 N.E. late, no haze. 3200 ft., 26·40 press.
" 27	29	Camp 29 . .	6	54	21	45	...	Cloudless all day, 1 S. early to 2 N.E. late, and cold. 2875 ft., 26·70 press.
" 28	30	KOLA-LENGAR	5	42	22	46	...	2 S.W. early, cloudless all day, later no wind. 2750 ft., 26·80 press.
" 29	30	"	8	44	26	41	...	Early 2 S.W., cloudless all day, later 2 N.E.
" 30	31	Camp 31 . .	6	40	18	47	...	Cloudless early, 1 S.W., later 3 N.E., 6 cumulo-stratus. 2900 ft., 26·70 press.
Dec. 1	32	CHAPAN KALDI	5	45	22	46	...	Early 1 S.W., later 3 W.N.W., 4 cirro-stratus. 2700 ft., 26·80 press.
" 2	33	VASH-SHAR .	10	43	28	53	...	Cloudless all day, early 2 S., later 3 N.E. 3000 ft., 26·60 press.
" 3	34	USHUR . . .	13	45	17	44	...	No wind early, 5 cirro-stratus, later 2 E.N.E., cloudless. 3000 ft., 26·60 press.
" 4	35	TATLICK-BULACK	12	42	31	...	...	Early 2 S.W., 7 nimbus for snow all day, later 1 N.E. 2850 ft., 26·75 press.
" 5	36	CHARKALICK .	11	37	27	41	...	8 nimbus for snow all day, much colder. Early 2 S.W., later 2 N.E. 3300 ft., 26·30 press. (Temperature taken here in an open *serai* 40 yds. sq., sheltered from the wind.) Winter has begun without much warning.
" 6	36	"	35	33	32	45	...	A wild storm from the N.W. followed by heavy snow; 2 inches fell in under two hours.
" 7	36	"	15	39	28	48	...	Heavy haze all day obscuring the sky. Sunny at midday, 3 inches of snow lying hard frozen.
" 8	36	"	17	39	27	35	...	Early bright sun but haze, view limit 2 miles. Later no wind, 4 cirrus.
" 9	36	"	22	28	22	40	...	Early 2 N.E., dull and obscure all day. No thaw except in sun at midday.

Date.	No. of Camp.	Name of Place.	Temperature. 6 A.M.	3 P.M.	7 P.M.	Max.	Min.	Force of Wind and Weather.
			Deg.	Deg.	Deg.	Deg.	Deg.	
Dec. 10	36	Charkalick .	8	35	18	42	...	Early cloudless. Heavy haze up to an arc of 30° round the horizon. 2 N.E.
" 11	36	"	6	36	17	40	...	All day cloudless, no wind. Heavy haze up to arc of 40° clearly defined.
" 12	36	"	7	32	17	...	...	Cloudless early, 1 S.W., usual arc of haze all round, later 5 nimbus for snow. 1 N.E.
" 13	37	Yundashkok .	7	...	19	...	...	Usual haze arc up to 40° all round, otherwise cloudless, 1 S.W., later 2 N.E., 4 cirrus. 2600 ft., 27·00 press.
" 14	38	Camp 38 . .	5	24	11	28	...	No wind all day, 3 cirro-stratus, haze as usual. 2550 ft., 27·25 press.
" 15	39	Tullick-Kulla	2	27	9	35	...	All day cloudless, 3 S.W. to W., usual haze, no wind at night. 2500 ft., 27·50 press.
" 16	40	Abdal . . .	3	32	18	35	...	7 nimbus for snow, early no wind, later 5 cirrus, 2 N.E. 2300 ft., 27·30 press.
" 17	41	Camp 41 . .	9	30	18	40	...	All day cloudless and sunny, early 1 S., later 3 N.E. 2400 ft., 27·20 press.
" 18	42	Camp 42 . .	14	34	18	29	...	Early no wind, 6 cirro-cumulus, later 4 N.E., 4 cumulo-stratus. 2400 ft., 27·15 press.
" 19	43	Camp 43 . .	1	25	14	36	...	Early 2 S.W., later increasing to 4 S.W., all day bitter cold. 2 cirro-cumulus, later 4 nimbus for snow. 2400 ft., 27·20 press.
" 20	44	Camp 44 . .	14	32	15	36	...	Nimbus for snow all day. Early 2 S.W., later 1 N.E. 2300 ft., 27·30 press.
" 21	45	Camp 45 . .	2	33	18	36	...	Heavy haze all round early, otherwise cloudless. 2 S.W.
" 22	46	Camp 46 . .	16	29	17	38	...	Comparatively a mild day, no wind, heavy haze arc up to 40° all round, otherwise cloudless. 2300 ft., 27·30 press.
" 23	47	Camp 47 . .	·5	29	11	34	...	Early 1 S.W., later 2 N.E. Another perfect day, cloudless and sunny, usual haze.
" 24	48	Christmas Eve (Camp)	—!*	28	15	31	...	* No thermometer left whole capable of registering below zero All minus readings noted thu: —! Same perfect day, cloudless witl bright sunshine, haze as usual, N.E. 2200 ft., 27·35 press.
" 25	49	Christmas Day (Camp)	—!	25	13	38	...	Biting wind, 2 S.W. early, lat 2 N.E. Cloudless, with sun a day. 2225 ft., 27·35 press.

Date.	No. of Camp.	Name of Place.	Temperature.					Force of Wind and Weather.
			6 A.M.	3 P.M.	7 P.M.	Max.	Min.	
			Deg.	Deg.	Deg.	Deg.	Deg.	
Dec. 26	50	Boxing Day (Camp)	—?	28	—?	36	...	No wind early, later 2 N.E., cloudy and sunless up to noon. 2150 ft., 27·45 press.
" 27	51	Camp 51 . .	—?	34	—?	33	...	3 N.E., 4 cumulus, biting wind, afternoon 2 N.E., cloudless. 2200 ft., 27·30 press.
" 28	52	Camp 52 . .	—?	24	—?	35	...	Cloudless early, no wind, later 4 cirro-cumulus, 2 S.W. 2375 ft., 27·20 press.
" 29	53	Camp 53 . .	—?	32	2	33	...	Cloudless all day, biting 3 N.E. wind. 2400 ft., 27·20 press.
" 30	54	New Year's Eve (Camp)	—?	30	—?	32	...	Cloudless all day, biting 2 S.W. wind. 2150 ft., 27·45 press.
" 31	54	"	—?	26	—?	34	...	Early 3 N.E. wind, biting cold, later 2 N.E., sunshine. 4 cirro-cumulus.
Jan. 1	55	New Year's Day (Camp)	—?	28	—?	33	...	Cloudless all day, bright sunshine, very cold early, later 2 S.W. 2200 ft., 27·40 press.
" 2	56	Tograck Kuduck	—?	24	—?	43	...	Early 7 nimbus with attempts to snow, 2 N.E., later cleared, bright sunshine, cloudless, 2 S.W. 2250 ft., 27·35 press.
" 3	57	Camp 57 . .	—?	34	16	...	...	Early 2 N.E., cloudless all day, later no wind, bright sun. 2500 ft., 27·10 press.
" 4	58	Camp 58 . .	4	29	—?	38	...	2 S.E., cloudless all day, sunshine. 2600 ft., 27·00 press.
" 5	59	Taltuk-Kuduck (Sweet-well)	—?	31	—?	...	...	No wind, extreme cold early, 3 cirrus, later 3 E., cloudless. 2900 ft., 26·70 press.
" 6	60	Camp 60 . .	6	31	19	35	...	Early no wind, 7 nimbus for snow all day, later 3 N.W., again 3 N.E. 3550 ft., 26·05 press.
" 7	60	"	11	23	10·	26	...	A terrific gale (Kara-Buran) last night from 9 P.M. to 2.30 A.M. 2 S.W. early, 7 nimbus for snow.
" 8	61	Camp 61 . .	9	20	4	28	...	7 nimbus for snow. 4 E., intensely cold wind all day. 2950 ft., 26·65 press.
" 9	62	Kara-Nor .	—?	20	—?	28	...	Forenoon 3 E., cloudless all day and very clear, dropping later to 1 E. 3000 ft., 26·60 press.
" 10	62	"	—?	22	—?	29	...	Cloudless all day, 2 E.
" 11	63	Camp 63 . .	—?	23	—?	...	...	No wind forenoon, cloudless all day, sunshine later, 1 S.W. 3100 ft., 26·50 press.
" 12	64	Tun Huan (Sachu)	2	...	...	...	...	3 cirrus, no wind early, bright sunshine, a beautiful day. 3100 ft., 26·50 press.

INDEX.